Jamestown REDISCOVERY 1994 - 2004

William M. Kelso   Beverly A. Straube

The Association for the Preservation
of Virginia Antiquities
2004

Dedication

2001

2002

2003

Graphics by Jamie E. May
Design and production by David Givens

Printed in The United States of America

ISBN: 0-917565-10-X

Forward

Jamestown Rediscovery 1994-2004 is the eighth in a series of updates on the historical and archaeological research known as APVA *Jamestown Rediscovery*, carried out under the auspices of the Association for the Preservation of Virginia Antiquities on its 22.5 acres on Jamestown Island. This volume however, is different from the rest of the series in that it is a synopsis of the last three seasons of excavation and a summary of what went on before it. Because the story of the excavation results has been an accumulative one, some of the text from the previous seven *Jamestown Rediscovery* volumes is herein reprinted but usually with updated discussion. So this more lengthy and comprehensive volume does not make the other issues obsolete. Rather if the reader wishes to understand the growing pains of the analysis over the ten year life span of the project, then a reading of all the issues is in order.

From the beginning in 1994, there were two major goals for the project: (1) find, uncover, and recover whatever might remain of the earliest settlement and the growth of the 17th-century town *and,* at the same time, (2) make that process of discovery as accessible to the visiting public as possible. For that reason the site and related laboratory work has been as visitor friendly as it can be, and considerable staff effort has gone into publishing the results of the research in a timely manner. Part of that publishing program is the *Rediscovery* series, which is literally rushed into print before the excitement of discovery fades. The downside of such a rapid publication program is that the time for full analysis to support conclusions is constricted, and therefore the meaning of discoveries is always subject to change through time. Therefore the reader should be advised that what appears in print is not necessarily a *conclusion,* but rather *a working theory* to be tested during future research. That, of course, is not really any different than any attempt to reconstruct and understand the past. However, the self-imposed deadline distills the process and renders most attempts to breathe meaning into the discoveries all the more tentative.

The first phase of the *Rediscovery* project was conceived to be a ten-year effort, 1994-2004, culminating in the production of both a comprehensive publication of the results of the research and a popular-level account of the historical background and APVA archaeological discoveries, both by 2005-2006. That still remains a publication goal. Along the way, periodical articles were planned as part of each year's work. In reality, the "articles" instantly grew into the more comprehensive yearly *Jamestown Rediscovery* booklets which were time-consuming in-house productions. This resulted, nonetheless, in time well invested in that each edition required archaeological and documentary background research that will ultimately prove useful in final interpretive works. This volume is one such work, "semi-final" in nature.

Acknowledgements:

The achievements of Jamestown Rediscovery are due in large measure to the many individuals and organizations who have provided leadership, generous financial support and scholarly advice and expertise.

Among the hundreds who could be acknowledged, we highlight a few here for special recognition:

Jamestown Rediscovery National Advisory Board: especially acknowledge the efforts of Dr. Warren M. Billings, chairman; Dennis B. Blanton, Dr. Edward Bond, Frederick Fausz, Dr. Jeffrey P. Brain, Dr. Cary Carson, Dr. Kathleen Deagan, Dr. Rex M. Ellis, Dr. Alaric Faulkner, Dr. William W. Fitzhugh, Ms. Camille Hedrick, Dr. James Horn, Dr. Jon Kukla, Dr. Douglas Owsley, Dr. David Orr, Mr. Oliver Perry, Dr. Carmel Schrire, Dr. George Stuart, Dr. Sandra Treadway, Dr. Edwin Randolph Turner, Mr. Robert Wharton, Roxane Gilmore, APVA's Trustees and Presidents Peter I. C. Knowles II and Ivor Massey, Jr., Executive Director Elizabeth S. Kostelny and APVA staff and membership for their constant interest and support.

Our partners, the National Park Service, Colonial National Historical Park. Among the most Generous Benefactors are: The United States Congress, The Commonwealth of Virginia, National Geographic Society, National Endowment for the Humanities and Public Policy, Virginia Foundation for the Humanities, James City County, Virginia, Colonial Dames of America in the Commonwealth of Virginia National Society, The Mellon Foundation, The Mary Morton Parsons Foundation, Jessie Ball duPont Fund, Richard & Caroline Gwathney Memorial Trust, Marietta M. and Samuel T. Morgan, Jr. Trust, The William H. John G. Emma Scott Foundation, William Byrd Branch of the APVA, The Colonial Capital Branch of the APVA, the Beirne Carter Foundation, the Eugene Holt Foundation, Mr. and Mrs. John H. Cronly III, Mr. and Mrs. William M. Grover, Jr., Mr. and Mrs. Thomas W. Hunt, Mr. Ivor Massey, Jr., Mr. and Mrs. Peter I. C. Knowles II, Elizabeth S. Kostelny, Mr. and Mrs. John A. Prince, Mrs. James W. Rawles, Alan M. Voorhees, Ms. Nancy Voorhees, Mr. Scott Voorhees, Mr. and Mrs. T. Eugene Worrell, Mr. and Mrs. Martin Kirwan King, and The Mrs. Mattielene T. King Estate. And Patricia D. Cornwell for underwriting special needs such as the annual field school, research travel, technical equipment and forensic anthropological research.

Staff: The Rediscovery Project has been very much a team effort from the start and now very much an experienced team effort. With an open mind to ways of improving the process, over the initial ten years of the project, the staff has had the opportunity to ever fine tune the way things have been done. I am especially grateful for their ability collectively to decipher the ever-widening archaeological story of Jamestown. I am indebted to senior curator Bly Straube's superior and ever-growing understanding of post-medieval material culture and for skillfully writing Chapters V and VI of this Volume; senior staff archaeologist Eric Deetz's ever growing mastery of field work, insight into post-medieval vernacular architecture and his unique ability to educate students and visitors; senior staff archaeologist and graphic artist, Jamie May, for her exceptional artistic eye on the computer and for her skillful reading of the archaeological signs in the soil of Jamestown; staff archaeologist and information technologist, David Givens, for his field experience, our GIS archives and for "constructing" this book; staff archaeologist Danny Schmidt for his ever growing field skills and commitment to the archives; Bob Berry for his conservation support and dedication to the *Jamestown Rediscovery* project; Douglas W. Owsley and Ashley McKeown for their insight and ability to unravel the art and mystery of Jamestown's skeletal biology; conservator/photographer Michael Lavin's ever more uniquely experienced conservation touches and photographic eye; Dan Gamble for his diligent and talented conservation work; Caroline Taylor for her careful artifact processing; Catherine Correll-Walls for accumulating the insightful Early Jamestown Biographies; and diligent and talented field work of archaeologists Carter Hudgins, Luke Pecoraro, Karisa Jacobsen, Cris de Triquet, and Tonia Rock. The efforts of the 2001, 2002, and 2003 University of Virginia field schools are especially recognized and appreciated as are the public relations and editing skills of Paula Neely, and proofing of Ann Berry and Betsy Ross Edison and the managerial talent of program co-coordinator, Ann Berry. Thanks also to Warren Billings and Sandra Treadway for help editing Chapter III and the helpful discussion concerning the Statehouses with Thad Tate and Carter Hudgins.

We are all grateful for the stalwart and ever encouraging Corps of APVA Jamestown interpreters and field and lab volunteers.

And for me, I am most grateful to Ellen, the steadfast "Mayor" of Jamestown, who gives meaning to whatever I do.

WMK, Jamestown, Virginia 2/5/04.

Introduction

It was not easy, and it did not happen overnight. In fact, for me it all began not even close to Virginia, but in Ohio over four decades ago in the library of my *alma mater*, Baldwin-Wallace College. Tired of memorizing names and dates for a history exam, one typical gray March day, I decided to cheer up by reading about Virginia where I heard the sun usually shines and American colonial history, second only to football as a passion in my life, was taken to be a serious subject. Somewhere among some faded back issues of *National Geographic*, an aerial photo of Jamestown Island spread out before me. I was totally mesmerized. The color image showed a network of open archaeological trenches casting a grid upon the landscape which laid bare the foundations of the buried town in a last ditch effort to exhibit its remains during the 350th celebration of its founding, in 1957. Until that moment, my Yankee-centric upbringing had never fostered much thought about what may have survived of the southern American colonial history. What I saw was certainly not the stereotypical northern image of the South: the pine barren hills of moonshine Appalachia. Rather here was a park-like place of hallowed ground, between unspoiled woodland and the spacious James River. The focus of the photo was the strict order of archaeological trenches crisscrossing the park. I was amazed that archaeology could even happen so close to my own time and place in history. Then, all my knowledge of archaeology had come from *National Geographic* photo essays on the pyramids. Never much of a spectator, I could not help imagining digging in that "ancient" Jamestown soil with my own hands. I was fascinated with

Figure 1. An aerial view of excavations at Jamestown conducted by the National Park Service in the mid 1950s. This grid of search trenches located a number of 17th century brick building sites, ditches, trash pits, and wells as preparation for the 350th year anniversary of the founding of Jamestown in 1957.

1

the accompanying story of the 350-year-old first settlement. I wanted to see it first-hand.

Eventually interest in early American history led me to graduate school at the College of William and Mary in Williamsburg, Virginia. So naturally my first stop was the ruins at nearby Jamestown Island in search of the 1607 fort that must surely have been uncovered in 1955. There, I was immediately drawn to the James River shore, the Association for the Preservation of Virginia Antiquities' moss-covered reconstructed church, the statues of Pocahontas and Captain John Smith, and a curious windowed exhibit in the side of the earthen Civil War fort nearby. The glass protected some exposed layers of dirt in the fort bank. It showed the actual soil surfaces that made up the bank: the Civil War zone complete with minie balls, on top of the dark band of "colonial" trash which was sitting on the deepest deposit, a lighter soil containing "arrowheads" and prehistoric Indian pottery. It was clearly a layer cake of time: pre-Jamestown 1607 at the bottom, the Colonial period in the middle, and the 1861-65 Civil War era on top. That seemed so simple; what is older is deeper, artifacts tell time and the earth can be an index of American history. Then I naively asked a Park Ranger where the old fort site was. I was surprised when he pointed to a lone cypress tree growing way off shore and said, "Unfortunately, you're too late, it's out there - and lost for good." Confused and disappointed I looked back at the dirt under glass that said "colonial" and asked again, "But what about here?" He thought for a moment, and replied with a shrug of his shoulders that I took as a "could be."

Figure 2. National Park Service archaeologist Joel Shiner next to the cross-sectional trench dug into the dirt bank of Jamestown's Civil War earthwork fort showing: A Civil War period, B Colonial Period, C Pre-1607 Virginia Indian Period (background) and a curious "L-shaped" excavated ditch (foreground right). This excavated cross-section was left visible to Jamestown visitors as an archaeological exhibit for some years after the 1955 digging.

A few decades and much fieldwork later, I had become an archaeologist specializing in the British Colonial America period, learning, with my colleagues, about the often forgotten American century, the 1600s. Most of our work focused on rescuing farm sites along the James River, which were being rediscovered by real estate developers and resettled by retirees. The more we learned from the earth about the 17th century, however, the more we thought

Figure 3. South church yard ca. 1928 showing original Pocahontas statue location where the installation of Jametown's first underground electric and telephone lines unearthed what eventually proved to be artifacts within the "lost" site of James Fort.

that the "colonial level" under that glass exhibit at the Civil War fort looked like a sign that the 1607 James Fort might be there. This seemed more likely when Nicholas Luccketti, Bly Straube and I restudied the field notes and artifacts from the 1955 National Park Service excavations that originally uncovered those exhibited layers and some disturbances in the soil nearby. These traces began to look like signs of the narrow slot trenches from early 17th-century wooden palisade defense "forts" we had all since found elsewhere on the James. Also the bits of iron and pottery found with them were old and military enough to have been part of James Fort. So when the APVA embarked on a campaign to do something significant with their property on Jamestown Island, such as archaeologically investigate it for remains of the first settlement by the 400th anniversary of Jamestown in 2007, I was certainly enthusiastically "offering" be chosen. Not that there was much of a line ahead of me, most archaeologists clearly discounted any chance of finding any trace of the early James Fort. At best they thought that there would only be clear signs that most or all of it had long since dissolved as the shoreline retreated before nearly four centuries of waves. In any event, the investigation began 100 feet from the site of the glassed-in cross section. Consequently, 33 years to the day when I first set foot on the island, Governor George Allen, of Virginia announced that the remains of the 1607 James Fort had been found. Fortunately for me, I did not have to miss out on digging at James Fort after all.

Figure 4. Ceramic German crucibles fused together during the making of glass in 1608? from the APVA collections found in the 1930's utility line trench near Pocahontas monument, south churchyard. The survival of this object with the tag describing where it was found helped determine where the Jamestown Rediscovery excavations would begin.

3

Prologue

The accent left no doubt they were British. "What are you doing?"

I was lost in the act of scraping loose dirt from a dark streak in Jamestown's yellow clay.

"Archaeology," I answered, hoping that would end the dialogue so I could get on with the digging.

No luck. "So have you found anything?" he said earnestly enough that I felt compelled to give a serious answer.

"Absolutely. See this black stain in the clay?"

"Yes."

"Well, that's what's left of a 1607 fort wall... James Fort."

"Really? Hmmmmm."

Silence for a moment, then she said, "You mean that's it? That's all there is? America, the last of the world's superpowers, began as... just dirt?"

"I never thought about it quite like that... but, yes, I guess it was...just dirt."

"But," she continued, "shouldn't there be a ruined castle or ...some marble columns ...or something real?"

"No....There was indeed... just dirt...but you know what else? I guess plenty of ...well...just hope."

"Oh...BRILLIANT," they said in unison. "Yes...brilliant indeed."

Figure 5. The first (1994) excavation summer season aided by visiting experienced professional historical archaeologists and University of Virginia field school students uncovering the first sign of James Fort, the dark soil line trace of a vanished upright log wall.

The British visitors moved on, but that brief encounter was a lightning bolt of insight, indeed brilliance, for all the players. On the one hand, the British visitors appeared to grasp the concept that global national stature was not necessarily synonymous with highly visible architectural ruins. The point was made that the USA began quite humbly in New World "dirt." It was that earth itself that ultimately gave the landless English immigrant a way to break into an otherwise closed English society, based forever on perpetuated family-owned estates.

I, on the other hand, gained an instant reverence for the "dirt" at my feet. In my mind, these humble marks in the clay are clear symbols of the fragile, yet enduring nature of Jamestown, Virginia, the site of the first permanent English settlement in North America. So much of what is left to testify to the solid expansion of English culture is indeed, "just dirt." Literally, these are the traces of a native people and the planting holes of immigrants, evidence that has survived amid the ground-disturbing activities of succeeding generations and the eroding effects of the adjacent James River. There was no gold; there was no short, all-water route to the riches of the orient, and the native population was often far from welcoming or willing to embrace the Church of England or to consistently feed the troops—all expectations of the sponsoring Virginia Company of London. But even though it would take some years to sink in, it was the land itself that would prove to be the saving grace of the colony.

The dirt at Jamestown has turned out to be "just" in other ways. Knowing that the soil contains so much of the remnants of the founding, struggle and antiquity of the "lost" Jamestown forges otherwise forgotten or misunderstood links in American history. For one thing, and contrary to the thinking of most Americans, this nation did not begin with the settlement of the pilgrims at Plymouth in 1620. Not only were the first palisades raised at Jamestown 13 years before Plymouth, but the English had settled much of the James River basin from the mouth of the Chesapeake Bay to as far west as within 20 miles of modern Richmond by the time the Mayflower dropped anchor. In fact, the southern Virginia settlement was so far flung, the Virginia Company felt it was losing control of its own colony. As a remedy, the Company established a centralized yearly meeting to bring the relatively freely elected men from the scattered settlements to James Town for a law-making session in 1619, the first English-style democratic representative governmental meeting in North America. For sure, Plymouth was more enduring, for it still exists as a city today, but what the Jamestown soil had obscured from view until now opens a long and unjustly closed window on the actual, deepest and most generally unknown European roots of modern American society.

For another thing, the same Jamestown soil has turned out to hold such a mixture of early 17th-century European and Native American artifacts, that it is now quite clear how significant a role the Virginia Indians played in the foundation of the first permanent English settlement. Clearly, North America was far from a culturally insignificant or otherwise empty continent when the Virginia Company adventurers filed onto the Jamestown Island shore of Virginia in 1607. This is not to say the English perceived that. They usually did not treat the Virginia Indians as anything more than "wildlife," nor did the English adopt the Indian way of life whole hog. But the recently turned archaeological Jamestown dirt "justly" leaves a strong impression that there was a solid early interdependence of the two societies.

As this volume will show, the soil also is telling a more just view of the talent of the initial players in the Jamestown story. Until now, in the words of one prominent American historian, Edmund S. Morgan, it has been mostly a tale cast as the "Jamestown Fiasco."[1] He makes a strong case:

> *The colony did not work out as the company envisaged it. The adventurers who ventured capital lost it. Most of the settlers who ventured their lives lost them. And so did most of the Indians who came near them. Measured by any of the objectives announced for it, the colony failed. And it failed ... because neither the Indians nor the English lived up to expectations.*[2]

It is true, as Morgan argues, that the Virginia Indians would not fit into what we can now know as a very naive Virginia Company settlement scheme. The Indians were supposed to become the farmers for the colony. False hope. For one thing, Indian women did all the things that Europeans considered work such as house building and farming while the men basically were out hunting and fishing. So the men did not turn out to be the worker bees the Virginia Company hoped for, and the women took their orders from the men. It is also true that half of the first group of English settlers were Gentlemen who by one definition were men who "*live idly... without manual labour.*"[3] Yet, Morgan admits, the Company had to send mostly gentlemen because they could pay their own way. Add to that, as Morgan points out, the loafing attitude of the original Jamestown laborers, then nothing positive got done; "*the idle* [were] *sent to teach the idle.*"[4]

Whatever these alleged incompetents did attempt, according to Morgan, turned out to be tremendous blunders such as not

Figure 6. In 1611, Ralph Hamor reports that "most" of the citizens of James Town were found at their usual pursuits of "bowling in the streets" much like the skittle players in this 17th-century Jan Steen painting. References like this led many historians to conclude that it was the "lazy" lifestyle of the gentlemen that turned the Jamestown settlement effort into a "fiasco."

building a serious fort at first or even getting around to unpacking their guns until **after** they were assaulted by the Indians. Then, even when they were starving they carried out a scorched earth policy toward the Indians, actually burning crops and villages. This effectively cut off the colonist's own food supply. So Morgan concludes *"the company, then, partly by choice, partly by necessity, sent to the colony an oversupply of men who were not prepared to tackle the work essential to settling in a wilderness."* [5] Morgan does admit that by 1617, tobacco, liberal government and individual land ownership turns the tide of fiascoism and Jamestown lives on after all. But there is little doubt that Morgan and generations of historians since the inception of America's Thanksgiving holiday, honoring 1620 Plymouth, Massachusetts, believe that Jamestown, the first permanent English settlement in North America, was a complete failure. And even if it did survive, so the story goes, it was certainly not as a result of **any** effort of the Virginia Company or the Virginia Jamestown adventurers.[6]

As this volume will show, what has emerged from the Jamestown soil offers a fairer story. "Fiasco" is a poor choice of words. The buried record of Jamestown's trials and errors is also the buried record of its trials and successes opening a newer, more positive spin on the traditional tale. For sure, it is a tale of a precarious attempt at planting English roots in the New World. But it is also a story of individual success and endurance by our nation's first founding "fathers," or more appropriately, founding "grandfathers." That Jamestown is the nation's first **enduring** English settlement is in itself proof of success regardless of the eventual financial demise of its sponsoring Virginia Company. Modern America took root for good at Jamestown. The pages that follow literally expose those telltale roots and the fair stories they can tell.

Chapter I

Founding Jamestown

The story actually starts with Columbus, who, as we all know, first sailed to the New World in *"fourteen hundred and ninety-two,"* and during his following voyage, began European settlement in America by establishing the town of La Isabela in what is now the Dominican Republic.[7] It requires no mathematical genius to calculate that 1607, the year England established its first lasting colony at Jamestown, is more than a century later. So clearly, England was a relatively late player in North American colonization. Why? There was a major problem. During most of the 16th century, the Atlantic Ocean was considered a Spanish Lake not to be ever seriously challenged by English navigators. Of course, that began changing when Sir Frances Drake, with his "unofficial" letter of mark from the daring Queen Elizabeth, hit hard at the Spanish gold and silver fleet and went on to bigger prizes by sailing around the globe. When the English and the weather smashed the Spanish Armada in 1588, colonization in the New World became a realistic English goal. For sure, the Armada's disruptive threat allowed the Sir Walter Raleigh-backed Virginia colony to get "lost" after 1587, but as the Atlantic shipping lanes opened up and the lesson of underfunded colonization became clear, the English got serious about starting what came to be an Empire upon which the sun never set. First came enduring Jamestown.

Figure 7. Defeat of the ships of the Spanish Armada by the English in 1588 ultimately opened the sea lanes to North America and Jamestown.

> *The soil was good and fruitful, with excellent good timber. There are also great store of vines in bigness of a man's thigh, running up to the tops of the trees, in great abundance...many squirrels, conies, blackbirds with crimson wings and divers other fowls and birds of divers and sundry colors of crimson, watchet, yellow, green, murrey and of divers other hues naturally without any art using.[8]*

So it was in May 1607. Virginia looked like paradise to the English *"gentlemen, artisans and laborers"* seeking a place to settle in the name of

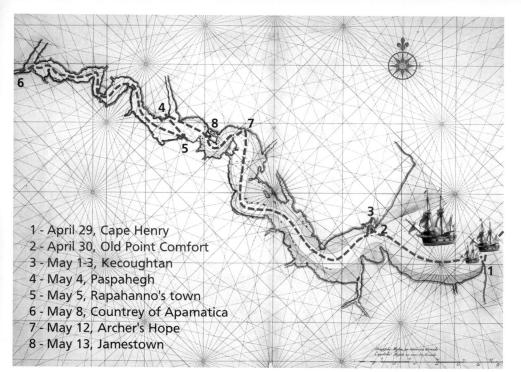

1 - April 29, Cape Henry
2 - April 30, Old Point Comfort
3 - May 1-3, Kecoughtan
4 - May 4, Paspahegh
5 - May 5, Rapahanno's town
6 - May 8, Countrey of Apamatica
7 - May 12, Archer's Hope
8 - May 13, Jamestown

Figure 8. Route of the James River exploration likely taken by the first settlers, April 29-May 13, 1607.

King James I and especially in the name of the Virginia Company of London, who paid for it all. Little wonder, these pioneers had left home during the gray, chilly English winter and spent most of the next four and one-half months astride the swelling Atlantic cramped aboard three ships that were, by today's standards, mere lifeboats. It was spring in Virginia, a time when the gentle seductive breezes and lush first growth camouflaged the inevitable deadly heat of the summer yet to come. The wildest dreams for the new world had come true. Surely a rich and genteel life would follow!

Entering the largest river of the Chesapeake, which they named after their king, James I, the ships sailed as far as 100 miles northwest to the Appomattox River before heading back toward the bay. Eventually they landed at Archer's Hope, George Percy's paradise of "*vivid and sundry colors.*" But while Archer's Hope seemed to be paradise, the ship channel was too far offshore for a permanent practical landing.

The next day, May 13, the group chose to settle a point of land that was actually an island at very high tide. Why there? Percy wrote that at Jamestown Island the Archer's Hope channel problem was solved. The deep water there was so close that ships could be tied to the trees.[9] Also, according to Virginia Company instructions, the colonists must not upset the Virginia Indians, especially by settling on land already occupied by them. Apparently Jamestown Island was vacant. They had more very specific instructions from the Virginia Company, the merchants and nobles who put up the money for the venture. The Company officials had advised their charges to settle at least 100 miles from the ocean as protection from what they thought would surely be Spanish reprisals for English privateering raids and punishment for muscling in on "Spain's" New World. Jamestown Island was, in fact, only 30 miles from the open sea, but if they did settle closer to the ocean, the Virginia Company advised the colonists to choose a naturally defensive place such as "*some Island.*" Certainly with only a narrow neck of land to guard against assault from the mainland Indians and with extraordinary visibility up and down the river to warn against surprise attack from the Spanish, Jamestown Island seemed all the more appealing. Its several "ridges" provided ideal sites for a fort, particularly the third ridge from the west, the highest point of land on the north shore of the river bend. It is also possible that although the Indians did not then occupy the land, they had been there in the not-too-distant past. By 1607, their cleared land might represent a fair-sized grove of straight, tall second-growth hardwood trees, ideal for building timber palisades and blockhouses.[10] These advantages apparently far outweighed the acres of mosquito-breeding marshes and lack of fresh water on the island.

So on May 14, 1607, just over 100 men and boys filed ashore from the *Susan Constant*, the *Godspeed* and the *Discovery*, onto what the English adventurers came to call Jamestown Island on the north shore of what they came to call the James River. The one eyewitness account simply explained

Figure 9. Captain George Percy (inset) describes his first look at the area near Jamestown (Archer's Hope) as paradise, but channel access and defense concerns brought the settlers to swampy and unhealthy Jamestown Island.

Figure 10. Jamestown Island from the west showing likely landing site on ground now underwater (foreground) but actual fort site surviving on land (arrow).

that Jamestown Island was their choice because the channel came near enough to the shore to moor their ships to the trees. This certainly made unloading supplies easier. While Captain John Smith and others left Jamestown soon after landing to explore the James River, the rest of the council—the new President Edward Maria Wingfield, John Martin, John Ratcliffe, George Kendall and Bartholomew Gosnold—were left to "*contrive* [design] *the Fort*," which apparently at first was no more than "*the boughs of trees cast together in the forme of a halfe moon.*"[11] Within a few days, this light defense became seriously inadequate to ward off Indian attacks. Thereafter, "*the President was contented the Fort should be pallisadoed* [and] *the Ordinance mounted.*"[12] By June 15, 1607, Percy described the finished fort:

> we had built and finished our fort, which was triangle-wise, having three bulwarks at every corner like a half-moon, and four or five pieces of artillery mounted in them.[13]

The only other detail we know about this early fort is that it had timber defenses made up of heavy "*palisadoes*" (upright side-by-side logs) planted in the ground.[14]

Whatever its form and degree of sophistication, most of the "*council's Fort*" did not last long. In January 1608, fire either seriously damaged or completely destroyed it. Yet by summer that year:

we rebuilt it...invironed with a palizado of fourteen or fifteene feet, and each as much as three or four men could carrie...we had three Bulwarks, foure and twentie peece of ordinance upon convenient plat-forms...[the overall plan] *reduced to the form of this ( )* [figure omitted but later called five-square].[15]

This five-square "James towne" seemed to prosper under Captain John Smith's strict leadership but soon after he left, in the fall of 1609, the colony began to deteriorate. By spring, when a supply arrived with the first governor, Sir Thomas Gates, and his future secretary, William Strachey, they basically found Jamestown in a shambles.

> *Viewing the fort [May 23, 1610] we found the palisades torn down, the ports open, the gates from off ther hinges...the Indians killed...our men* [if they] *stirred beyond the bounds of their blockhouse.*[16]

Figure 11. The appearances at Jamestown of Sir Thomas Gates in 1610 (above) and Lord Delaware in 1611 (below) save Jamestown from failure after the "starving time."

Food began to run low without hope of resupply. Things got so bad that Gates ordered an evacuation of the town. On June 7, 1610, "*we...buryed our ordinances before the front gate which looked into the river*"[17] and the survivors sailed downriver. Much to their surprise, but in reality part of a plan known to Gates, they soon met an advance party from the incoming supply fleet of the new Governor, Lord Delaware. Thus after only 30 hours respite from Jamestown, the demoralized group had to backtrack and prepare for the arrival of the new governor. Thereafter, the new leadership and especially the new supplies quickly seemed to rejuvenate the town. So, Strachey's next description of the fort is considerably more positive than his first and remains the most exact that is known to exist. Only three days after his return to the abandoned town, Strachey saw:

> *the fort growing since to more perfection, is now at this present in this manner: ...about half an acre...is cast almost into the form of a triangle and so palisaded. The south side next the river (howbeit extended in a line or curtain sixscore foot more in length than the other two, by reason the advantage of the ground doth require) contains 140 yards, the west and east sides a hundred only. At every angle or corner, where the lines meet, a bulwark or watchtower is raised and in each bulwark a piece or two well mounted....And thus enclosed, as I said, round with a palisade of planks and strong posts, four feet deep in the ground, of young oaks, walnuts, etc...the fort is called, in honor of His Majesty's name, Jamestown.*[18]

Figure 12. *Eyewitness accounts are the basis for this 1950s model of James Fort.*

Collectively these eyewitness accounts establish with little doubt that the fort was not quite a triangle ("*triangle-wise*" or almost a triangle) with watchtowers and/or bulwarks at each of the three angles where ordnance was mounted. This seems to agree with what appears to be a serious yet minuscule sketch of the fort on a map of Virginia delivered to King Philip III of Spain in 1608 by his ambassador to England, Don Pedro de Zúñiga. Some believe it is a tracing of an early John Smith map. In any case, each bulwark of the fort has a different plan, some possibly representing Strachey's watchtowers. And while there were three sides, or *curtains*, between the bulwarks, only the south and east sides appear to be equal in length, and they form a right angle with each other. This figure therefore certainly is "*triangle-wise*." The Zúñiga map also shows a much out-of-scale flag which may be in reality a rectangular plan for an extension to the town or an enclosed garden area to the north.

Figure 13. *Percy's 1607 description of the first days of occupation at Jamestown island fits this 17th-century Dutch image of soldiers at their camp in the Low Countries.*

In 1611, another eyewitness chronicler, Ralph Hamor, arrived in the colony from England and later published a description of

14

Jamestown which may or may not indicate a change in the form of the fort and the layout of the town:

> *The Towne* [James Town] ...*is reduced into a handsome forme, and hath in it two faire rowes of houses, all of framed Timber, two stories, and an upper Garret, or Corne loft high, besides the three large, and substantial Storehouses, joyned together in a length some hundred and twenty foot, and in breadth forty, and this town hath been lately newly, and strongly impaled, and a faire platforme for Ordence in the west Bulwark raised.*[19]

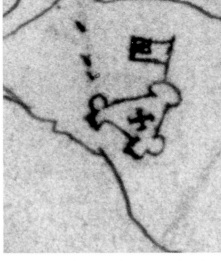

Figure 14. *The only known 17th-century plan of James Fort 1608 (?) as depicted on the Zuniga Spanish spy map.*

His glowing account of the "*handsome forme*" of the town and the "*faire rowes of houses*" seems to paint a picture of a renovated and seriously expanded fortified area. On the other hand, Hamor never really says the town plan expanded outside the limits of the original fort in any particular direction, however, he does mention houses scattered beyond the town.

Contemporary descriptions of James Fort's first "faire" private and public buildings are vague but suggest that for months the town must have looked like a temporary army camp. At first, the settlers "*cut downe trees to make place to pitch...Tents,*"[20] which were described as "*castles in the air.*" As late as September 10, 1607, there are "*no houses to cover us, our Tents were rotten and our* [thatched roof] *Cabbins worse than nought.*"[21] Three years later, however, things seemed to have improved some. Strachey described the houses in the fortified town:

> *to every side, a proportioned distance from the palisade, is a settled street of houses that runs along so as each line of the angle hath his street. ...The houses were all burnt by a casualty of fire the beginning of the second year...which since we have better rebuilded though as yet no great uniformity, either for fashion or beauty of the street.... The houses have wide and large country chimneys* [wood, clay covered?]...[they] *cover their houses now (as the Indians) with the barks of trees, as durable and good proof against storms and winter weather as the best tile...before in sultry weather would be like stoves, whilst they were, as at first, pargeted and plastered with bitumen or tough clay.*[22]

Regardless of how improved these shelters became, it is clear that they were never intended to last long anyway. According to Strachey:

> *We dwell not here to build us bowers.*
> *And Halls for pleasure and good cheer:*
> *But halls we build for us and ours,*
> *To dwell in them whilst we live here.*[23]

15

Figure 15. Sydney King's 1950s hypothetical view of Jamestown as it may have been expanded to the east by 1611.

And apparently they only existed at all as long as there was a constant repair and replacement program: "*we were constrained every yeere to build and repair our old cottages, which were always decaying in all places in the Countrie*," while at the same time the "*pallizadoes* [were] *not sufficient* [at Jamestown?] *to keepe out hogs.*"[24] These so-called "*cottages*" may have been prone to decay but they were not scarce. By summer 1608, "*we had about fortie or fiftie severall houses warm and dry.*"[25] The town houses increased to "*some fiftie or sixtie*" a year later, which, if the figure is not exaggerated, meant that some of them had to be outside Strachey's 1.75-acre fort dimensions.[26]

There were no other documentary clues to the physical appearance of James Fort until 1995. Then the existence of a detailed chart of the James River from its confluence with the Appomattox to the Chesapeake Bay came to light. This chart, drawn from ca. 1617 ship's logs is one of 156 included in a world-wide *Atlas of the Dutch West India Company*. It shows Jamestown, individual houses around modern Hopewell, and two other early Virginia forts: Fort Algernon at Point Comfort and Charles Fort at nearby Strawberry Bank. The map maker, Johannes Vingboons, illustrates both downriver forts as attached gable-end buildings, three at Algernon and two at Charles Fort.[27] He depicts Jamestown in an identical way—attached buildings—and locates them about one-third of the way from the western end of the island. These charts, intended as navigational guides, usually show buildings as they would appear from a distant ship, not as mere symbolic structures. So it seems that either each of these forts had prominent multi-section storehouses "*three large storehouses joined together in length*"[28], or the chart symbols depict blockhouses or watchtowers, clearly the most visible features of forts from a distance. If they are defenses, then

Jamestown and Fort Algernon appear almost identical: three blockhouses each, while Charles Fort had only two and perhaps a palisaded "yard." In fact, the Jamestown Island buildings are labeled *"Blockhouse Jamestown."* And if the triple houses mark the exact location of the town, as it almost certainly does, then the fort was clearly not built on the western, and subsequently eroded, end of the island. In fact, allowing for distortion in scale, the storehouse or blockhouse symbol appears to be precisely where the church tower stands today.

Figure 16. Caert [chart] Vande Riuer POWHATAN [James River] Geleg in Niew Nederlandt [Virginia] Atlas of the Dutch West India Company by Johannes Vingboons. Apparently drawn after ca. 1638 from a ca. 1617 ships log. Details: Jamestown Island and vicinity (above left) with "Blockhouse Jamestown", settlements near modern Hopewell area (below right) and forts Algernon and Charles (above right).

There is very little record of James Fort after the Dutch navigators produced the 1617 chart. A last-minute warning saved the fort from damage during the disastrous Indian uprising of 1622, but apparently a year and a half later, James Fort, other forts, and a number of the houses in Virginia were all very much at risk:

> August or September, 1623... *James Citie*... [and elsewhere in the colony] *have been suffered by the Colony of late to grow to such decay that they are become of no strength or use...there are no places fortified for defense & safetie...the plantations are farr asunder & their houses stand scattered one from another, and are onlie made of wood few or none of them beeing framed houses but punches sett into the Ground And covered with Boarde so as a firebrand is sufficient to consume them all.... The fortifications antientlie used were by Trench and Pallizado and (which now are all gone to ruyne* ...[lined out] *and diverse blockhouses made of timber...* [lined out] *great Tymber built uppon passages and for scouring the Pallizadoes: all which now are gone to ruin.*[29]

So their well-known but scant eyewitness accounts give a traditional view of early Jamestown and its principle players. But we can also know more about the historical background of the Jamestown adventure, the settlers who left England in those early years, and the other lesser known but critical players in the drama: the Virginia Indians, English women and the Spanish.

Figure 17. 1610 map of London area showing Blackwall, the point of embarkation for the original Jamestown settlers, and the Sir Walter Raleigh House at Blackwall, traditionally known for housing settlers in the 16th and 17th centuries (now demolished).

It is technically false that the first ships disembarked from London as most history books state. Rather, the settlers last trod English soil at a place called Blackwall slightly downriver from London adjacent to a foreboding sounding place known as the Isle of Dogs.[30] Blackwall in the early 17th century amounted to alehouses and churches supporting the docks of the emerging English maritime trade. Today, at the end of a street known as Blackwall Way, is a place known traditionally as Blackwall Stairs where the remnants of apparently very old wooden stairs are visible at low tide. Local lore has it that the Virginia legion of men and boys boarded the three ships for Virginia there in December of 1606. Nearby and standing until at least 1897, was what the local historians call the Sir Walter Raleigh House, a Tudor half timber structure that served as an Inn where travelers, presumably once Sir Walter himself, awaited transport out of the Thames.[31] This is conceivably the freshest memory of an English house that most of the future Jamestown settlers would carry with them during the tedious unending crossing to the New World. There must have been great longing to return to that rugged inn and the alehouses of Blackwall when the three supposedly outbound ships lay becalmed in bone-chilling weather near the mouth of the Thames for over a month. So the hopeful 108 colonists got *nowhere* for almost half of the anticipated entire length of the voyage.[32] Who were these shivering, frustrated men and boys waiting for the winds and their fortunes to change?

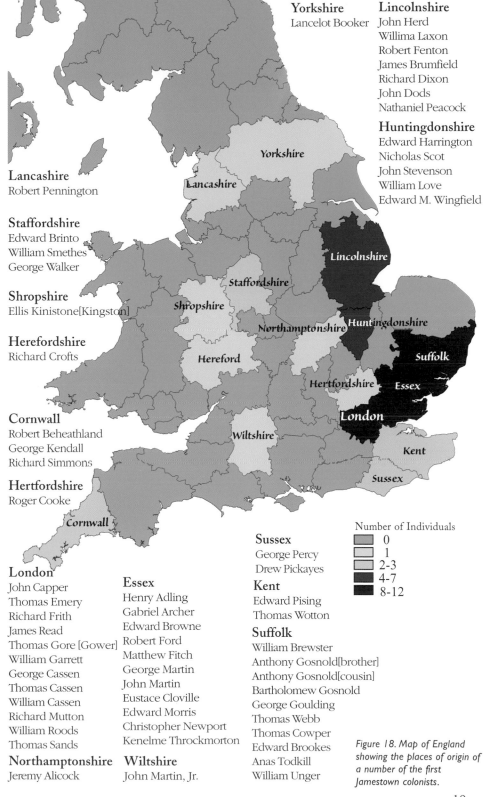

Yorkshire
Lancelot Booker

Lincolnshire
John Herd
Willima Laxon
Robert Fenton
James Brumfield
Richard Dixon
John Dods
Nathaniel Peacock

Huntingdonshire
Edward Harrington
Nicholas Scot
John Stevenson
William Love
Edward M. Wingfield

Lancashire
Robert Pennington

Staffordshire
Edward Brinto
William Smethes
George Walker

Shropshire
Ellis Kinistone[Kingston]

Herefordshire
Richard Crofts

Cornwall
Robert Beheathland
George Kendall
Richard Simmons

Hertfordshire
Roger Cooke

London
John Capper
Thomas Emery
Richard Frith
James Read
Thomas Gore [Gower]
William Garrett
George Cassen
Thomas Cassen
William Cassen
Richard Mutton
William Roods
Thomas Sands

Northamptonshire
Jeremy Alicock

Essex
Henry Adling
Gabriel Archer
Edward Browne
Robert Ford
Matthew Fitch
George Martin
John Martin
Eustace Cloville
Edward Morris
Christopher Newport
Kenelme Throckmorton

Wiltshire
John Martin, Jr.

Sussex
George Percy
Drew Pickayes

Kent
Edward Pising
Thomas Wotton

Suffolk
William Brewster
Anthony Gosnold[brother]
Anthony Gosnold[cousin]
Bartholomew Gosnold
George Goulding
Thomas Webb
Thomas Cowper
Edward Brookes
Anas Todkill
William Unger

Number of Individuals
0
1
2-3
4-7
8-12

Figure 18. Map of England showing the places of origin of a number of the first Jamestown colonists.

19

Figure 19. Otley Hall, Suffolk, England, the moated manor house of Bartholomew Gosnold's uncle, possibly the meeting place where Gosnold, Edward Maria Wingfield, Christopher Newport, John Smith and Richard Hakluyt planned the Jamestown voyage and settlement. The meeting room (right) with former owner Nicholas Hagger (left) and author (right).

Of course, certain biographical facts are commonly known about some of the Jamestown leaders. We know, for example, something of the members of the first council selected by the Virginia Company before the voyage and made known to them when they opened a sealed box upon reaching the Virginia shore: Edward Maria Wingfield, John Martin, Captain George Kendall, John Ratcliffe, Bartholomew Gosnold, and Captain John Smith.[33] They all had military/combat experience either acquired in the 80-year wars in the Netherlands, privateering, or during the establishment of the English plantations in Ireland. Captain John Smith had the Dutch experience, plus he fought in France and Transylvania. Gosnold led the capture of a prize of a Spanish Galleon and took a colonizing party to briefly settle off Cape Cod in 1602. Except for Smith, they all were gentry, some urban and some rural. What is not so well known are their ages, which ranged from the oldest, Wingfield, who was 57, to the youngest, Smith, 27. The rest of the Council were in their 40s, except Gosnold, who was 36 and Kendall 37. Their average age was 40. At a time when 56 was the average life expectancy, these men were primarily "seniors."[34] So the younger, commoner Smith does not seem to fit the norm. The rest of the party, for whom biographical data has been determined so far, ranged in age from the 46-year-old Christopher Newport of Harwich to 9-year-old James Brumfield of Lincolnshire. The average age of the non-council men was about 25.[35]

The settlers' home parishes and probably their family seats were overwhelmingly either the greater London area, including the Kent/Sussex counties to the southeast and Essex; Suffolk; the greater Peterborough area, and John Smith's Lincolnshire. The greatest number of all the original colonists for which a place of origin could be possibly determined are the 12 who came from the city of London, but an equal number came from the greater London area and East Anglia. There seems to be a difference between the greater London area and East Anglia in ages at the time the Virginia fleet sailed, with the younger individuals coming from the river "port" town areas of Suffolk, Norfolk, Lincolnshire and Cambridgeshire. A small percent came from other towns or counties but not from any one other particular region in England. Fourteen came with relatives: cousins, father-sons, and brothers. Six had some kinship with Gosnold.[36]

From these statistics, admittedly determined from cursory research still in progress, one still might speculate how and why these men and boys wound up filing down those Blackwall stairs to begin their Virginia adventure. Of course, the prospect for finding gold was considered to be a realistic expectation, but there were also promises of assignments of land in Virginia to planters or adventurers.[37] It is logical to assume that many of the immigrants were the younger sons of gentry, with little prospects of inheriting the family lands in England. Where it can be determined from records so far, that was the case for at least six of the gentlemen and probably for a majority of the remaining 22 for whom older siblings could

Figure 20. Otley High House, Suffolk, the manor of Gosnold's father, Anthony.

not be determined. For example, the gentleman Bartholomew Gosnold had an older brother. Prospects for acquiring land in Virginia must have been appealing to these younger gentlemen. That seems to have been true of immigrants well into the 17th century.[38] But it seems that land could not be the primary consideration for many others. At least three other gentlemen, including Wingfield and Martin, were the eldest sons in their families.[39] Clearly, they were gentlemen with other motives, perhaps just the adventure of it all in its own right.

But obviously, the men and boys had to at least learn about the voyage before they could possibly sign on to go. How did the word get out in an age when only one in ten could read and where the roads were hardly passable? The distribution patterns of geographic origins may be a clue.[40] They suggest that getting the word out can be attributed to the principle leaders. It is logical to assume that the settlers from London simply learned of the venture through the promotional program of the Virginia Company based there. In fact, Gosnold's cousin was Thomas Smythe, the London merchant, *"whose wealth and influence played so large a part in the formation of the first Virginia Company,"* and who may have had a personal hand in collecting the London recruits himself.[41] It is clear that Gosnold gathered the leaders and many of the other first settlers from among his East Anglian friends, neighbors and relatives. He must have been a particularly effective promoter, as he, like few others, could tell firsthand of what the Atlantic voyage would be all about and describe "Virginia." It was indeed Gosnold who was the admiral of the 1602 Cuttyhunk colony near Cape Cod. Despite the fact that the colony only lasted a month, it is almost certain that Gosnold would have been able to assure his listeners that the new Virginia adventure would be different. He had learned from the Norumbrian (New England) shortcomings and successes. He could well have said with conviction that the south of Virginia was a paradise in comparison to the northern latitudes.[42]

John Smith does credit Gosnold with being the principle promoter of the Virginia venture.[43] Born in 1571 near Ipswich, Suffolk, Gosnold with his brother Anthony and sisters Elizabeth and Margaret attended school at his uncle John's moated manor, Otley Hall, likely the site of future Virginia colony planning sessions. His uncle became secretary to the Earl of Essex, and it was through this family connection, that Gosnold became a daring mariner, venturing to the Azores in 1597 and privateering against the Spanish where he accumulated his booty. Essex next intended to fund a New World voyage to include Gosnold, but Essex's implication in the 1601 Essex Rebellion and his ultimate execution left Gosnold no support for the trip. It was not until the following year that the Earl of Southampton, Wingfield's cousin, stepped forward to fund the Cuttyhunk colony. But despite that rather limited attempt at colonization, Gosnold became known as an outstanding mariner and immediately began planning the attempt to sail to the southern coast of America. By 1605, the plans for a southern colony led by Gosnold were much advanced, and by then included Wingfield, Gosnold's cousin, and Gosnold's friend, soldier, traveler, John Smith. In on the planning as well was Richard Hakluyt, the nearby vicar of All Saints Church, Weatheringsett and the King's official geographer. It was Hakluyt who put into print the most vivid accounts of the English explorations in the New World and the most forceful and convincing arguments for founding English colonies. Otley Hall may have been used as the forum for the planning meetings of these promoter/ friends and as a base for recruiting men from the vicinity. Judging from the way the East Anglian hometowns cluster on the map of Southeastern England, it is logical to assume that Gosnold was an accomplished recruiter for the Virginia venture from the environs of Otley.

When the fleet sailed, however, Christopher Newport became the commanding admiral, and Wingfield, a chief stockholder in the Virginia Company, an aspiring governor. It was the experienced mariner, but second in command, Gosnold, who had to watch helplessly as the fleet floundered in the mouth of the Thames for almost the entire first month of the voyage. Gosnold also must have been frustrated enduring Newport's long southern route to Virginia via the Canary and West Indian Islands when he already knew the benefit of the faster northern route. It was, in fact, at their first stop in the Canary Islands that Gosnold's friends, John Smith, Stephen Calthrope, and apparently a John Robinson, were implicated in a mutiny. Smith was "*restrained*" probably in chains and by the time the fleet got to Nevis in the Virgin Islands, Newport ordered gallows to be constructed to hang him. The hanging never happened, possibly because of the intervention of Gosnold.

We pick up the Jamestown story again in Virginia. Unfortunately, after lingering for three weeks, the talented Gosnold died of an unknown illness at Jamestown on August 22, 1607, and was buried in or near James Fort with full military honors.[44] By the fall of 1607, according to Smith, 67 of the original 108 settlers had died, and George Percy recorded the deaths of 24 Gentlemen, one laborer and two others during the months of August and September 1607.[45] The greatest number of the gentlemen, 11 of the 16 who were reported by Percy as having died, came from London.[46] The rest of the summer, those who died had come to Virginia from just about every other region in England. It is perhaps significant, however, that the men Captain John Smith took with him during his two voyages of "*discovery*" that summer, one to the Falls of the James and the other into the Chesapeake, included the men and boys from his home area of Lincolnshire and Norfolk. They were apparently among those who survived the summer death toll. At least George Percy did not add them to his death list. Of course they were away from Jamestown Island during the real heat of the summer, sailing on the open water which gives more

Figure 21. Probable boundaries of Powhatan's influence known as Tsenacomacah.

credence to the assumption that Jamestown Island with its marshes and no fresh spring water caused the demise of so many so fast. On the other hand, perhaps Smith chose the strongest and healthiest of the group to go with him, thus culling out the people who could just as well have survived had they stayed at the fort.

The story of Jamestown traditionally focuses on the story of Smith and other leaders, so much so that a number of people whose actions affected the settlement immeasurably became invisible. John Smith listed 213 settlers' names among the first few Jamestown voyages and dismissed the rest of the unnamed people as mere "*diverse others.*"[47] Then and later, there were indeed a number of traditionally anonymous "diverse others" who were essential during the early Virginia Company period to assure that Jamestown would be permanent: the Virginia Indians, eventually the English women, and surprisingly, the Spanish. The archaeology of James Fort certainly testifies to their presence and a focused look into the records, as meager as they are, can tell more of their stories than one might expect.

The choice of the site of Jamestown has long been maligned by historians, owing to the unhealthy nature of the low-lying marshy island and the fact that it lay deep within Powhatan's territory. Those negatives are both so true. The island is so low-lying today that 80 percent is below the predicted 100-year 8 ½' flood level. [48] There also were no springs, so only brackish river water or shallow wells could serve the colony, a fact often listed as contributing to Jamestown's high death rates. So why choose this place? Percy claims proximity to the channel, but it is clear that the experienced military leaders saw some high ground and the surrounding water as a natural defense against the real and the perceived enemies: the Tsenacomacans and the Spanish.

The Tsenacomacans? In 1612, William Strachey, who became Secretary of the colony, wrote:

> *The severall territoryes and provinces which are in chief commaunded by their great king Powhatan, are comprehended under the donomynation of Tsenacommacoh, of which we may the more by experience speak being the place wherein our abode and habitation hath now well neere six years consisted.*[49]

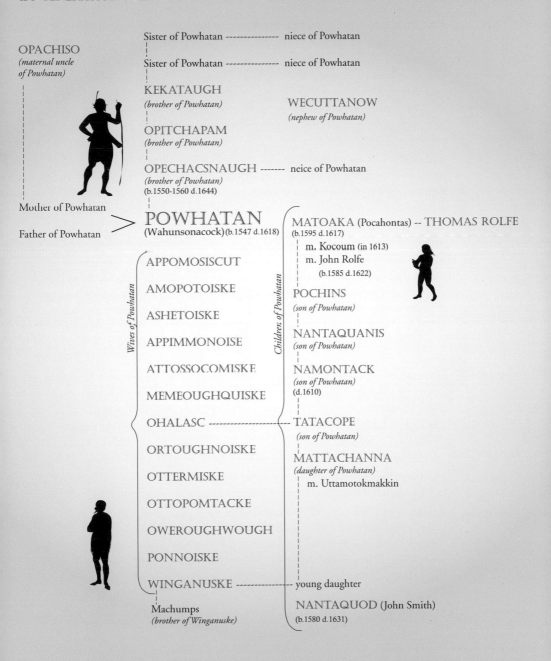

1ST GENERATION   2ND GENERATION   3RD GENERATION   4TH GENERATION

OPACHISO   Sister of Powhatan -------------- niece of Powhatan
*(maternal uncle
of Powhatan)*   Sister of Powhatan -------------- niece of Powhatan

                        KEKATAUGH
                        (brother of Powhatan)   WECUTTANOW
                                                          (nephew of Powhatan)
                        OPITCHAPAM
                        (brother of Powhatan)

                        OPECHACSNAUGH ------- neice of Powhatan
Mother of Powhatan   *(brother of Powhatan)*
                        (b.1550-1560 d.1644)

Father of Powhatan   > POWHATAN   MATOAKA (Pocahontas) -- THOMAS ROLFE
                        (Wahunsonacock)(b.1547 d.1618)   (b.1595 d.1617)
                                                            m. Kocoum (in 1613)
                        APPOMOSISCUT   m. John Rolfe
                                                              (b.1585 d.1622)
                        AMOPOTOISKE
                                                          POCHINS
                        ASHETOISKE   *(son of Powhatan)*

                        APPIMMONOISE   NANTAQUANIS
                                                          (son of Powhatan)
                        ATTOSSOCOMISKE
                                                          NAMONTACK
                        MEMEOUGHQUISKE   *(son of Powhatan)*
                                                          (d.1610)
                        OHALASC ----------------------- TATACOPE
                                                            (son of Powhatan)
                        ORTOUGHNOISKE
                                                          MATTACHANNA
                        OTTERMISKE   *(daughter of Powhatan)*
                                                            m. Uttamotokmakkin
                        OTTOPOMTACKE

                        OWEROUGHWOUGH

                        PONNOISKE

                        WINGANUSKE -------------- young daughter

                        Machumps   NANTAQUOD (John Smith)
                        (brother of Winganuske)   (b.1580 d.1631)

Figure 22. Hypothetical Powhatan family tree based on English sources.

25

Tsenacomacah presumably was the Native American name of the territory under the control of Powhatan, or the native name of the part of "Virginia" explored and first settled by the English. The native people then are Tsenacomacans. But not so to the English. To most Englishmen, the people they met at various places along the banks of the rivers were called variously: savages, salvages, naturals, natives, barbarians, heathens or Indians. Today many refer to the native people as Powhatans, which makes about as much sense as referring to people living in England then as Jamesians. They were in fact Tsenacomacans. But the traditional names would not do. The Powhatan River, became the King River named for King James I.[50] Of course the King also claimed all of Tsenacomacah and beyond to the western sea and north to modern New Jersey, as long as no other "Christian" nations had any settlements there. Thus, English names really replaced Tsenacomacan terms as a first phase of the establishment of an English population to replace the Tsenacomacans themselves. To rename places with English names meant conquest. After all, in the eyes of many of the English, the land was vacant except for the "savages" who were more like other forms of wildlife on the "untamed" landscape. But quite to the contrary, Tsenacomacah to the natives was a very real "nation" with a sophisticated language, customs, government and economy. They had their own names for themselves, their villages, their rivers and even the new English arrivals, Tassantasses (King James and his people). [51] We can know this only and ironically, from English accounts even though by their very nature they are observations of a biased "foreign" culture. Nonetheless these "snapshots" of Tsenacomacans, even if viewed in a cultural-centric "western genealogical" framework, become a profile of a very significant group of players in the Jamestown story. Doing this adds a more balanced ethno-historical and humanistic quality to the beginnings of Anglo-America.

The southern-most river in Tsenacomacah was the Powhatan (modern James River), named for the long-time native leader of the united chiefdom that greeted the English colonists in 1607. Who was he? Some speculate he was the cousin of Don Luis, who met the Jesuit settlers of the Chesapeake in 1570.[52] It was Don Luis who went to Spain with the Jesuits and upon return led a massacre of the missionaries. Regardless of his cousin's identity, Powhatan is almost invariably characterized by the English as the single-most powerful chief among the Virginia Indians.

> He is of parsonage a tall well proportioned man, with a sower looke,
> his head somewhat gray, his beard so thinne that it seemeth none
> at al, his age near 60; of a very able and hardy body to endure any
> labor. [53]

Powhatan (Wahunsonacock) was the head of a huge family for which we can know some measure of genealogy. A variety of records, mainly Smith's *General History*, and Strachey's *Historie of Travell Into Virginia*

Britania, list the names of 30 of Powhatan's relatives and in-laws (see Figure 22).[54] Of his three named brothers, the most can be known of Opechancanough, werowance (chief) of the principle village on what the Tsenacomacans called the Pamunky River (modern York River). Upon Powhatan's death in 1618, Opechankanaugh became ruler either after or along with another brother, Opitchapam. Opechankanaugh led two devastating assaults against the English in 1622 and 1644. When he was over 90 years old, Opechankanaugh was shot and killed at Jamestown where he was imprisoned after the 1644 attacks on the English settlements.[55]

One source claims Powhatan had "...*many more than one hundred*" wives. The names of at least a dozen of them are recorded.[56] One wife, Oholasc, served as Queen of Quiyoughcohannock. The names of seven children of Powhatan's five sons and two daughters are also on record. Three sons were werowances and the fourth, Nantaquawis, was described by Captain John Smith as the "...*manliest, comliest and the boldest spirit I ever saw in a salvage*."[57] Smith was himself an adopted son of Powhatan, who named him Nantaquoud.[58] Much is known, of course about his favorite daughter, Pocahontas. And while the other daughter, Mattachanna, is only mentioned by Smith, it is known that she married Uttamkokmakkin (Tomocomo), a priest who traveled with Pocahontas and her English husband, John Rolfe, to England in 1616-1617.[59] Tomocomo was not impressed with the land of the strange Tassantassians, but apparently, Pocahontas was. Lord Carew, in a letter to Sir Thomas Roe in 1616/1617, wrote that she waited "*reluctantly*" for favorable winds for her return voyage, though sorely against her will. In the end, she died before sailing to Virginia.[60] She is buried at St. George's church, Gravesend, presumably under the chancel of the church that burned in the early-18th century. Because of that fire and the rebuilding of the church, Pocahontas's exact burial spot remains a challenging puzzle for archaeologists and interested direct descendants of the Jamestown colony.[61]

Besides Uttamtokmakkin and Pocahontas, there are records that a number of individual Tsenacomacans spent time with the English. Kemps, an Indian prisoner in the fort, taught the colonists to raise corn, and while he was a slave of George Percy, he guided the English during raids on the "*Pasbeheans and the Chiconamians*."[62] Pepasschicher also guided the English. Mantiuas, also called Nantaquawis, a son of Powhatan, traveled with them, and Muchamps was "*sometyme in England*." Powhatan had Amarice killed for staying in the fort without his permission.[63] It is a fact that Pocahontas married John Rolfe in 1613. Her first husband was an Indian named Kocoum.[64] In asking permission from Sir Thomas Dale to marry, Rolfe seems to be indirectly saying that this was both frowned upon by the English and/or an intercultural marriage would be unusual. The fact seems to be that indeed intermarriage was officially scorned. But un-

Figure 23. Oderatus by Frederik Bloemaert, b. 1610. Reminiscent of Mistress Forest and her maid Ann Burras who were the first English women to come to "Blockhouse" Jamestown, 1609.

officially, there is strong reason to suspect considerable mixing of the two cultures: the all-male population of the settlement during the first 16 months, the fact that the Spanish reported in 1612 as many as "*…40 or 50 of the men had married with the salvages…*" and the quantity of Tsenacomacan artifacts found archaeologically in good historical desposits in the earliest features at Jamestown. [65]

Despite the co-mingling of the Tsenacomacans and the Tassantassians of either gender, disaster almost wiped the colony out during the Starving Time of 1609-10. Some Virginia Indians besieged the fort that winter, and it was so effective that "*…it is true that the Indians killed as fast without, if our men stirred but beyond their bounds of their blockhouse, as famine and pestilence did within.*"[66] Recent recognition of a serious drought in Virginia 1606-1613 may have been the reason the Tsenacomacans stopped supplying food to the settlers. On the other hand, it may be that the arrival at Jamestown of 20 women and children on the *Blessing* sent too strong a sign to the locals that the English were here to stay.[67] Extermination of the invaders may have appeared to be the only course of action. Whatever the effect the immigration of women and children had on Tsenacomacan "foreign policy," they constitute another group of anonymous "diverse others" who deserve credit for the permanence of the colony.

The first English women, Mistress Forrest and Ann Burras, came to the colony in the fall of 1608. They were not the only English women in town for long, however. According to the Spanish ambassador to England/spy, Pedro de Zúñiga, there were 100 women (among) the 400 or 500 men in the Gates 1609 flotilla to the colony.[68] Of course, the *Blessing* women accounted for twenty of these, but we can be reasonably sure that perhaps half the remaining 80 arrived as the remains of the fleet limped into the Jamestown port during the summer of 1609, and with the Bermuda ships *Deliverance* and *Patience* that arrived at Jamestown in May 1610.[69] The names of the Blessing women are not known, but Temperance Flowerdew, wife of the future Governor, Sir George Yeardley, came in 1609 as did Thomasine Cawsey, Elizabeth Joones and Amtyte Waine. They were all apparently in town with the 20 or more women who came with the *Bless-ing* and other supply ships just in time for them to experience the "starv-ing" winter of 1609-1610. The list of named women grows to 35 by 1618 if the dates and the census of 1624-25 are reliable.[70] Sir Thomas Gates and his daughters, Margaret and Elizabeth, arrived in 1611.[71] There must have been hundreds of anonymous "diverse other" women who braved the crossing and the "seasoning time" of a Virginia summer. It is likely that the three female burials uncovered by archaeologists beneath the third and fourth statehouse foundations on the western edge of the town site, may be evidence that few of that group could survive at Jamestown for long. All three were dead before the age of 34.[72]

The siege of James Fort almost ended the colony, for the two Bermuda-built ships came not only with women, but with far too few provisions for a starving colony and themselves. So by June 1610, Gates decided to move the survivors out of Jamestown and set sail for England. Thanks to what has been characterized as last-second divine intervention, an advance vessel followed by the arriving Governor De La Warre and abundant fresh sup-plies turned the deserters back to Jamestown in what seemed to be the nick of time. But a more careful reading of De La Warre's account of that so-called chance meeting reveals that "after" he had met the two depart-ing Jamestown ships, he learned that Gates knew De La Warre was on his way, and Gates was going to wait for him for "*ten days at Cape* (Point) *Comfort…*" at the mouth of the James. After that time he was to "*…oth-erwise so to go for England…*" with whatever he had left on board of his 30 days rations.[73] This waiting period made good sense. Upon his arrival in the James from Bermuda two months earlier, Gates found 30 people with Percy at Point Comfort, literally healthy as clams, living off the seafood there. They had thrived while their fellow colonists held the fort and died like "*dogges.*" So it would be fair to conclude that even if De la Warre ar-rived 11 days later than he did, Gates and the migrating Jamestownians, revived by the Point Comfort seafood, would have chosen to wait longer for De La Warre. Why chance an ocean crossing with meager supplies or risk sailing north to the Grand Fishing Banks with only a hope of finding food and a flotilla home to England? In any case, believing that luck alone saved a failed Jamestown seems to be an exaggeration.

It seems probable that the Tsenacomacan siege of James Fort and the alarming death rate during the Starving Time winter was to some degree

Figure 24. Diplomatic maneuvering of King Philip III (left) of Spain and King James I (below) by chance and by design allow early Jamestown to survive and take root.

brought on by the serious drought. No one could grow food. And surely the arrival of the English women and children was a clear sign to the Indians that James Fort was no mere trading post. There is another group of "*diverse others*" playing or actually *not* playing significant roles in the early James Fort events, the Catholic Spanish. It is clear from the eventual archaeological recovery of a Catholic crucifix, rosary beads, and medallions that Spanish Catholics were probably represented somehow in town. Of course, the first president, Edward Maria Wingfield, and perhaps other Englishmen had strong Catholic backgrounds, and the arrest and execution of Captain George Kendall seems to have been carried out because he was a suspected agent of the Spanish.[74] It is also clear that the Spanish King, Philip III, received a steady stream of secret information he was getting directly from a "*confidential person on His Majestie's* [English] *Council*" concerning Jamestown events and details.[75] The settlement was in a precarious place indeed according to the Spanish. A letter from the Spanish ambassador in London, Don Pedro de Zúñiga reported to Philip details of Zúñiga's conference with James I, whereby he claimed King James himself said that if the Spanish want to "*punish*" (remove) the Jamestown colonists, "*neither he nor they could complain.*" In fact, according to Zúñiga, King James called the Jamestown colonists, "*terrible people.*" Zúñiga was almost certainly exaggerating, trying to maneuver Philip to send troops to wipe out the colony, for in all his surviving letters he consistently urges Philip III to do this.[76] Regardless of what James did say and his stance on Jamestown, there was clearly a desire on the part of the Spanish to erase it from their "Indies." On January 17, 1608, Philip III endorsed a plan proposed by his Council of War whereby he "*command*[ed] *that there should be prepared whatever was necessary to drive out the people who are in Virginia...*[and] *not to let anyone hear what is being done.*"[77] Presumably the plan was to send a fleet that was then lying at the Windward Islands and had been preparing for some time to sail to Jamestown to annihilate it. But there seems to have been another "final solution" proposed to the King, which would involve a double agent at Jamestown.

In another letter to King Philip, written in March, 1609, Zúñiga refers to his dealings with Baron Arundel, a disgruntled English Catholic, who proposed to act as a spy for the Spanish by sailing on the pretext of a voyage of discovery, chose a man in Puerto Rico whom the King needed to appoint to be the real spy at Jamestown, take him to Jamestown and instruct him about the geography of the James River region and the nature of the English forts there so that he could relate to King Philip: "*by what means those people can be driven out without violence in arms.*"[78] What "*means*" to erase Jamestown the Baron had in mind without firing a shot is a mystery. One theory is that a Spanish agent be sent to secretly lace the common kettle with arsenic. This would explain the periodic mass deaths at Jamestown.[79] This of course cannot explain the deaths that occurred before March 1609, (66 in 1607 summer, and 13 in 1608).[80] Also what Arundel proposes is really a *plan* about a *plan*.

Plan One is the proposition that as soon as the King gets around to approving the plan (two months for letters to go to and return from Spain-May 1?) Arundel would be sent trans-Atlantic (6 weeks, June 15?) to pick up the King's handpicked agent in Puerto Rico. From there they would sail to Virginia (1 month, July 15?) to spy on Jamestown and the English and their fortifications (1 month? August 15?). Then after all that time, Arundel had to inform the King either in person or by letter that the spy mission was complete, which, in either case, requires yet another trans-Atlantic voyage back to Spain, (2 months, October 15?). Only then could the English be removed without recourse to arms which is really Plan Two. But before Plan Two could be implemented, it would involve yet another approval of the King whose message of "yes" or "no" would then have to cross the Atlantic again (2 more months, December 15?) to be either carried out or not carried out by agent X and possibly Arundel (unknown amount of time). So this entire scenario would require nine months at best (March-December), provided 1609 was a rare non-hurricane year. Granted there still could be enough time for agent X or Arundel to poison all but 60 of the 215 people left at Jamestown, January-April, 1610.

But Philip III also wrote after he read of the proposed Arundel scheme that he did not approve of dealing with Arundel. He replied to Zúñiga that he should act with *"great caution with the Baron of Arundel."*[81] Over the next two years, the King merely kept asking for inside information about the colony without giving the green light to crush it.[82] It is speculation, but it is possible that Arundel knew that the population of the colony probably had had enough of Virginia, and any offer to be ferried back to England might look far better than an impending winter without Smith's negotiating talents with the Indians.[83] Or maybe he thought it possible to gain enough of Powhatan's trust to persuade him to stage a more concerted siege of the fort. Then Jamestown would indeed be wiped out without resorting to Spanish arms.

The fact that the Windward Island fleet never sailed to Virginia and that the Spanish let Jamestown take root by neglect, by chance or design, has turned out to be one of the greatest diplomatic success stories in the history of the English nation. And thanks to what these *"diverse other"* Spanish did not do, Jamestown survived.

Figure 25. The Somerset House Conference 1604. This historic meeting between Spanish and English diplomats ended 20 years of fighting among the English, Spanish and the Dutch. The resulting peace treaty removed a good measure of the threat of Spanish sea power from the challenges of English North American colonization.

Chapter II
Finding James Fort

Figure 26. Aerial view of James Fort site with archaeological plan overlay.

So clearly the Jamestown documentary story is disappointingly lean during the reign of the Virginia Company, 1607-1624. There is precious little to go on besides the relatively meager accounts of Percy, Smith, Strachey and Hamor. Attempts to reconstruct the growth and development of the colony under the Virginia Company from documents alone are frustrating. It is true then that, in the words of one prominent Jamestown historian, "whatever we can learn that is new about early Jamestown will have to come from archaeology."[1] So from the beginning in 1994, the overall goal of the *Jamestown Rediscovery* excavations was to locate and uncover any remains of the first Jamestown settlement, especially traces of James Fort as it was originally constructed, and how it evolved to accommodate a growing population during the Virginia Company years, 1607-1624.[2] This seemed to be a mission impossible. It was the opinion of various visitors to Jamestown Island beginning as early at 1837, and most archaeologists, that all traces of the James Fort settlement had been washed away by the James River shoreline erosion.[3]

Figure 27. View of Jamestown Island showing extent of agricultural fields prior to 1930.

Now it is clear after ten seasons of digging that the exact opposite is true: the archaeological remains of the early settlement are essentially intact. It took ten challenging seasons, but by July 2003, excavations have uncovered enough surviving traces of James Fort to define the complete triangle. To be so positive about the fort's archaeological survival took the sum total of almost every shred of evidence found during that decade of digging. Since most people were so sure, and so sure for so long, that the fort had been located on the extremely eroded western end of the island, proof to the contrary had to be extraordinarily conclusive. The case had to be backed up by the unearthing of a clear architectural form that fit 17th-century eyewitness descriptions, meager and ambiguous as they were. The discovery of palisade wall fragments here and there, scattered building remains, and a few deposits of artifacts of a military nature dating to the 1607 period would not be enough to prove anything. After all, those remains could be evidence of a fortified area that grew up somewhat later than the original 1607 palisaded structure. Yet, a concerted effort over the years has recovered enough large and meaningful segments of the remains of palisade walls, military-type building sites, and the sealed deposits of thousands of English and Virginia Indian artifacts dating to the late-16th and early-17th centuries to prove, beyond reasonable doubt, that the early fort site still existed on dry land.[4]

This archaeological proof could only be mustered by a deliberate, ever-expanding excavation going from one excavated area to an adjoining area where the apparent pattern of fort period fragments led. What happened on the Jamestown site in the century after 1699 when the capital moved to Williamsburg and most occupants abandoned the buildings and the town, both helped and hindered that step-by-step archaeological process of excavation. During those years the land slowly reverted to agricultural fields. On the one hand, that was good news for future archaeology. With the exception of the construction of a Confederate earthen fort in 1861, no extensive post-town, ground-disturbing construction took place to destroy the buried evidence of occupation. No modern town, such as Plymouth, Massachusetts, for example, grew into and over the original town site to eventually obliterate and conceal whatever 17th-century remains might be there to discover. On the other hand, the eventual plowing of the Jamestown site was bad news for archaeologists. Plowing the land for farming on Jamestown Island blended the upper foot or so of the heretofore intact layers of 17th-century town remains. Objects left on the site through the 17th century were mixed together in the plow zone as one layer, making it difficult to determine what came before what, in time. So archaeological removal of the "plow zone" exposes all surviving bits of James Fort and other 17th-century features all at once, regardless of the sequence through time of the events that created them. For example, a 1607 period hole that once held a wall post and a filled-in drainage ditch that once marked a 1680 property line would appear archaeologically to be from the same moment in time. Plowing destroyed any evidence of soil levels, deposited one on top of the other, that could have proved that the 1607 post hole and the 1680 property line were from different periods of time. But not all was lost. The plow only went so deep, usually a foot or so, a level that could be shoveled off and the artifacts retrieved in screens relatively quickly. This made possible an excavation process that could be categorized as the "quilt" method. That is to say, once the digging has lifted the plow zone, the excavation progresses by adding one 10' square at a time, revealing the nature of the original town design and direction of walls, buildings, ditches, pits, and graves.

The quilt method literally "followed" the trail of the Jamestown remains. Then, as the excavated angles of walls and buildings datable to the first quarter of the 17th century took on a triangular form, Percy's 1607 "*triangular-wise*" palisaded fort with "*half-moon*" bastions took shape. The archaeological evidence was accumulative and, finally, as conclusive as it can get in historical archaeology. Ten excavation seasons have uncovered over 300 "patches" of the quilt, one discovery laying the groundwork for the next. Bit by bit, from 1994-2003, James Fort emerged from its earthen shroud.

Deciding where to begin in the first place was the key to eventual success. Twenty-two and a half acres of the island, acquired by APVA, were no small shroud. Three theories narrowed the field. First, it made sense that churches rarely move from original locations sanctified by prayer and human burials. Why should the church at James Fort be any exception?

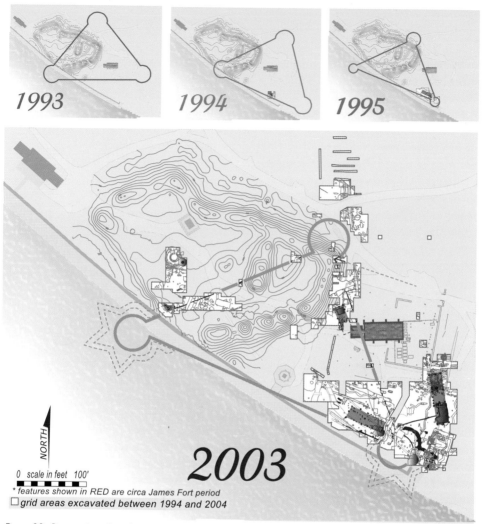

2003

NORTH

0   scale in feet   100'

* features shown in RED are circa James Fort period
□ grid areas excavated between 1994 and 2004

Figure 28. Progression of predictive models of James Fort based on documentary
sources corrected over time as discoveries honed in on its precise location in 2003.

The Jamestown church according to one eyewitness was in or near the
middle of the triangle that was the fort. If that were true, then initial digging between the shore of the river and the church tower, which is the
only above-ground remnant of 17th-century Jamestown, should intersect
the fort's south wall line. Another obvious assumption was that the
Jamestown Rediscovery groundbreaking ought to be located where military and industrial objects datable to the first quarter of the 17th century
had already been found. In fact, by chance and by design, military and
industrial artifacts have been found in the vicinity of the church tower at
various times during the first 60 years of APVA ownership. And finally,
documentary descriptions and a sketch from ca. 1608 support a theoreti-
cal fort plan in enough detail that it could be transposed upon the modern churchyard landscape, and give some guidance for the initial digging.

The measurements recorded by William Strachey set the scale for the initial digging, with the assumption that Strachey's measurements were the distances of what he called the fort's curtain, which is technically defined as the distance of a fort's walls between the usual extended corners or bulwarks.[5] Assuming also that the bulwarks were large enough accomodate cannons on record (50' in diameter) then the hypothetical fort became 1.75-acres in size. The central church served to anchor the hypothetical fort to the modern landscape.

As fragments of the actual fort were unearthed, however, the superimposed size of the estimated fort migrated west and finally shrank from its assumed church-tower center and 1.75-acre size. In other words, ongoing archaeological discoveries corrected and re-corrected the hypothetical fort model until it finally fit precisely onto the modern landscape. The process evolved in time as follows.

The first discovery in 1994 was a section of palisade trench along the river and a parallel line of postholes close to the trench. This discovery served to anchor the hypothetical south wall of the document-based plan, but the fort still floated hypothetically on the land in all three remaining directions.

By September 1996, the discovery of a moat and curved wall trench and segments of a palisade trench extending to the north formed a corner of the fort (bulwark), thus anchoring the plan to the east. Discovery of this bulwark and east wall also provided enough evidence to conclude that the fort did indeed exist on land and that most of it could be uncovered in time. Still the size and extent of the fort to the north and west remained open-ended. But determining the bounds in those directions had to wait.

The appearance of another early palisade striking off to the east of the bulwark and a related building site attached to it claimed several excavation seasons of work to trace and determine what role this additional fort period construction played in the overall fortification scheme (1997-1999). At the same time, attempts to skip along the projected east wall line in search of a north bulwark produced some more of the wall but no bulwark (1999-2001). It was not until the last possible projected segment of east wall and extensive area within the Civil War earthwork were opened up, that the model and the ground could be brought together with precision (2002-2003). The hypothetical model and the actual site became a perfect fit at last.

Over a span of the ten seasons (1994-2003), all the angles and corners found on the ground transformed the model from a guess to the real thing. But mere "claims" to finding something as important as ground zero of the "genesis" of the United States of America needs detailed proof. That case follows, piece by piece.

Again, the first season of excavations found remnants of the south palisade. In the wall section that survived, appearing as a distinct black streak

Figure 29. The site of James Fort as it appeared below the plow zone in the South church yard, October, 1994.

in the surrounding yellow undisturbed clay, careful excavation showed clear impressions of decayed circular or beveled upright timbers 5" to 1' in diameter. There even appeared to be a pattern in their diameters as one progressed along the line—large, medium and small—as if each tree had been sectioned into thirds and erected accordingly. At three positions along and just inside the line, postholes and post soil marks appeared, undoubtedly signs of larger support or buttressing posts for the line. This strongly suggests that the palisade was a high, heavy wall. Importantly, the trench was also straight-sided, and flat-bottomed, which are requirements for a trench dug to firmly support palisades rather than a ditch for drainage.

The form of the wall trench, and the soil stains left by decayed posts in the main wall trench, leave little doubt of the former existence of a palisade there. But whether or not it was the wall of James Fort depended on establishing its date of construction and how long it lasted. Finding datable artifacts in fill deposited during construction and destruction was the key. Excavation of 30 feet of the soil where logs in the fort wall and one support post had decayed recovered a few artifacts, all dating no later than ca. 1610. A very crude clay tobacco pipe and a ceramic crucible base found in the fill of a support post appear so similar to those found at a 1585 minerals lab workshop site at Fort Raleigh, North Carolina, that they likely dated to the early James Fort years.[6] A 15th- to early-17th-century Venetian glass trade bead (Nueva Cadiz), a late-16th-century Scottish snaphaunce pistol lock, and a Hans Krauwinckel (1586-1635) casting counter (German calculating token) were found where some of the palisade timber once stood as well. These artifacts suggested that the palisade

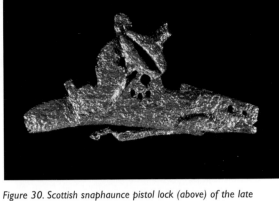

dates to the earliest years of settlement. And these artifacts are even
more convincing of an early date
for the wall line when one consid-
ers that the palisade objects came
out of the space once occupied by
the individual palisade posts, not
the soil packed around them during construction. Only occasional
bits of prehistoric pottery came
from that construction fill. This
means, in all probability, that only
pre-1607 Virginia Indians and not

Figure 30. Scottish snaphaunce pistol lock (above) of the late 16th century, Hans Krauwinckel casting counter, and Nueva Cadiz beadfound in the fill of the south palisade line.

English settlers had ever occupied the site before
palisade construction began. The palisade then is old
enough to be part of James Fort. And a line of individual postholes found six feet north of the palisade
likely supported a platform for musketeers, perhaps
added in 1610. Discovery of a number of tobacco
pipe stems, and brick and glass in these holes all in-
dicate that this platform was related to the original fort but constructed a
few years later in time.

Expansion by more ten-foot squares moving east from the riverbank
wall line of the fort uncovered another palisade trench curving from south
to north and a larger and deeper trench that mirrored the curve of the
smaller trench, nine feet to the north and east (see Figure 28). It is clear
from the parallel nature of the narrow and wide trenches that they are parts
of the same construction. The palisade trench could be identified as such
because it had the required shape: straight sides and flat bottom, and some
post stains were clearly visible. But unlike the south wall line, the bulwark palisade trench did not penetrate very far into subsoil, hardly deep
enough to support upright timbers. The trench ranged from five inches
deep where it was cut by the foundation of a 1922 Pocahontas Monument base, to one-half-inch deep at a point where some sort of grading
wiped it away nearest the river bank. It is therefore likely that along and
close to the original riverbank, considerable original soil is missing, probably as much as two and a half feet, or more. Yet all along the south edge
of the site the plow zone became progressively deeper above the clay subsoil while along the upper section of the curved palisade trench, what
appeared to be old topsoil actually survived below the plowed soil. The
palisade trench cut through this layer establishing that this was close to
the original ground surface when the palisade was constructed. The palisade trench itself held only Indian pottery, further evidence that this trench
was put up on historically virgin ground (1607).

39

Figure 31. Artifacts associated with signs in the ground of fort configuration prove old and military enough to establish construction as early as 1607. clockwise: 17th-century cabasett helmet, 15th century breastplate; silver English sixpence, 1602; late 16th-17th-century English Border ware jug.

Actually, the apparent confusing existence of a thick plow zone and survival of old topsoil can be explained if an earth wall or a rampart once stood over and along the curved palisade. That is where the dirt wound up that came out of the nearby entrenchment. This also created two and a half feet or so of depth of soil necessary to support the palisade logs. Digging and piling up such an entrenchment-rampart would be standard procedure in fort construction; the idea being that an attacking enemy would have to struggle through the entrenchment, then scale the rampart before getting to the palisade. In any event, that dirt embankment explains the survival of original topsoil below the depth of the James Fort earthwork. The embankment kept the plow blade always above the topsoil, even as the plowing gradually leveled the earthwork. In other words, the later plowing, perhaps as much as 150 years in duration, gradually took down the embankment until it reached the old topsoil level and the last few inches of the palisade trench.

Fortunately, acquisition of the property by the APVA in 1893 ended cultivation, or this bulwark footprint would never have survived. This, however, does not explain why grading erased not only the topsoil but the palisade trenches along the riverbank.

Captain William Allen owned and farmed Jamestown Island during the middle of the 19th century. It was his slaves who built much of the earthwork that the Confederate Army planned to use to stop Union ships from sailing up the James River and capturing Richmond. The surviving earthen shore gun embankment is imposing today with some embankment mounds still standing as high as six feet above the original pre-battery grade. The question is, where did the dirt come from for this construction?

The likely answer is from the immediately surrounding area, from the digging of moats, and from scouring inside and along the nearby riverbank. Some of the James Fort dirt then is in the embankment mounds of the Confederate fort. In fact, there are reports that during the fort construction, the builders found old burials and 17th-century armor. Also, it makes sense militarily to grade down the adjacent elevated shoreline to water level, effectively eliminating cover for any Union amphibious landings. Post-Civil War drawings of the church tower shoreline area do clearly show dirt mounds and the cliff.

Figure 32. Southeast James Fort bulwark site excavation in 2003 showing John White's house/warehouse (ca. 1644 building foundation) overlying the ca. 1610 James Fort demi-lune ditch (arrow). Log posts mark previously discovered and backfilled palisade trenches.

Figure 33. Overhead view of the demi-lune ditch (arrows) beneath the White building brick-work, facing south (James River).

The Civil War grading theory is all the more plausible when considering the shallowness of the palisade postholes, again strongly suggesting that dirt is missing. These postholes in size and filling materials seem to form an arc inside the palisade line. It is possible that they supported a wooden retaining wall holding earth to form a platform for mounting cannon. The space between the palisade line and the posthole line seems to be enough to mount, fire, and maneuver a 17th-century falcon or a falconette, the type of cannon ammunition found on the site.

Excavations to the east of the curved palisade trench and the "dry" moat eventually uncovered a right-angled extension of the ditch suggesting a more complicated bulwark design. The ditch deviates from the quarter-circular pattern to a straightened course for 30 feet where it makes a slightly less than 90 degree turn toward the river. Most of the extent of this angled ditch existed beneath the remains of a burned building likely post-dating the existence of the fort by at least two decades. The 46' x 30' building which once stood on a foundation of cobblestones had an English basement (probably originally only three to four feet below surface) and included two exterior brick chimneys, one each in the two 23-foot-wide basement rooms. Original construction of the basement and one of the chimneys cut into the already backfilled moat extension, but since it had become so deep, the moat still survived to a depth of two feet. Uncovering and recording the building ruins, likely the house/warehouse of merchant/politician, John White, required months of excavation beneath a protective shelter and resulted in recapturing the commercial waterfront landscape of mid-17th-century Jamestown.[7] But what remained of the fort-period moat beneath this important ruin contributed significant insight into the true fort design.

The digging beneath the White building indicated that the moat originally was at least four feet deep below the estimated original fort-period ground surface and perhaps originally six feet wide. The moat clearly marked the location of an advance earthwork which may have consisted of a three-point defense known as a demi-lune. Thus it is apparent what Percy's description of the triangular fort with three bulwarks at every corner meant. Percy also adds *"like a half-moon"* which could mean demi-lune, a military term for circular work with chevron-shaped forward projections.[8] In any case, only the point of one outwork seems to have survived with the possible symmetrical additional points destroyed by erosion and seawall construction. Excavations south of the "point" of the ditch uncovered a palisade trench as well, extending south from the point. That additional palisade confuses understanding of the precise design of the outwork. Still, it is clear from what survives that Wingfield, Gosnold, and the other Captains, who were left by Smith and Newport to *"contrive"* (design) the fort, knew enough up-to-date military architectural design elements to produce a James Fort more in keeping with contemporary European standards.[9] That being the case, the James Fort design, heretofore based on documentary descriptions alone, has unfairly cast the knowledge and talent of the Jamestown leaders in unfavorable light. They were experienced military men, having served in the Netherlands or Ireland and were more capable militarily than many have supposed. This design element of the demi-lune speaks to that.

Besides the ca. 1640 John White building ruin, the bulwark area excavation revealed that layers from the building's occupation and destruction spilled south and west from the foundation. Those levels also accumulated on top of a deposit of sand and domestic trash that increased in depth toward the river. This appeared to be an attempt to extend the shoreline behind some type of bulkhead perhaps

Figure 34. Circular pit inside southeast bulwark; possibly a place to store powder near the bastion guns.

now lost during the concrete seawall construction. A ten-foot-wide wide doorway centered on the White building ruin on the riverside and exterior postholes suggests that this area was used as a loading dock, perhaps the reason for the 17th-century shore reclamation effort. In any case, the

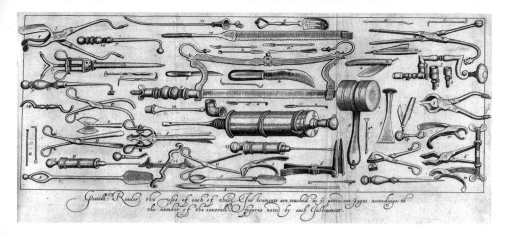

White building debris and the shoreline material extended southwest until they rested upon a circular pit, filled with washed-in clay and dark organic soil holding scores of artifacts dating to 1610. This collection included a number of gun parts, 1602 Irish halfpennies, an ornate horse bit, and a medical instrument, known as a spatula mundani, which was used to treat constipation. This medical implement turned out to be quite precisely datable to 1609, as there was record of it being sent to the colony with a chest of other medical instruments in that year. The pit itself may have originally functioned as a relatively safe place to store gunpowder for the bulwark cannons. How it fit into the overall scheme of the demi-lune bulwark is problematic. It is located in a position that would have been in the path of the circular palisade if it had ever originally completed its circular form suggested by the palisade trench that survived and the ca. 1608 Zuniga map. That being the case, perhaps both the magazine and the demi-lune were not original to the first fort design but rather part of changes made in 1610 reported by Strachey as "[the fort] *growing…to more perfection.*"

Figure 35. Early 17th century surgical tool (spatula mundani) devised by English surgeon John Woodall and his illustration of it along with the other tools of his trade, 1617 (above).

Once the southeastern bulwark and south wall lines appeared to be archaeologically established on the ground, the likely place to find any surviving evidence of the east wall became the focus of the excavations. As the southeastern bulwark began to take shape to the north a relatively faint linear soil stain, actually found during the very first season of excavation, began to take on increasing significance. The stain was old enough to be from the fort period because it had been severed by the digging of a ca. 1620s drainage ditch. Tracing it back toward the bulwark area established that it was straight as an arrow, it was indeed a palisade trench and it terminated opposite the upper path of the bulwark palisade. Construction of the original Pocahontas statue base in 1928 destroyed the ending point of the curved palisade but the fact that it did not connect with the east line on the west side suggests that there was a fort gate located there. Once it was clear that the trench was part of the bulwark design and likely the east wall of the triangle, four spaced trenches were dug at intervals along the projected line. These trenches, except the northernmost, all uncovered the trench left from what at first appeared to be the decayed palisade wall. Since a section of these tests looked vaguely like the signs of decayed upright timbers in a slot trench found along the south palisade line, it was logical to conclude that the east line held the same evidence. That did not turn out to be exactly true. While the slot trench was there, there was no clear evidence that the upright timbers decayed in place. This became very disturbing, in that while the 45-46 degree angle between the east and south wall trenches would fit to make Strachey's overall dimensions, without evidence that timbers stood in the trench, it would be hard to prove that this was part of the fort at all. Yet the age and lack of artifacts in the upper reaches of the trench strongly suggested that this was an original and early part of the settlement.

Dissection of a section of the palisade slot trench offered an answer to the missing timber stain mystery. The test trenches near the church determined that unlike all of the other areas excavated in the James Fort vicinity to that point, this area had never been plowed. It is logical to assume that plowing near the only visible monument of Jamestown during

Figure 36. Lateral exposure of the east palisade trench showing evidence of its removal in the early 17th century.

the later 18th and early 19th century, the church tower and graveyard, was off limits owing to the possibility of disturbing burials. Again it must be noted that while plowed soil can have its advantages archaeologically, uncultivated ground preserves soil layers in their original configuration from the time of their deposition up to the present. This means that, in theory, the entire depth of the original palisade trench was left undisturbed along some of the east line, offering the possibility of viewing a complete unplowed palisade cross section.

Excavations to that point had dissected the palisade line literally from top to bottom. On the south, that method was logical in that each stain left by the timbers could be removed individually, leaving the shape (earth mold) of each post. In fact, that line was so clear that it was possible, after excavation, to fill the excavated timber cavities with cement and so produce a positive reproduction of the bottoms of the posts. That could not be done on the east line; there were no post stains visible to dig out. So an attempt was made to examine the east line by digging, not top to bottom, but from the side of the trench stain, which had a good chance of revealing evidence of each post undetectable from the top down. Not so. What this digging angle revealed was that while the original slot trench did indeed once hold timbers upright, they were removed by digging around them until they could be pulled out of the trench.

A test trench put into the side of the Confederate earthwork along the projected line of the east palisade suggested the same scenario. Only a ditch filled with mixed soil was found in alignment with the other sections of the east line but no post stains. It was also clear from the nature of the soil layers above the backfilled palisade trench that the Confederate earthwork was constructed from dirt re-deposited as soldiers or slaves dug out the moat next to it. That explained why there were two soil layers holding only 17th-century artifacts on top of the palisade slot—one building up soon after the palisade stood there. The other soil layer, the re-deposited 17th-century town level, wound up on the earthwork to the south as Captain Allen's slaves and Confederate soldiers began digging the adjacent moat. Trenches into the same earthen wall nearer the church in subsequent seasons also revealed the reversed-in-time soil levels above the palisade trench which could be traced continuously, except where a road graded it away. Be that as it may, the disturbed palisade itself raises the question of why the settlers dug up and removed the east wall of the James Fort. And, why did they do that so soon after it was built, a fact suggested by the telltale early Indian artifacts, in the trench fill?

A possible answer lay in the discovery of yet another related palisade trench and a closer look at 17th-century eyewitness descriptions of the town's defenses.

Removal of plowed soil north of the southeastern bulwark revealed an additional palisade running from the east wall line at its southernmost end.

This line extended 60 feet where it came to an end at a sizable soil stain with related postholes, remains of an apparent backfilled cellar in a post supported building. Excavation a few inches below the plow zone along the length of the palisade revealed the clearest stains of decayed upright timbers yet found. Testing, again from the side, of a four-foot section of the line revealed the earthen molds of decayed timbers anchored side by side in two-foot-deep trenches. This and the digging along the aforementioned east palisade line in the unplowed ground near the church supported the conclusion that the standard depth of two feet for the palisades was the norm. While this seems shallow and hardly the four-foot depth reported by Strachey, recent experimental raising of palisade sections on the site to mark the archaeological discoveries clearly prove that trenches only one-foot six-inches deep can rigidly support adjacent and pinned logs and rails.

The extension of the apparently triangular fort was a part of the early fortified area as, again, only prehistoric Indian artifacts appear in the fill which should come as no surprise.

The writings of John Smith, William Strachey, and Ralph Hamor leave little doubt that the triangular James Fort did not encompass all of James Town for long.[10] Their descriptions, read in light of the extended palisade, may also explain both the quick removal of the east fort palisade and the eventual location of the church, directly next to and outside the east wall. After Smith was appointed President (September 10, 1608), he wrote that, "*James*

Figure 37. "Town" palisade trench showing soil stains of original decayed palisade posts after removal of plowzone (left). Removal of clay originally tamped around the up-right town palisade posts, leaving a perfect soil cast of each side-by-side unhewn timber (above).

towne being burnt, we rebuilt it…environed with a palizado of fourteen or fifteene feet… [the overall plan] *reduced to the form of this ( ) figure* [omitted but later called *"five-square"*]."[11] The word "reduced" is the key to understanding what Smith describes. Today the word clearly means "made smaller," but some uses of the word in the 17th century meant "changed," "restored back" or maybe even "made larger." It must have meant "changed" to Smith, because he reports that by the summer of 1608, Jamestown consisted of 40 or 50 houses, far too many structures to fit into Strachey's sub-two-acre triangular fort.[12] It only makes sense to conclude that another palisaded enclosure, probably rectangular in shape, was attached to the original triangle, perhaps to form Smith's pentagon. This plan must have offered much more space for house construction. Perhaps the palisade trench found extending east from the triangle is Smith's 1608 line. A more substantial palisade seems also to be a part of Strachey's description of the walls that were either constructed as additions or were reconstructed and/or repaired by Sir Thomas Gates and his men after Lord De La Warre arrived in 1610: *"enclosed with a palisade of planks and strong posts, four feet in the ground."*[13]

This palisade probably secured both the original triangle and the same housing area in Smith's five-sided town and Hamor's later town that was *"reduced into a handsome form* [with] *two faire rows of houses…newly and strongly impaled."*[14] Of course, if the extended eastward line is either the one reported by Smith or Strachey, then attaching it to the triangular fort just north of the southeast bulwark still allowed the bulwark to be defendable by design. Cannon placed in the protruding bulwark and the forward demi-lune-like cannon entrenchment could still provide cover fire for attacks made on the extended town. But Strachey's 1610 description of the fort, apparently the most precise of eyewitness accounts, clearly seems to contradict the archaeological evidence of palisade removal along the eastern line. One must conclude that the east line stood until Strachey could measure it in 1610, but went down as the town expanded thereafter as Hamor describes.

Nonetheless, these later archaeological signs of the changing palisade configuration may also suggest why the east side of the palisade was dismantled. It wound up inside the expanded palisaded area and therefore no longer served as a barrier to attacks from outside the compound. It had become obsolete. The expanded palisaded town also explains later church locations on or near the obsolete east fort wall. The church simply kept its position at the center of the new town, moving from the center of the triangular fort/town to the center of the expanded pentagon. In other words, the church had to be moved east to remain at the hub of the larger community. Then finally, when the fort no longer stood, almost certainly after ca.1630, the tower wound up built against a standing church with no regard for the removed palisade line that left its construction and de-

struction trench beneath it. This may suggest that if the later churches are at the center of the earliest expanded town and the expansion was rectangular, then the expansion to the east resulted in tripling the area of the palisaded town (a total of 4-5 acres). At this point, the palisade extension is known to turn north of the cellar building, but trenching north of this last sign of the wall determined that the line changed course again somewhere in the present walled church-

Figure 38. Pattern of support postholes and the cellar (left) and pit complex of holes of Structure 160 (right), the barracks (?).

yard burial ground. To wind up as Smith's expanded form and large enough to enclose all the 40 to 50 houses that he reports, the line would likely make a right turn to the east. Another extended line appeared attached on a slightly less than 90-degree angle to the junction of the north bulwark and the east wall of the fort which would form a very asymmetrical "rectangle" around the east section of the fortified town. It will take future excavations to explore that theory.

Excavations have located three James-Fort-period building sites (designated Structures 160, 165, and 166), all of strikingly similar design. The archaeological evidence of all these buildings consists of irregularly spaced rectangular post configurations aligned with the nearest palisade; they are all one- room-wide but multiple rooms in length, and they all have a cellar at one end. Two of the structure sites are located within the original triangular enclosed area exactly ten feet from the adjacent palisade. Describing the fire of January 8, 1608, Smith says the buildings were 8 or 10 YARDS from the palisade,[15] but judging from the archaeological evidence of these buildings, his memory must have dimmed. The buildings' alignment with the adjacent palisade walls puts them at a 45-46 degree angle to each other. This is actually the proof that these are indeed all pieces of the James Fort footprint as Strachey describes it: *"To every side[of the fort] as proportioned distance from the palisade, is a settled street of houses that runs along, so as each line of the angle hath his street."*[16]

49

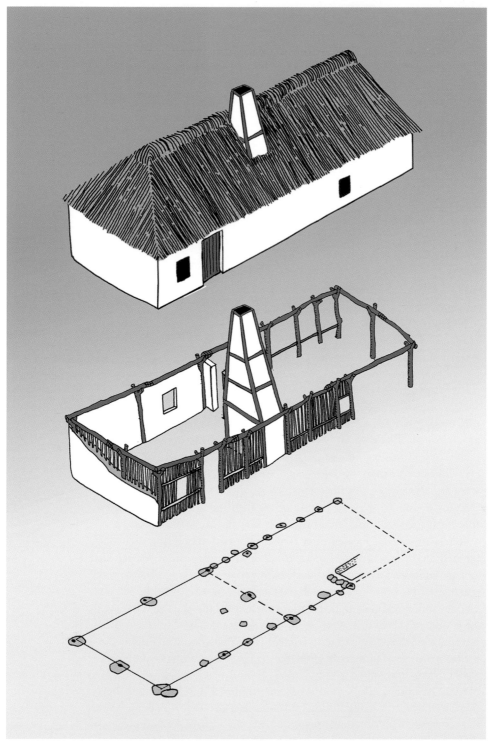

Figure 39. Site plan of Structure 160 below an interpretation of it as a mud and stud building.

Strachey also reports that the buildings in the fort were all burned in the fire of 1608 and were then rebuilt and improved. Excavations did indicate that the west end of the southern building was built twice, as indicated by a structural posthole cutting into another structural posthole along the wall line of the western end of the building. Strachey also indicates that the original buildings, presumably the ones that burned, had clay walls. Indeed some of the second-period posthole fill held burned clay daub apparently from the fire. The improvement to the buildings by 1610, according to Strachey was the adoption by the English of Virginia Indian building techniques and materials. The thatched roofs and apparently even the mud walls were replaced with bark shingles "as the Indians."[17] Again the clay-covered houses apparently were too hot in summer compared to the Indian-like lodges that replaced them. The fill in the second period postholes and the holes to what appear to be the attachment of at least two rooms onto the structure to the east, did not contain any daub, suggesting they were indeed related to a phase-two bark-covered construction.

The cellar/pit in the easternmost "room" of the building included an original symmetrical section that experienced a number of somewhat randomly appearing alterations through time. The original cellar was about five feet wide, aligned along the south wall of the easternmost room of the building. That cellar accumulated fill and some discarded objects before it was disturbed by the digging of the more randomly shaped holes that culminated in a small square shaft. It is somewhat unclear as to whether or not the post-cellar digging took place when the building was still standing, and therefore was some sort of a cellar expansion, or was a pit dug into the previous building site, perhaps to serve as a reservoir, clay quarry and/or a place to mix daub. But some particularly adhesive clay in the pit contained the impressions of decayed cut marsh reeds, clearly remnants of tempering material that could be a sign of daub processing. It is possible then that after the building went down, the pit became a "pug mill" (mixing pond) for making daub with the deeper hole serving as the water source.

Fill in the other later pit/cellars generally consisted of a bottom occupation level with some washed in clay/sand then a marked deposit of dark humus mixed with lumps of clay subsoil suspended in it, and contained virtually no artifacts. Above these lowest fill layers were numerous garbage and trash-laden deposits filling the hole to the modern plowed surface. When this same pattern of fill appeared in other fort-period cellars on the site, and as it became clear that the early buildings were of a type of construction known in England, specifically in Lincolnshire, as "mud and stud" construction, it is almost certain that this humus/clay mix is in fact from the fallen mud walls.[18] Mud and stud construction requires only a crudely aligned light frame of young trees seated in the ground and ver-

Figure 40. Whitt Cottage, Thimbleby, Lincolnshire, England, a classic example of a surviving post-medieval mud and stud building a traditional building, a technique "transported" to early Jamestown.

tical smaller "studs' between them to support walls of mixed earth. Both the mixed humus/clay layer near the floor levels of the pit/cellars and the almost random and slightly out-of-line support postholes found on all the sites strongly suggest this traditional Lincolnshire folk-building tradition. It is also not surprising that Captain John Smith, who directed much of the building at the fort, and William Laxon, a carpenter, were both from Lincolnshire and certainly familiar with the mud and stud tradition.[19]

The siting of the three fort-period Structure 160, 165, and 166, which are exactly parallel with the fort palisades, certainly suggests construction and use during the first years of James Fort. The dates of the artifacts recovered from deposits made during the lifetime and abandonment of the buildings follow suit. A single clay tobacco pipe bowl with a teardrop-shaped heel design lay on the earthen cellar floor of Structure 160, beneath fill that accumulated there after the building was no longer in use. This pipe bowl shape is known to have a manufacture/use date of 1590-1610. This same type of pipe bowl appears at Jamestown with regularity in contexts with late 16th- to early 17th-century coins and other precisely datable objects. Bowls with the same shape have been discovered at the site of Fort Saint George in Maine, which had an occupation date of 1607-1608, and on the wreck of the Jamestown supply ship, the *Sea Venture*, which sank in 1609.[20]

The upper levels of fill in the pit/cellar of Structure 160 held over 44,000 artifacts. Military arms and armor of the late-16th early- 17th century, including an intact helmet, comprised the majority of the metal objects. Artifacts which are precisely datable included: three coins ranging in date from 1590 to 1602, casting counters dating as early as 1580, Elizabethan lead to-

Figure 41. Overhead view from church tower of James Fort and Structure 166, the "soldiers' house," showing some support postholes of the walls (white line) and cellar. Red line marks the west Fort wall line uncovered during previous excavations.

ken from the 1570s, and a lead cloth seal which dates no later than 1603.[21] Like the palisade excavation, the posthole fill of Structure 160 produced only prehistoric artifacts showing that only pre-1607 occupation existed there before the digging and filling of the pit. This suggests construction in 1607 or very soon thereafter. Based on these finds, the remains of Structure 160 may be the earliest known Anglo-American building.

Building remains of Structure 166 along the east palisade reflect the same characteristics as the others. The cellar was about as large as the original cellar in Structure 160. The framing holes were about as randomly spaced as well, and the width was a uniform 17' wide. This building site suffered considerable post-fort-period damage, probably starting with the growth of an oak tree next to the cellar, then grading during the erection of the adjacent Civil War earthwork in 1861, grading to establish a road in the late 19th century, and finally the erection of a fence around the 1907 reconstructed church. It is amazing that any trace of Structure 166 survived all of this disturbance.

Being so near the 17th-century brick church tower may have saved parts of the building features. Again, plowing seems to have avoided the church site. In any event, the survival of an unplowed portion of overburden gave the first indication of the original depth of postholes for these mud and stud structures with the

Figure 42. Structure 166 wall postholes and cellar (left), musketeer's pouch (lower right) and dagger, food remains, and Venetian trade beads near the cellar cooking fire (upper right).

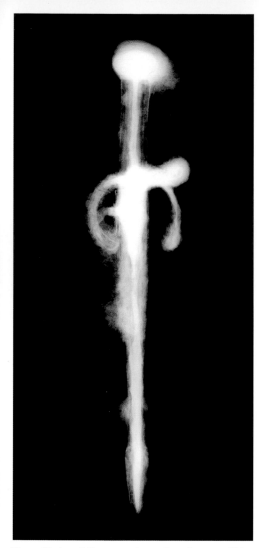

Figure 43. Late 16th-century dagger from Structure 166 cellar in its sheath as revealed by digital x-ray.

cellars as deep as four feet. The mud wall collapse survived in the cellar above about six inches of a deposit that must have accumulated during the time the cellar was in use. This "occupation" level held artifacts scattered about the cellar floor that appear to have been abandoned at one instant in time. In one corner, a fire once burned upon which someone was about to or was once in the process of cooking a cut of pork, or a combination of pork and turtle, in a Virginia Indian pot. A butchered hip-bone of a pig and a butchered turtle shell lay near the cooking fire, suggesting the pork and turtle menu. Near the Indian pot, lay a large Venetian trade bead. Was the cook a Virginia Indian woman?

The identity of the cook cannot be known, but whoever was cooking was doing so while surrounded by weapons. A sheathed dagger was found within arm's reach of the cooking fire, and behind it were found a musketeer's bag of gunflints, lead balls and powder. And why or even how someone could burn a fire on the floor of a mud and stud cellar which presumably had a wooden ceiling (below the first floor) is puzzling. Also in question is why the cellar had a lightly constructed, wooden dividing wall, against which the occupation level accumulated, a question which is equally hard to explain. So too are the presence of four shovels left on the floor of this apparently make-shift kitchen.

The great number of Virginia Indian artifacts, the dagger, and copper objects date the cellar to the first few years of settlement just as its association with the east wall of the fort suggests. In any event, the remains of Structure 166, like Structure 160, mark the beginnings of Anglo-American houses.

The third mud and stud "longhouse" is Structure 165, which was found attached to the end of the 50' palisade extending the fort to the east of the southeast bulwark (see Figures 44 and 45). Structure 165 is the most sophisticated of the three mud buildings found so far. It was the largest, 72' long, but retaining the "standard" 17' width. It was divided into at least three and perhaps four rooms. The southernmost room was built over a sizable, partially wood-lined cellar constructed in two phases under a superstructure that was supported by fairly irregular-spaced upright posts. The palisade attached to the building at what appeared to have been the original southwest corner post, but at some point the cellar was enlarged by digging beneath the superstructure to form an L-shape.

The cellar also had a series of entrance steps descending from the west and fanning toward the south, so that the room could be entered from the north. It was also clear that the cellar once had a timber lining on the east and north walls. Cavities left where wall timbers decayed were filled with regular deposits of distinct, sandy clay. The wall on the east held back a mixed clay "liner" presumably packed in there behind the timber to water-proof the wall closest to the actual wall line of the superstructure above. The west wall did not need the waterproofing, as it was well under and away from the outside western wall line. By the same token, the original south wall would also not require water-proofing clay as it too was well underneath the superstructure.

Natural subsoil clay in the L-addition made up the cellar floor, but a mixture of sandy clay leveled the floor in the north half of the structure. In that section, the flooring fill contained two barrels buried upright in the northeast corner of the room. The barrels apparently served as sumps whenever the cellar took on water, which, judging from the lower few inches of washed sand on the floor and the washed sand in the barrel, happened on many occasions. No barrel wood survived, but the dark stain left where the wood decayed formed a perfect mold in the sandy fill around and in it. The washed layers and the installation of the barrel also suggest that the cellar was in use over an extended period of time.

A fire had also burned in this cellar along the west wall. There, charcoal on the floor, and clay heated enough to turn red, clearly pinpointed a fire "place." There was no evidence along the clay cellar wall above the fire area that there had ever been a flue. Here again was a puzzle: how can a fire exist in a basement below what had to be a wooden floor without setting it on fire?

The answer might lie in the discovery of small postholes found in a line cutting into the subsoil below the dirt floor south of the cellar stairs, suggesting that some sort of partition existed there before the floor level was raised. A wall there does not make much sense unless there was need, as in a prison, to secure the cellar space at times from access by the stairs. That barrier and the fire make sense in light of one John Smith tale. Smith tells of putting one of two Powhatan brothers in a "dungeon" until the other brother returned a stolen pistol by sun-up.[22] Failure to comply would result in the execution of the prisoner. That night, taking pity on his prisoner, Smith allowed him to burn a charcoal fire. The fire was apparently flueless as it rendered the prisoner unconscious by the time the brother returned

Figure 44. Structure 165, the "store/workshop", attached to James Fort by palisade showing wall postholes and three rooms: cellar with stairs and drainage barrels (foreground), central room and "workshop" (background) with three brick hearths.

the pistol. Thinking him dead, the brother loudly and justifiably cried foul, at which time Smith told the conscious man that if he promised to end the thievery of arms forever, he would bring his brother back to life. A stiff shot of alcohol did the trick, and, according to Smith, he thereafter had little trouble getting his way with the Indians. He had the power to raise the dead, or so they thought.

A flueless charcoal fire that perhaps burned only once, and the inner security wall at the base of the steps in the cellar, seem to identify the site as Smith's dungeon. But jail or not, it is clear that the cellar did serve as part of the Jamestown defense system. Shelves cut into the north and south walls could have been built there to serve musketeers. These shelves would have given an elevated firing position through a ground-level opening, which makes all the more sense when it appears that the cellar and its superstructure extend so far beyond the palisade wall that it could act as a bastion. In that case, a musketeer could provide flanking fire toward anyone assaulting the palisade.

Like the other two fort-period cellars, the outer building (Structure 165) held three distinct types of fill, laid in this sequence: washed sandy clay at the bottom; above that, the aforementioned fill that washed in along the floor from the south and on into the barrel sump; on top of that, a deposit of what has to be the collapsing of mud and stud walls, a rich vein

Figure 45. Structure 165, the store cellar, showing layers of collapsed mud walls (arrow) below major deposit of garbage and trash holding over 37,000 domestic, industrial and military artifacts from ca. 1610.

of trash and garbage spilling in from the south and east. Finally, brown loam leveled the resulting depression, presumably so that eventually the abandoned fort's outbuilding site could easily be plowed.

Three of these layers represent the end of the life of the cellar: the wall collapse, the trash and garbage, and the leveling loam. This sequence is almost identical in the fill of the cellars of all three fort-period buildings. The exception is the eastern fort building which does not have a trash layer. It may have had such a deposit, but it was destroyed during the 19th-century earthwork and roadwork.

What these layers tell is a regular story of construction, use and demise. The story of the building unfolds like this. First, as the light wall supports went in the ground, the builders dug a cellar, presumably stockpiling the mixed topsoil and clay. As a network of lighter studs lined the walls between the major upright poles, the stockpile fill was spread (pargeted) onto the frames. A light sapling roof frame could have been built first then raised up as forked pole wall posts went into place. The light roof was hipped for strength. When the mud walls were dry and stable enough, thatch was added to complete the roof. The empty cellar then came into use for a concentrated period of time, likely during the stressful first three years, 1607-1610. Simply explained, this is the building's "life" story. But it is not so easy to explain the trash layers on top of the fallen mud walls. To explain this, two scenarios make sense.

First there may be what can be called the De La Warre cleanup. It seems that all the cellars with the trash layers and indeed the fort moat and the circular magazine were apparently filled at one time. A convincing number of pieces of the same ceramic vessels fit together from the four sources to support that conclusion. The nature of the collection from the four deposits was, also, almost identical: scrap copper, jettons, armor, weapon parts, broken pottery (especially delft drug jars), and food remains. Another similarity is that the most recent artifacts in all the features date to no later than 1610; therefore, all four features seemed to have a similar backfilling date.

So because of the nature of the fill and the same backfilling date, it is tempting to ascribe the cultural levels to the massive clean-up ordered by Governor De La Warre upon his arrival with the men and supplies that saved the colony from abandonment in June of 1610.[23] However, it should be noted that the date of the deposits can only be said to date sometime after 1610, not necessarily in 1610.

Even with De La Warre's reported commitment to revitalizing the fort, it is difficult to explain why all of the major subsurface footprints of the fort buildings and moat, and thus the fort itself, would be abandoned and filled. This is especially difficult given William Strachey's description of the fort as still triangular in form, just as Percy and Smith had described it earlier. Yet Strachey also made the point that the fort was "lately brought to perfection," presumably by the efforts of Lord De La Warre's men. Remember that Strachey held that the 1610 fort was a triangular shape with two 300' sides on the north and a 420' side on the south made of "*planks and strong posts.*"[24] Perhaps the explanation lies in Strachey's earlier description of the town, written about what he saw on May 20, 1610, the day he arrived with the previously shipwrecked party from Bermuda. Strachey makes a strong point that the town was in shambles with the main gate off its hinges and the houses and palisade torn down and cut into firewood.[25] It is significant that previous excavations have indicated that the east wall of the fort seems to have been purposely removed, possibly resulting in the expansion of the town (but some removal itself could well have been a result of this desperate gathering of firewood).

Of course the palisade razing, even in part, left the whole settlement wide open to attacks from the Powhatan, unless the east palisade had already become an interior wall, rendered obsolete by the "*five-sided*" fort built after the 1608 fire. In any case, if an exterior wall were down, then it is understandable, as Strachey remarks, that the Indians would kill anyone who ventured from the "*blockhouse*" (to which the survivors may have been confined because it was the only place left secure enough to protect anyone).[26]

The "blockhouse" could mean, of course, the blockhouse built near the isthmus at the extreme western end of the island, or the blockhouse on Back River. But it is also possible that some settlers were seeking safety in the cellar building, or buildings in the fort which had become in a sense a blockhouse or fort house after the palisades were gone.

Strachey also remarks that the surviving settlers were suffering from pestilence from within the blockhouse. If they were in fact trapped inside the buildings for their own safety, then it is not beyond the realm of possibility that their garbage and trash could wind up in the cellars below them. Under siege by the Indians, who would risk an appearance beyond the protection of the blockhouse walls, just to get rid of rubbish?

While that might explain the garbage and some of the trash in the cellars, it does not account for the industrial waste from glass-making, pipe-making, metallurgy, and the reworking of armor, nor does it explain the essentially artifact-free clay in the lower levels of each of the fort cellars. The starving and trapped settlers would hardly bide their time by busily manufacturing things and dumping the industrial waste in the cellar below. Nor could they dig new holes elsewhere beyond the security of the blockhouse walls and bring the spoils back for disposal in the cellar. Indeed, the redeposited clay layer must have gone into the cellar hole as a result of the mud wall collapse. So it seems, then, that the blockhouse confinement brought on by the Indian siege is not a convincing explanation for the cellar garbage at all.

What is left is what could be called the Ghost Town Theory. The fort may have been primarily abandoned fairly early on, in favor of the improved two streets of handsome houses described by Hamor in 1611. That being the case, the fort would begin to fall in from abandonment and neglect as the colony experienced a long period of peace with Spain back in Europe and with the Indians in Virginia. During this time of semi-desertion, the fort and its smaller extension begins to erase itself, any holes and ditches such as moats and cellars would erode in, and finally, in the case of buildings, the mud walls would cave into the cellars.

Descriptions of the fort during those years of peace with the Powhatan give the distinct impression of a ghost town.[27] This could at least account for the mixed clay (mud and decayed stud layers) above a relatively thin occupation zone. Then finally as the fort reaches a hopeless state of decay, and the settlers adopt a disastrous, false sense of security (right before the 1622 Indian "massacre"), the useless fort is totally abandoned. The cellars become convenient trash dumps for refuse lying about from the early occupation years. The fact that the dates of the trash are so consistently early, 1607-1610, and that so many of the fragments from the same vessels are scattered among the various features, suggest that this trash came from a common source. All of the pieces from broken and discarded objects were thrown together at first, only to get scattered in the backfilled cellars later. These earlier objects, of course, then go into the cellars on top of the collapsed mud walls. This would explain why all the artifacts are so consistently datable to the very early occupation years, but were perhaps re-deposited so much later, possibly as late as the middle 1620s.

A vast quantity of discarded food remains and animal bones was found in the cellar fill of this extension building, as it was in the Structure 160 cellar/pit. At this writing, only the bones from Structure 160 have been comprehensively analyzed, giving vivid testimony to the struggle for survival at Jamestown during those first precarious years, 1607-ca.1610.[28] This dating for the deposit can be fairly precisely determined owing to the number of objects datable stylistically or historically, and the number of dated coins recovered. Actually some of the bones turned out to be the most precisely datable evidence of the collection. How so?

Strachey reports that he and the shipwrecked Bermuda contingent arrived at Jamestown in May 1610 with provisions that were collected during their nine-month shipbuilding stay in Bermuda. One of the Jamestown cellars held the bones of birds and among them were the bones of a cahow, a bird found only in Bermuda. The collection also contains Bermudan conches, a number of tropical fish common only to those islands, and some pieces of Bermudan limestone. There is no other record from any other time of supplies coming into Virginia from Bermuda, other than in 1610. It follows then that these uniquely Bermudan food and other supplies were brought to Jamestown in May 1610 by the ex-*Sea Venture*

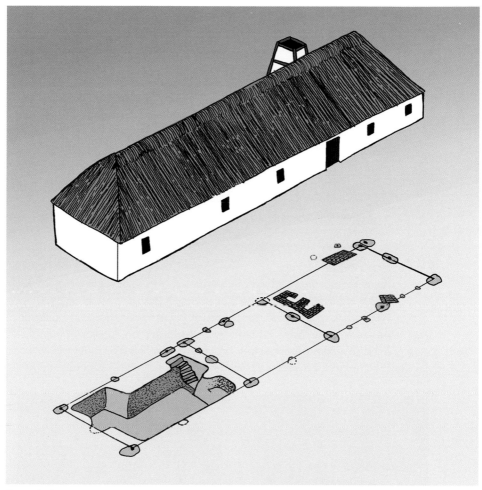

Figure 46. Archaeological plan (below) and mud and stud conjectured reconstruction of store/workshop, Structure 165.

passengers, supplies which were eventually cooked and eaten by them and by the surviving settlers of the "Starving Time" at Jamestown, after which they discarded the bones in the fort cellar.

It also appears that the voyagers were not carrying many extra supplies on their trip from Bermuda to Jamestown, as they had no way of knowing that they would find a starving Jamestown. Upon landing, Sir Thomas Gates took over leadership from George Percy and immediately saw the urgent need to realistically assess the ratio of population to provisions. Gates concluded, at first, that the Bermudan food supplies should be kept in reserve for a possible retreat voyage back to England while he, in the meantime, would send parties out to forage among the Powhatan, hopefully to gather enough food to get the colony back on its feet. Having no luck with that plan, Gates figured that at that point there would be enough food for the colonists to survive at Jamestown for 16 days if he rationed two cakes (possibly a type of dried fish cake) per person per day.[29] If no supplies could be found during that period of two weeks plus, they would abandon the colony.

No food materialized. They would have to leave. On June 6, the settlers buried the ordinance and whatever else they had hopes of reclaiming if they ever came back. Then with everything else that was of saleable value, they headed down river toward the open ocean, their interim destination the Grand Fishing Banks off Newfoundland.

It should be again stressed that Gates and the retreating Jamestown settlers <u>did</u> plan to stop at the Charles and Algernon Fort area and wait at least ten days for possible English supplies to arrive.[30] There, for the short term, they knew they could live off shellfish, like the healthy party of original settlers there had been doing, who had greeted them on their way in from Bermuda. But before they had been away from Jamestown for just over a day, an advance boat arrived from Lord De La Warre's ship to bring the announcement of the imminent arrival of the new governor, Lord De La Warre, with enough new men and supplies to save the day.

In ant case, besides dating the collection with evidence of the Bermudan provisions, the discarded food bones from the fort cellar graphically underscore just how serious the "Starving Time" was for those who tried to hold the fort during the winter and spring of 1609-1610. The presence of

Figure 47. Collection of discarded food bones and shells from the barracks' (Structure 160) cellar/pit, some of which is a grim reminder of the "starving time" diet, 1609-1610.

poisonous snake vertebrae and musk turtle give some indication that life at Jamestown had reached crisis proportions, but butchered horse bones, and the bones of the black rat, of dogs, and of cats powerfully demonstrate how dire the condition of the colonists must have become. For example, fifteen bones or bone fragments of a large dog or dogs were recovered from the fill in the dry moat of the southeast bulwark. These did not show signs of butchering, but being with the other bones that did, may indicate that while these animals were brought to Virginia as hunters or "weapons" of war, they may eventually have become a food source.

It is significant, too, that x-rays of skull fragments found show that dogs at Jamestown lived hard lives even before they may have wound up on the dinner table. The radiograph shows a small piece of lead shot imbedded in the skull. This was not, however, the cause of death; the x-ray also shows that the bone had healed around the shot. It seems logical to assume that the injury may have come from combat after the Powhatan acquired muskets, as early as 1608 according to John Smith.[31] Documentary sources indicate clearly that the Indians realized the strategic importance of the colonists' dogs, even before the Powhatan had the use of muskets. Gabriel Archer reports as early as May 1607, that while the settlers themselves escaped harm, one Powhatan attack on the Jamestown settlers resulted in the killing of *"our dogs."*

Of course the Indians may have had nothing to do with the shot in the skull of the once wounded dog. It is perhaps just as likely that the lead wound up there as the result of a stray hunting shot. But here again may be another sign of extreme hunger: that the starving colonists may have resorted to killing and eating one of the very key means they had to hunt successfully and more easily live off the wilderness.

Of course if the settlers were confined to their *"blockhouse"* as Strachey reports, then domesticated animals, such as dogs and cats and anything else living *"inside"* (even rats) would become the only source of food for the besieged colonists. So Percy apparently is not exaggerating when he writes that, during the *"Starving Time"*:

> *"Then having fed upon horses and other beasts as long as they lasted, we were glad to make shift with vermin, as dogs, cats, rats and mice."*[32]

The exact species of the lead-carrying dog with the head wound is not precisely known, but it has characteristics of a mastiff.[33] There is no question that this dog was relatively large, perhaps in the 45- to 55-pound range. According to record, grey hounds and mastiffs were at Jamestown, and perhaps this skull comes from one of those breeds. Chances are this is not the skull of a Virginia Indian dog. A rendering of one "local" Indian dog suggests that they were relatively small with very distinctive skull shapes. Some believe that relatives of these Indian dogs, the Dingo, still roam free in the backwoods of coastal North Carolina.[34]

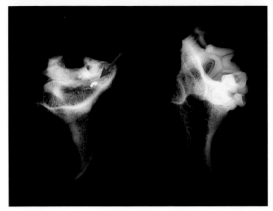

Figure 48. X-Ray of dog (Mastiff?) mandibles showing gunshot lead (arrow) in healed wound.

In any case, things were so bad during the "Starving Time" at Jamestown that Strachey reports only 60 of the 500 people at Jamestown survived.[35] A combination of numbers from several eyewitness accounts, however, suggests that while the death rate at Jamestown was appalling, it has been exaggerated. By adding and subtracting population estimates, using accounts of individual and group deaths, and numbers arriving on various ships, one can estimate that by the fall of 1609 which was the beginning of the "Starving Time" there were 215 people at Jamestown and 30 living in the environs elsewhere.[36] By the time of the arrival of the group from Bermuda then, there were 90 left alive in the colony, with 60 of these living in the town. So the number of deaths during that time was less than half the total reported by Strachey (155 compared to 440). However, with the influx of the estimated 135 *Sea Venture* survivors, the totals at Jamestown jumped to 195. No wonder that they quickly ran out of food and had no choice but to leave. When the De La Warre entourage arrived in the nick of time, the Jamestown population could well have been 345. So if De la Warre actually brought provisions to support the total population for a year as reported, then his ships must have been heavily laden indeed.

It goes without saying that the nature and extent of the artifact and food remains from the backfilling of the cellar probably has very little to say about what human action took place in and around the extension building. But artifacts found in the sub-floor and relatively thin occupation layer may tell the tale: a Nuremburg jetton (tokens made for mathematical calculations), a fragment of a French ceramic flask, and a 1573 silver English sixpence, all dating to the late 16th century. The cellar was in use then in the very early fort period, which is more evidence too, that the expansion of the fort occurred soon after the original triangular enclosure went up.

The question is, however, not so much when the cellar was in use, but whether or not the artifacts are any clue to the use of the building. Apparently the answer is yes. When they are considered in light of the floor plan and the fact that some were found in occupation levels in the northernmost rooms of the complex. There, over 100 jettons were found in the plow zone and scattered across the top of, and imbedded in, a thick clay floor. Also, a James I 1607 silver halfpenny was found in the plowed soil, presumably the tilled remnants of the original floor. And perhaps the most telling of all, a fragment of a glass alembic (a domed vessel used in distilling) was found in the floor, almost certainly broken off the alembic re-

Figure 49. Minute James I rose and thistle silver halfpenny, 1606-1608, found at the store/workshop Structure 165 site. Coins and over 100 coin-like copper jettons from on and above the workshop floor could be evidence of trade in that same room.

covered from the trash levels in the cellar under the southernmost room (see Figure 50). There, a ceramic boiling vessel known as a cucurbit rested in the fill with the alembic. The alembic and the cucurbit are the two main components of a distilling operation. These objects and other specialized ceramic vessels found with them including crucibles, a distilling dish and a dipper are all implements required for the detection and refinement of precious metals. These artifacts may be the only clue to the purpose of the three brick fireplace hearths in the north room as no other evidence of industrial waste appeared in any of the occupation fill.

The largest hearth showed evidence of two periods of construction and that the fire was hot enough to partially melt the brick surfaces. Distilling only requires enough heat to boil liquid, so either something else was being heated there or the continuous fires took their toll on the surface of the brick.

Distilling is still the most likely use of the rooms, or at least one use. The process also requires a collection vessel at the end of the line, and it is likely French Martincamp flasks were used for that purpose. Jettons would not have been used in distilling, so their presence in the northern room in such great numbers is rather puzzling. If the jettons were used for the purpose for which they were made, their presence seems to be suggesting that the northern room was some type of accounting office. Or, perhaps, this room was the space occupied by the Cape merchant, the man appointed by the Company to keep track of the supplies and any material that could be shipped home to turn a profit. If an accounting office is the identity of that space, then the James Fort Cape merchants who were responsible for the Virginia Company "store" were based there in 1607-10.[37]

As for the jettons, it is also possible, and probably more likely, that settlers used the jettons for a currency, assuming that official coinage was not readily available that far away from England.[38] If that is the case, then what were people buying there? And, if the jettons had intrinsic value, then why did they wind up lost and scattered on the floor in such great numbers? Perhaps the jettons were used for trade with the Virginia Indians for food and, if so, the transaction may have occurred in a building that would have been somewhat secure yet outside the actual triangular fort.

Figure 50. Ceramic "boiler" or cucurbit and the base of a glass globe-shaped chamber (alembic), two parts of a "still" found in the cellar of the store/workshop show that scientists with the early settlers had the equipment to test for gold and other precious metals.

In any event, understanding the use of the northern room(s) was difficult enough considering plowing disturbances, but that turned out to be a minor problem because the churchyard burial ground extended across the building site. Over a dozen burial shafts pierced the earth floor, especially in the northern room, so that only segments of the original surface between the burial shafts remained intact. Fortunately, most of the hearths survived the burials and the surviving earthen floor also contained artifact caches in small shallow holes. One such hole contained a curious collection of virtually intact objects: an English Border ware candlestick and a square glass-case bottle full of pebbles. Perhaps these were simply hiding places, or a 17th-century attempt to ward off evil spirits, especially witches.

Just north of the extension building another cellar-like pit existed during the early fort period. It first appeared beneath the plow zone as a circular discoloration about 8' in diameter. This had all the signs of a backfilled well. Wells are particularly valuable archaeologically for a number of reasons. During use, objects usually accidentally fall into the shaft and the water cushions the impact, so that unbroken artifacts accumulate at the bottom. The water also acts as a preservation agent. Permanently wet environments inhibit rust of metallic objects and can preserve organic materials such as wood, leather and plant remains in a waterlogged state. Then, once wells are abandoned, they are filled with garbage and trash, usually over the space of a short period of time. This backfill can present the opportunity to recover a primary deposit of artifacts and food remains in a time-capsule-like condition. The discovery of a well from the fort period also offered an opportunity to test Strachey's 1610 statement that the well was:

> "Six or seven fathom deep, fed by the brackish river oozing into it;
> from whence I beliefe the chief causes have proceeded of many
> diseases and sicknessess which have happened to our people who are
> indeed strangely afflicted with fluxes and agues and every particu-
> lar infirmity." [39]

As excavation proceeded, the fill did indeed look like the well's time-capsule (see Figure 51). The upper three feet of the well fill held trash-laden layers containing apothecary jars (one complete jar and many nearly complete), sheet copper waste, jettons, fine glass buttons, a case bottle, fish hooks, much ammunition and small powder flasks known as bandoliers, traces of cloth preserved by contact with copper, a Scottish James VI coin of 1597 and a Groningen (Netherlands) token dated 1583. The fill also contained considerable quantities of Virginia Indian artifacts including mendable pots, arrow points and stone flakes from point manufacture, and a section of a reed matting. The stone flakes are numerous and, because some are of the same stone type as one of the finished points, it appears that the manufacturer, i.e. Virginia Indian, was producing the points in

Figure 51. Probable cellar from another "town" house east of James Fort which contained considerable quantities of European military objects and Virginia Indian artifacts. These include a section of a mat made of reeds fastened together with bark fiber cord preserved below copper.

the fort.[40] The matting, made of marsh grass held together with bark fiber cord, survived because it wound up buried immediately under copper waste and ammunition bandoliers. The copper salts in effect acted as a sterilant, fending off organisms that normally would decompose the reed fibers.[41]

The collection from this pit/cellar gave one of the clearest signs of non-trade related Virginia Indian presence at the fort, and probably the earliest deposits yet found on the site. But it seems that from the beginning, there was little chance that most of the natives would accept the English who they felt "*were a people come from under the world to take their world from them.*"[42] Clearly some Indians did not belive that of the English men.

But in the early weeks of the 1607 summer, Captain Gabriel Archer reported native attacks at the fort. One day Archer counted 40 incoming arrows and the death of a dog at the hands of the Indians. On four other days, he mentions that long grasses and reeds stood along the fort palisades and bulwarks and that the Indians would hide in them and take aim at the colonists. "Sunday [May 30, 1607] they [Indians] came lurking in the thickets and long grasses, and a gentleman one Eustace Clovall unarmed stragling without the fort, shot 6 arrowes into him." *Clovell died a week later.*   Soon after, Archer writes that "3 of the [Indians] *had most adventourously stollen under our bulwark and hiden themselves in the long grasses...."* [43]

Amazingly, it seems that the Indians themselves offered a solution to the long-grass sniper problem: *"He* [Indian] *counselled us to Cutt Downe the long weedes rounde about our fforte...."*[44]   Apparently, the Powhatan war policy of attrition was not a particularly unanimous decision. In any case, by August 1607, cutting grass must have become a very low priority, for the sick and dying soldiers.

Excavations have recovered over 200 arrow points inside the footprint of the fort, along the palisades, around and in the bulwark, and in the bulwark ditch. Their shapes and sizes date them primarily into two periods: the Archaic, 8000-1200 B.C. (30%) or the Late Woodland, 900-1600 A.D. (68%).[45]   Likely, the ancient Indians living on or hunting at the Island left the archaic 8000-1200 B.C. points.

The predominant Late Woodland points comprise a unique assortment of shapes, sizes, and stone types together, suggesting that they came from a wide area of coastal Virginia and North Carolina. A great number were found buried with 1607-1610 European artifacts, suggesting the possi-

Figure 52. Artifacts arranged by upper to lower levels of deposits in "town" house cellar? Fill taken together appears to comprise one of the earliest deposits on the expanded James Towne site.

Figure 53. Some of the over 200 Virginia Indian stone projectile and knife points found in historical deposits at James Fort. Evidence of their manufacture within the Fort and the recovery of Indian/settler period pottery found with them reflects a strong native presence within the early community.

bility that they were being used by Indians taken into the fort or reused by the settlers, who may have adopted use of the local bows and arrows. Smith reports that in exchange for bells, the Massawomeks gave him "*venison, beares flesh, fish, bowes, arrows, clubs, targets, and beares skinnes.*" But clearly, some arrows arrived in the fort during battle. A few of the points may even be from the rain of forty arrows seen flying into the fort by Archer.[46]

Thus recovery of so many Virginia Indian artifacts within the suspected well offers valuable insight into first contact at Jamestown. As excavation proceeded below the top three feet, however, the circular shape pit began to become more rectangular. Finally, below a concentration of oyster shells, the shaft bottomed out onto a fairly level earth "floor." The discovery of a fort well would have to wait for another day.

This "floor" was more likely yet another trash-filled cellar, likely lying beneath yet another mud and stud building, and constructed on the same axis, west of north, as Structure 165. But there was no other surviving evidence of a superstructure here. That was probably because the many 17th-century churchyard grave shafts surrounding the cellar destroyed any related building postholes if they had ever existed there. So here was an early building apparently lying just outside of the extended palisade. It is tempting to conclude that this structure, with all its Virginia-Indian-related fill, marks an area reserved for Indians, thus keeping the triangular section of the town separate and more secure. That might be true. But again, the trash-laden levels in the cellars do not have any obvious connection to the use of the cellars, but rather appear to be just a means to level-up the ground after the buildings disappear. The alignment and close proximity to the palisaded cellar building, Structure 165, suggests that future excavation to the north of the pit may determine that this cellar was indeed inside the extended fort and that it attaches to an as yet undiscovered wall line turning east from the churchyard. In that case, the artifacts do speak to the close relationship between Englishmen and some Virginia Indians inside the fort more loudly than few have imagined.[47]

But discovery of the south wall line, its shot platform addition, much of the east wall line, the surviving southeast bulwark and demi-lune, and

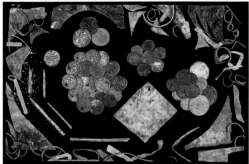

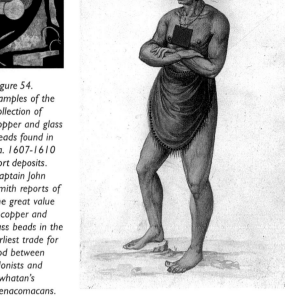

A cheife Herowan.

Figure 54. Samples of the collection of copper and glass beads found in ca. 1607-1610 Fort deposits. Captain John Smith reports of the great value of copper and glass beads in the earliest trade for food between colonists and Powhatan's Tsenacomacans.

three and possibly four fort-period buildings, still left the actual size of the fort unknown. That remained a mystery until digging began inside but directly under one rampart of the Civil War fort, the last possible key area that could have been obscuring the elusive north bulwark. By design and by luck, this vital remnant of the fort design turned up during the 2003 summer excavation.

Until the summer of 2003, Strachey's apparent 1.75-acre model was leading nowhere. Until then, digging precisely in the places where his dimensions led, had uncovered only a single palisade trench that made no sense as part of the missing bulwark. That wall line ran straight north into the marsh. A bulwark would not take that course, as by definition it had to form some sort of a closed-in protected space. Instead, the straight trench looked more like the 1608 Zuniga map "flagpole," that strange fort "flag" which could actually have been the plan of an enclosed garden attached to the fort with a single palisade line.[48] Until the summer of 2003, the only significance of the sole palisade trench seemed to be how it formed a curving right angle near where the bulwark should be. There, it disappeared into an area seriously disturbed by modern road grading. In any event, removal of a corner of the Civil War earthwork just east of the Zúñiga "flagpole" finally solved the long-sought-after riddle of the whereabouts of the north bulwark. Before that, skipping ahead directly along a projected line of the east wall came up empty, assuring that a look beneath the Civil War rampart had to produce some sort of end, or key change in direction, of that east wall. Sure enough, there the palisade curved northeast as the bulwark wall should do. Enough survived the adjacent road

Figure 55. Excavation below the Jamestown Civil War earthen fortification (background) revealed junction of the James Fort east palisade wall trench (red arrow) with the north bulwark (white arrow) and another slightly later palisade (green arrow) protecting the "town" to the east.

grading to give assurances that this was indeed the "corner" of the triangle. Our model, which had been based on believing that Strachey's 100-yard measurement meant only the space between bulwarks (technically the fort's "curtain") was too big, leading the Jamestown archaeologists to search in vain, literally on the wrong side of the road. And it was at this same spot that another, later extension of the palisade to the east turned up as well.

The oversized estimate based on Strachey's fort description led excavators to an area inside the Civil War earthwork where the missing west wall should have been. But a digging season there found only very shallow postholes on that projected line. However, the effort was far from wasted. Instead of finding the telltale palisade trench along its predicted western route, the long-sought-after, fort-period well appeared instead.[49]

Again note that a well from the fort period offers time-capsule artifact opportunities: a tight time period and pristine preservation. The subsequent excavation proved that these were realistic expectations (see Figures 56, 57, and Chapter V). Digging first revealed a brick-lined shaft partially surviving at the surface and encased within a sizable construction basin which had been dug but then immediately filled-in during original construction. Backfilling of the basin had to be immediate because original below-ground courses of the circular brick lining, built with rectangular bricks and interspersed wedges, required the force of the exterior basin backfill to hold it together. This exercise in construction physics, of course, was essential in building the shaft and for keeping it open to the water table, reached at a depth of nine feet. But more significant for future archaeologists was the fact that datable objects inadvertently wound up within the construction basin fill, thus establishing the time of construction.

Based on the dates of a number of artifacts found within the construction shaft, the well was built during the first 15 years or so of Jamestown settlement, within the fort period. The ceramics and pipe bowls were types known to have been made as early as the beginning of the 17th century. The collection also includes fragments of a Spanish earthenware ceramic costrel (handled jug), a type found elsewhere in Virginia after 1619 (However, since no other site in Virginia was settled as early as 1607, this may not mean that what was found elsewhere has any relevance to the date of this well.).

It is safe to say that this well was a water source for the occupants of James Fort sometime during its formative Virginia Company years. Precisely what those fort period years were, and exactly when the upper brick lining collapsed and put the well out of use, is difficult to say. Some things did wind up at the bottom likely by accident during its use, notably a hardly corroded, late-16th-century pewter drinking mug known as a flagon, complete with the initials of a married couple whose surname began with the

Figure 56. A brick-lined well in the original parade ground, Smithfield, known to be just west of James Fort (left) beside apparent Civil War storage shaft (right).

initial "P" and whose Christian names began with "R" and "E."[50] Also by chance or accident, "used" containers may have slipped into the functioning well including a pewter wine jug known as a measure, a Portuguese (Merida) jug and an early 17th-century German stoneware Bartmann jug. Many iron implements were also lost in the well including the well bucket swivel handle and a number of hoes and axes probably once tied to the bucket to act as counter weights.[51] Much also went into the shaft after the well head collapsed and the well was abandoned, including a curious collection of what appears to be most of one man's armor: a burgonet type helmet, front and rear gorgets to protect the neck, a breast plate and a number of tassetts or frontal hip and thigh protective plates. Apparently these were discarded perhaps either because they had become obsolete in favor of the lighter and less restraining "jackets" or, perhaps, because enough years of peace with the Virginia Indians before the uprising in 1622 lured the settlers into thinking such protection was no longer necessary (see also Chapter V).

The discovery of a red-oak wooden curb beneath the brick shaft at the bottom of the well reveals how the shaft was constructed, and could eventually be the key to an exact time of construction. Again, evidence shows that the settlers first dug a 12' wide basin from the colonial ground surface to a convenient depth for accessibility. Then builders narrowed the basin diameter, creating a step. They then continued digging downward another four feet until reaching wet soil at the ground water table. At that point workers seated the wooden ring-like curb on the surface and built a chest-high cylinder of bricks. Their next step was to dig inside and under the curb, allowing the section of brick shaft to slide downward. Then the process was repeated: brick courses were built on the partially lowered shaft, then gradual lowering of the shaft was done by more under-cutting and so on until reaching a depth where enough water could accumulate to make the well operational.

It was necessary to employ this seemingly overly-complicated process because at the water table level and on down, there was no other way to go deeper and still have the brick shaft hold back the soft, sandy clay sides of the hole. Once the soft water-bearing walls below the water table were secure, the shaft could be built up, from **above** the water table to the surface. Levels of brick fragments, dropped by the masons as they formed and implanted the small wedges, indicate that the shaft went up in chest-high increments followed by the packing of backfill outside it, until it reached the 17th-century surface. At that point, the well builders mortared the well head above ground as the deposit of mortar-encrusted bricks deep in the shaft fill indicate. This top down/ water table up well-building method was common in England and Virginia.[52]

The presence of the waterlogged wooden curb was not only the key to learning the construction process, but more importantly, it can date the well construction more precisely than other artifacts. How so? The curb wood was in such good condition that it was possible to still see growth rings which were produced each year throughout the life of the original tree. Yearly growth-ring width in trees depends upon the amount of rainfall, wider in wet years, narrower in dry years (see Chapter 2). Hence, comparison of the pattern of the curb rings with the known ring sequence for the Jamestown region can determine when the tree lived and when it was felled. That analysis is now in progress. In the meantime, the ca. late-1610-20s construction date and a 1620s backfilling date stand as the well's lifetime.

But even more significant than its well-preserved artifacts is the opportunity the well presents to test Jamestown well water and Strachey's discussion of wells in 1610. Strachey's depth estimate appears to be correct: six ancient fathoms (18').[53] The shaft only stood 14' as found, but the missing four feet probably disappeared during the Civil War grading in 1861. Strachey also blames the rash of deaths during the "Starving Time" winter of 1609-1610 on the brackish and polluted water in the well. So chemical testing of the newly discovered fort-era well was in order. To do that, water samples were taken to be tested.

What would this test of the modern Jamestown water table find? If anything, the ground water at Jamestown should have proven more contaminated than it was in 1607. For example, today's water should be more highly saline than it was

Figure 57. Brick-lined well with half excavated construction shaft. Artifacts from the deposit date the construction of the well to the later Fort period, ca. 1620.

four centuries ago, given an estimated sea-level rise of four feet. Also, given modern industrial river pollution and over one hundred years use of the APVA Jamestown septic system on the Island, one could reasonably expect the tests to find much higher levels of pollution in the water table than existed during the Fort period.[54]

The salt levels, however, proved negligent. This indicates that the nearby brackish river and swampy wetlands have no effect on the water table in the well. In fact, the testing found that the Jamestown water is clean enough to meet modern drinking water standards after removing the contaminants from the modern excavation.

So was Strachey wrong about the Jamestown well water salt content and if so, why? Explanation may lie in the probable source of his information. In his preface to *The History of Travell*, wherein he discusses the allegedly polluted well, Strachey credits Percy as his source: *"from [whom] these Commentaries and observations, I must freely confess I have collected these passages and knowledges.*[55] It is likely that Percy, who was acting-governor of the settlement during the "Starving Time," would blame all the deaths under his watch on something other than shortage of food. After all, it might have appeared that Percy could have prevented death by starvation by his own abilities to negotiate for food. Percy may have also had an incentive to discredit his old Jamestown enemy, Captain John Smith, who had already reported digging the first well at Jamestown in 1609 which, reportedly, held only "sweet water." Perhaps today the "sweet" ground water that was scientifically found at Jamestown may help historians ferret out just who was telling the truth in some of the 17th-century eye-witness accounts of the fort period. This brings into focus what may be otherwise obscure in documents. Strachey relied unquestionably on Percy's reports. But at least some of Percy's information may have had what today might be called a positive "spin" on reality.

At first, finding a well where Strachey basically said the west fort wall was located seemed to suggest further Strachey error. Perhaps he had underestimated the size of the Fort, in which case, the well found was actually inside and not outside the original triangle. Or, it began to seem plausible that slaves or soldiers constructing the Civil War earthwork around the long-abandoned well site had scoured out the interior so deeply that the palisade wall trench had been destroyed.

While this well did appear to wind up outside the original triangle, it was also logical to assume that just as the fort was expanded to the east, so too it could have been expanded to the west. In that case, a relocated west wall would lie beyond the present western limits of the excavation. Consequently, this well would lie within the expanded fort walls. But if that were the case, then it was logical to assume that the well would be located near the center of the expanded fort: so either Strachey had underestimated the fort size by half, or a later expanded fort had doubled the size of the structure after he wrote about it in 1610. That being the case, then, this well would likely be a replacement of the first well reported by Smith in 1609.

At that time, logical thinking suggested the following questions: Are Strachey's accounts just plain false? Could the discovery of a fort-period well in the area where Strachey's dimensions suggest the west wall line should be, just prove another Percy error in fact?

These questions are asking whether the well location, as found, is actually more evidence that Strachey relied on other self-serving Percy details such as the size of the fort. This inference does not necessarily follow, unless Strachey never really got to Jamestown at all. If Strachey did come to Jamestown, why would he rely on Percy's description of things he could clearly see for himself?

The tone of Strachey's text suggests that he is writing firsthand as an eyewitness at Jamestown. In fact, the archaeological discovery in the southeast fort bulwark of a brass signet ring with a version of the Strachey family crest engraved on it is unusually clear proof of his actual presence at Jamestown. Still, for Strachey to credit Percy for the "*observations*" (dimensions) might well mean that Strachey did not personally measure the fort but, perhaps, just took notes while Percy gave him more, and possibly incorrect, statistics. If this latter scenario were true, then the well location as found might mean that the Fort was larger than the 1.75 acres that would have been enclosed by the length of Strachey's three walls. But remember, the discovery of the north bulwark in 2003 established, in fact, a smaller fort.

While it was fairly clear, before the 2003 season began, where the missing link in the east wall/north bulwark had to be, and which direction to dig from, the fort-period well was a puzzling tossup. If the well location meant the fort was larger than the Strachey-inspired model, then further north and west seemed the way to go. But there remained the strong possibility that the Civil War scouring had erased the west wall exactly where Strachey had seen it; so digging north and west could go on forever and never find the vanished wall line. Clearly, what needed to be established was how deep the scouring went in 1861 and/or to find soil levels that had escaped that disturbance.

The first archaeological look at Jamestown soil under the Civil War earthwork 45 years earlier was a reminder to the *Jamestown Rediscovery* team that archaeologists since 1954 had known that the 17th-century layers lay unscathed there. This then would be the area in which to establish the pre-1861 soil level.

The objective was to see if the pre-1861 soil level was more than two feet higher than the present surface inside the earthwork. If not, then clearly the west wall evidence there would be gone. Also, under the earthwork would likely be the only place where the west wall trench would

Figure 58. Late-16th, early-17ᵗʰ-century pewter flagon at the "moment of discovery."

be preserved if the scouring had gone deeper than the 1607 trench. This suggested digging from the well toward the river.

That effort in the summer of 2003 turned out to be barren. The last place to dig then would be toward the southeast, right into the height of the Confederate earthworks.[56] Disturbing the Civil War landscape had always been a last resort, as it was an original piece of Jamestown Island history which was a part of the Island's significance. Also the thought of having to remove from four to eight feet of modern to 1861-deposited soil, before getting the answer to the 1607 grade question, was daunting. Almost equally as daunting was the 1907 statue of Captain John Smith which had been erected near the earthwork in that direction. Just before the *Jamestown Rediscovery* project began, Dr. John Cotter, the distinguished Jamestown archaeologist from the 1950s excavation of the Civil War earthwork, jokingly mused that John Smith was gazing out into the river looking at his vanished Fort.[57] In other words, take heed future archaeologists: the Fort is truly gone. Yet, even if truth be known, and despite years of evidence to the contrary, until the third leg of the triangle could be found, there was still some chance that Cotter was right. But finally, excavation at last proved once and for all that the John Smith statute peered from a secure place **within** the Fort. Much to everyone's surprise, the Fort wall appeared within this new test trench!

Multiple excavation trenches followed along the west line, tracing it to the bank of the river where the seawall construction had ended river erosion around 1901. Digging then continued intermittently on each side of a mound of earth left from a Civil War bombproof, for a total of 200'. Once established, the entire triangle became a known entity. Extending each angle line until it intersected another, gave the true dimensions of the fort's triangular shape: 304+-' on each land side (100 yards +-) and 425+-' (140 yards+-) along the river, enclosing a total of 1.1 acres. Now it was clear that Strachey had in fact given accurate measurements, but it was technically describing not the "curtain" of the Fort, but rather where the angle lines of the walls intersected. Actually the sentence following his dimensions were meant to tell us that he had measured that way. He writes that he considered the curtain to end *"where the lines meet,* [where] *a watch tower or bulwark was raised…"* but we misread him. Consequently, the fort model was more than a half acre too big, fostering a considerable amount of almost fruitless digging on the north and west side of the actual wall.

Figure 59. View of west palisade wall trench (arrows) and apparent west bulwark trench at the point where pre-concrete seawall river erosion ended in 1901.

Yet in the end James Fort was found at last. From that day forward, there has been no frustration and no head scratching when it comes time to begin adding another 10'-square patch to the James Fort "quilt." Now there is no doubt that removal of parts of the Civil War earthwork inside what we now know is the James Fort triangle will reveal the true first town plan. Stay tuned.

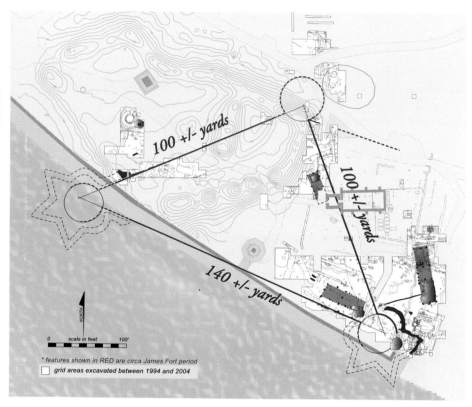

Figure 60. Extensions of the three James Fort palisade wall trenches found by archaeologists are identical to William Strachey's 1610 figures proving that he measured between bulwarks from points where the lines of the angles met, 300 yards X 300 yards X 140 yards.

Chapter III

Forging Democracy

There is more to the *Jamestown Rediscovery* archaeological story than finding James Fort. There is a political dimension. Just as Jamestown claims its place among America's premier historic sites as the first enduring English settlement in North America, it also rates national prominence for being the place where the first elected representative government met in English America. The story of the origin and growth of American democracy begins with the meeting of the first General Assembly in 1619 at the Jamestown Church, and ends in 1698 with the burning of the Jamestown Statehouse Complex.[1] It is a story of evolutionary growth, reflected in the nature of the Jamestown meeting places.

Symbolically the story begins in borrowed space in a building designed for worship, and winds up in its own space in a building complex designed specifically for self-government. That structure, with its attached and largely public-owned living spaces, is arguably the largest Colonial public building (23,000 square feet) ever built in what would become the United States of America. Like the final Statehouse built of brick, self-government at Jamestown in the 17th century grew solid.

Both the church and the Statehouse sites are on the APVA part of Jamestown Island, the church on the east and the Statehouse Complex on the west. Full archaeological and architectural study of what is probably the very first General Assembly site, at the now reconstructed church, remains to be done. But excavations of the Statehouse Complex spanning more than a century can now unveil the rather dramatic 33-year story of that last Jamestown Capitol.

During the initial construction of the Jamestown concrete seawall by the Army Corps of Engineers in 1901, the engineer in charge, Samuel Yonge, noticed a brick building foundation protruding from the eroded river bank along the western side of the APVA's 22.5-acre portion of the Jamestown site. In his book, *The Site of Old Jamestown, 1903,* he describes the foundation excavation that followed.[2]

Yonge traced the entire extent of the brickwork by digging along the walls uncovering remains of five contiguous buildings built over time from the river side eastward. He also discovered the foundations of six chimneys and two additions with cellars to the north. Yonge excavated the cellars, finding a three-foot square, and a three-foot-deep brick-lined pit in the bottom of one of them, which he thought was a well. Charred debris led him to conclude that the building had burned. He also thought that the eastern section of the five-part building fit documentary references to the Jamestown Statehouse which was first built at public expense in 1663-

Fort Site

Statehouse Complex

Figure 61. Samuel Yonge (far upper left) his 1901 excavation of
the Statehouse Complex (lower right) and the marked State
House Ridge Foundation, 1920s (center).

65, burned in 1676, was repaired
by 1685, and was burned again
and abandoned in 1698.[3] While
the excavation was crude by mod-
ern standards, this work and his study of erosion rates of the shoreline
and land records throughout the town site were remarkably thorough and
insightful. For example, he was one of the few who prophetically thought
remains of James Fort still could be found on land in the vicinity of the
church tower.[4]

　　In any event, it appeared that his digging at the Statehouse Complex
cleared away some of the debris from its destruction by fire in 1698 and/
or from the 1676 Bacon's Rebellion fire. The foundations were eventu-

Figure 62. Yonge's excavation plan of the State House Ridge.

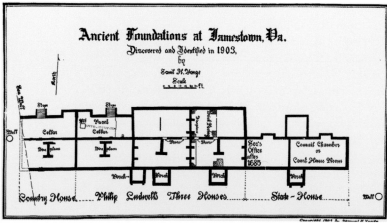

Ancient Foundations at Jamestown, Va.

Discovered and Identified in 1903,
by
Saml H. Yonge
Scale

Country House — Philip Ludwell — Three Houses — State - House

ally capped with concrete and the cellars rebuilt from bricks salvaged from them.

Yonge recovered a number of artifacts from his Statehouse Complex excavations, particularly from the cellars. This collection survives in the APVA archives.[5] Yonge found a number of iron hinges and a distinctive door lock plate, identical to a lock found at 1665 Bacon's Castle. The cellar floor was also littered with a number of military items including a number of hand grenades, bills and cannon balls, evidence consistent perhaps with public use of the building. Yonge also found a distinctive type of decorative brick known as a mullion brick which is usually used in church windows.

As a contribution to the 350th celebration of Jamestown's founding, the APVA and the National Park Service seriously considered reconstruction of the easternmost unit of the Statehouse Complex, identified then as the "third and fourth State House." This goal required two major investigations of the eastern end unit by National Park Service archaeologists.

Figure 63. Some of the artifacts from Yonge's excavation of the Statehouse Complex cellar including building hinges, a door lock (bottom, left) and 17th-century bills (center) and grenades (top).

Louis Caywood led the first excavation of the Statehouse Complex in 1954.[6] He basically dug along the exposed eastern end of the foundations, opening trenches three-feet wide on either side of the brickwork. Caywood found evidence of a partition wall undetected by Yonge, burned floor joists, some roofing tiles and slate. He also recovered bones from six graves.

Joel Shiner, took over the Statehouse excavations the following year, to explore the burial ground component of the site.[7] Shiner cleared away all of the topsoil and whatever accumulated building debris Caywood had missed, and dug down to the top of pre-building subsoil in order to locate and test additional graves. Shiner found 70 grave outlines and uncovered the bones from seven. He also recovered a large number of artifacts across the actual Statehouse footing, and tested an area adjacent to the chimney foundation in Building 1.

Artifacts from these excavations are mostly building materials. Domestic objects are distinctly sparse, perhaps more evidence of public use. Shiner also recov-

Figure 64. Dated window leads from 1956 excavation, 1678 and 1686.

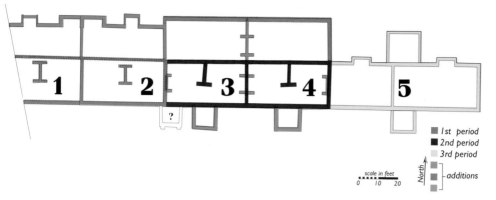

Figure 65. Statehouse foundations showing building sequence.

1st period
2nd period
3rd period
additions

scale in feet
0   10   20

North

ered lead from casement-type windows in a disturbed soil area outside Buildings 4 and 5 bearing dates of 1678, 1683, and 1686. These were likely installed during repairs or from a rebuild in the later 17th century.[8]

Excavation and re-excavation of the masonry footings of the Statehouse Ridge Complex in 2000-2002, and subsequent archaeological and architectural interpretation of those building remains, draw a clear picture of the original structure.[9] The sequence of construction of the various building units through time, certain masonry and frame details from unit to unit, and an architectural survey of English and American brick buildings of the same time period and scale, together offer a convincing basis for a conjectural reconstruction of the complex.[10]

Jamestown Rediscovery excavations of the Statehouse Ridge Complex, confirmed Yonge's conclusion that Buildings 1 and 2, 3 and 4, and 5 were built from west to east. The brickwork of each successive foundation abutted rather than bonded onto its predecessor, confirming the west to east building campaign.

The first two double units in line, Buildings 1 and 2, each had continuous foundations, indicating that the two were built at the same time. The mortar used in the two double units was identical. Therefore they were almost certainly built close in time to each other.[11] It is uncertain how contemporaneous the double unit Buildings 3 and 4 are with double units 1 and 2, but identical mortar in 3 and 4 indicates that they were built close in time, one onto the other.[12]

Buildings 1 and 2 were doubled in size and cellars added, but whether this happened before or after Building 5 existed at the eastern end of the line of buildings is not evident. No artifacts excavated in 1903 can be reliably ascribed to deposition during construction, so a precise time for the addition remains unknown. Also the relatively scant fragments of builder's fill that survived the 1950s excavations along the Building 5 foundation produced nothing datable. Nor were datable artifacts found in the original construction scaffold holes recently excavated, with one exception. A probable repair scaffold hole produced a fragment of Virginia-

made pottery, Challis type, which dates to ca. 1690. There is a preponderance of "early style" flat clay roofing tiles on the site of Buildings 1
and 2, and yet a shift to a preponderance of curved pantiles from the area
of the footings of Buildings 3 and 4 could suggest some separation in time
between the construction of Buildings 1 and 2, and construction of Buildings 3 and 4.

The relative chronology of additions is clear: Buildings 3 and 4 were
constructed <u>after</u> the addition to Buildings 1
and 2 . This was determined by the fact that
the lowest courses of the foundations of
Buildings 3 and 4 were stone, suggesting a
later construction time-period than the all-
brick addition to Buildings 1 and 2. Also the
Buildings 3 and 4 footing abutted rather than
bonded into the Building 2 footing, proving
that this addition was the final major structure adjoined to the original Buildings 1-4
core. Building 5 had two additions to the
original main body of the structure, a porch
chamber on the south and a massive stair
tower on the north. How soon after the original construction these were added could not
be determined.

It is clear that the main body of Building
5 had an original brick cross-wall dividing the
building into two unequal sized spaces. The
interior plans of the other buildings suggested
by their original H-shaped, back-to-back
fireplaces indicate equal sized rooms and
lobby entrances south of the chimneys. Tests
into the interior fill of Buildings 2, 3 and 4
indicated that they had all burned and that
the H-shaped chimneys in Buildings 3 and
4 were removed and replaced by end chimneys. Scaffold holes apparently from the new

Figure 66. Brick bonding sequence showing that
Building 5 was built onto and therefore after Building 4. The same non-bonded footings appeared
between Buildings 2 and 3, and the two rear additions.

end chimney construction at the east end of Building 3 were found inside
and cutting through burned levels in Building 2, indicating that Building
2 was in ruins when the alteration took place in Building 3 next door. Also
the discovery of a re-used decorative gauged (rubbed smooth) brick, a type
not used in Virginia until the late-17th century, suggests that the move
from central to end chimneys took place toward the end of the 1600s.[13]
The stair towers centered on Buildings 3 and 4 also abutted the main body
of the buildings, showing that they were later additions, probably added
as part of the late-17th-century remodeling.[14] Foundations of central fire-

85

Figure 67. Trade token dated 1667 from the Globe Tavern on Chancery Lane, London. Found in fill inside Yonge's mystery "porch foundation."

places were also found to be additions to the partition walls in Buildings 3 and 4 additions, probably remains of cooking hearths for each complex. Partition walls may have typically divided the main block of Buildings 3 and 4 into two unequal sized rooms, the hall and parlor. Future excavation of the fire and occupation levels tested so far should provide concrete evidence for this supposition.

Yonge reported finding an additional "porch" foundation which he proceeded to cap in concrete as he did all the other footings. Since its location, straddling the union of Buildings 2 and 3, makes no logical architectural sense, this footing was excavated further in 2002. No brick footing was found under the concrete. This is puzzling because Yonge clearly understood the other footings. He guessed that this odd footing belonged to some earlier structure. The datable artifacts from this so-called footing, however, dated with unusual precision to the last third of the 17th century, including window leads of 1671 and 1686, a tradesman's token from the Globe Tavern dated 1667, and Green Spring and Challis pottery, ca. 1660-1710. Artifacts from disturbed contexts over Building 2 produced the earliest materials from the site including types of local tobacco pipes and a sword pommel from the second quarter of the 17th century.[15]

An in-depth architectural study produced a conjectural reconstruction of the entire Statehouse Complex.[16] Details of the reconstruction are based on the foundation floor plan, some building remains, parallel contemporary buildings in England and mortar analysis, the latter determining that the exterior walls were painted solid red (see Figure 68).

Sorting out the documentary history of the Statehouse Complex enlightens its archaeological/architectural story, giving historical meaning to the physical remains. But that has not been an easy task. To what specific buildings the documents actually refer requires myopic scrutiny of the entire documentary trail of "state house" references, going back to the original meeting place, the Jamestown Church. Without this more complete chronological story, the meaning of some documents and the story of the later Statehouse prove to be extremely difficult to pin down.

For example, there appears to be a reference to a Statehouse on the western ridge as early as 1656, but other archaeological data and an alternate reading of that document do not support the existence of a building that early on the ridge. Indeed, that particular document could be quite logically read as a reference establishing the location of the Statehouse, at that time, far to the east, in the New Town section of Jamestown.[17] At any rate, and despite some difficulty resolving apparent gaps and discrepancies in the records, piecing together a logical scenario for the Jamestown meeting places of the General Assembly is possible, from its inception in 1619 until it officially moved to Williamsburg in 1699 (see Cotter map, page 88). But first, because the story of the buildings is so interwoven with the evolving nature of the General Assembly over the course of the 17th century, a thumbnail history of that body is in order.

The first assemblies comprised a unicameral body from 1619 to 1643 and consisted of the governor appointed by the crown, the 12-member council appointed by the governor, and the burgesses elected from the various plantations and Jamestown. These earliest assemblies were not modelled on the English Parliament but on the Virginia Company's governing body, and had quite limited authority. Only gradually did the General Assembly of the Virginia colony take on more meaningful characteristics of a representative legislature, after the London Company went bankrupt in 1624.

In 1643, Governor Berkeley encouraged the burgesses to sit apart from the Council of State, and thus was born the House of Burgesses. This, of course, required a separate space for each body to meet, and possibly separate buildings. Once split into the two bodies, the governance model in the colony became more like the English Parliament, though there were still profound differences between the General Assembly in Jamestown and the Westminister legislature in London. The General Assembly in far-off Virginia grew largely independent of direction from London, and reached its zenith of power in the 1660s and 1670s. The 1676 uprising against Virginia's governor, Sir William Berkeley, and the subsequent burning of Jamestown during Bacon's Rebellion, caused the Crown to interfere in the Assembly's business thereafter with the result that the assembly lost much of its independence. The principal business of the General Assembly became the enactment of statutes that governed a great variety of the business of the colony, but through the process of legislating the colonials acquired the skills to govern themselves.[18]

The first elected burgesses at Jamestown met July 30-August 4,

Figure 68. Hypothethical reconstruction of the State House Complex.

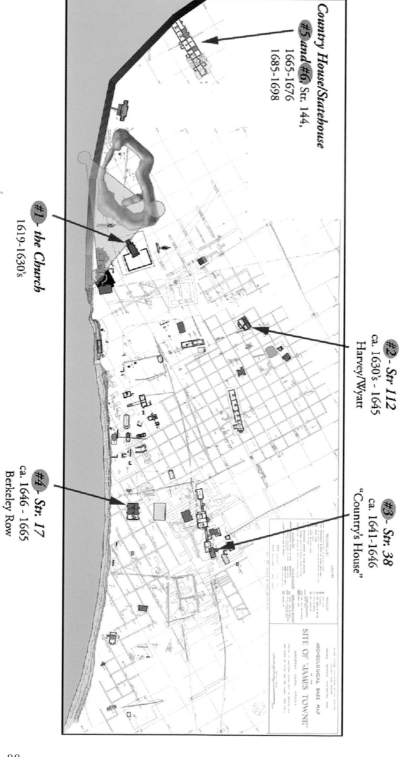

"State Houses" 1619-1698

Country House/Statehouse
#5 and #6 Str. 144,
1665-1676
1685-1698

#1– the Church
1619-1630's

#2– Str. 112
ca. 1630's - 1645
Harvey/Wyatt

#3– Str. 38
ca. 1641-1646
"Country's House"

#4– Str. 17
ca. 1646 - 1665
Berkeley Row
"late/Old State Houses"

Figure 69. Mary Jeffrey Galt (upper left) and her Jamestown Church excavation, 1901.

1619, in the only building large enough at the time to accommodate a sizable group meeting, the Jamestown Church, where *"...the most convenient place we could finde to sit in was the Quire of the churche."[19]* Tradition places that first Statehouse/Church immediately adjacent to and east of the 17th-century brick church tower that is still standing. It seems clear that the church in 1619 was not built of brick, nor is the existing tower originally a part of that early church. Actually the first reference to the construction of a brick church appears in 1639, [20] and the building seems to have been under construction until as late as 1646.[21] The original church was a mere sail cloth awning which evolved into a more permanent timber structure in 1608. As the 1608 timber structure appears to have seen a number of years of neglect, it was rebuilt in 1617.[22] This rebuilt 1617 church then was the site of the First Assembly two years later. Archaeological evidence that the church of 1617 was technically the first "Statehouse" may have been found during excavations adjacent to the tower, led by a founder of the APVA, Mary Jeffry Galt, from 1893-1903.[23]

Galt uncovered two brick foundations next to the standing tower. She wrote that *"with her own hands"* she had uncovered two brick foundations: a larger but shorter 2nd-period foundation, and a slightly narrower and longer and earlier brick-on-cobblestone footing. Galt decided that since

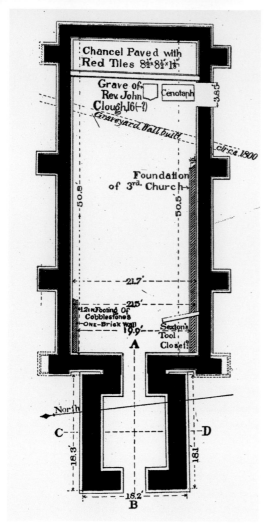

Inside the figure:
Chancel Paved with Red Tiles 8½"×8½"×1½"

Grave of Rev. John Clough 16(-?)

Cenotaph

-3.85

Graveyard Wall built

circa 1800

Foundation of 3rd. Church →

50.8

50.5

←---- 21.7' ----→

---- 25' ----

12 in Footing of Cobblestones

ONE-Brick wall

19.9'

Sexton's Tool Closet

A

North

C --------+------- D

18.3'

18.1

---- 18.2' ----

B

Figure 70. Yonge's plan of Jamestown Church Foundation excvation, 1901.

the dimensions of the brick/cobble foundation matched those specified in 1608, then this footing must have once supported the church built by Christopher Newport's sailors in that same year.[24] This, Galt concluded, was the place where the General Assembly first met. That representative body continued to gather in the choir loft until it outgrew the space.[25]

If you can believe the Virginia governor, Sir John Harvey, by 1629 some or all governmental meetings wound up taking place in his house. He complained in 1632 that "his" house had served as the colony's Statehouse at his expense for three years running.[26] This might also mean that he held the quarterly council meetings there while the once-a-year full Assembly met in the church (until construction of the new brick church commenced in 1639). But despite Harvey's objections, there is good reason to suppose that Harvey's house continued serving the government as "State house"(his words) throughout his tenure at Jamestown, and even after he left office and Virginia.

In 1641, the Virginia government bought his home lot which included a "...tenement now used as a courthouse and one piece or plot of ground lying and being on the west side of the said capital."[27]

Recent land plat research suggests hypothetically that the Harvey house/ "State house" was located where a substantial house foundation appeared during National Park Service excavations 1954-56.[28]

Labeled Structure 112, the excavations indicated that this had been a sizable building for Jamestown at the time. The digging revealed a construction date during Harvey's governorship, during the second quarter of the 17th century. That this was Harvey's house/ "State house" is also strengthened by the archaeological recovery there of a plaster leopard's head; that symbol was part of Sir Harvey's family coat-of-arms.[29]

Figure 71. Park Service excavation of Structure 112 (left), likely Governor Harvey's house/Statehouse (below).

In 1639, King Charles I of England instructed Sir Francis Wyatt, Harvey's successor, to build *"...a convenient house for the meeting of the council and dispatch of public charge."* [30] Until 1643, the burgesses and the council had met together, so this building is apparently intended as the one meeting place for the Virginia government per se. There is no direct evidence that Wyatt carried out this mandate. In fact, as late as 1644, a land patent to a merchant/burgess, John White, for half an acre of land relatively close to Structure 112, bordering on land *"appertaining to the statehouse"*...on the east, suggests that the former Harvey house and lot, located northeast and apparently contiguous to the White property, still functioned as the Statehouse. [31] Or, the Harvey house could have been put back in government service in 1643 after the governor, Sir William Berkeley, had the burgesses agree to meet separately from the council. [32] After 1643, the separated House of Burgesses needed its own meeting space, which could have necessitated a totally separate building. It is possible that another building, referred to as the *"country's house"* (belonging to the *"country of Virginia"*), may have served the council and court, while Harvey's old house now public-owned (Structure 112), likely would have been used by the new House of Burgesses.

In any event, land records and archaeological excavations in 1934-41 appear to locate the *"country's house"* some 350 feet from the river toward the western end of New Town. [33] The 53'x 20' foundation of a brick house found there (labeled Structure 38 by National Park Service archaeologists) could well be the remains of this *"country's house"* which served as a meeting place for the Virginia colony's council and court until it was named in a 1652 directive to be repaired *"...and the cellars[let] for the public benefit."* [34]

The relatively scant remains of Structure 38 are difficult to interpret because the construction of another but slightly smaller and later 17th-century Structure 31 disturbed the original building remains. [35] What does remain, however, suggests that like Building 112, for Jamestown at this time Structure 38 was a sizable and permanent brick building.

Figure 72. Structure 38/31 foundation during 1950s excavation, likely the "country's house" of ca. 1640s.

So the *"country's house"* and Harvey's house may have served as the major governmental meeting places while the next governor, Sir William Berkeley, established himself at Jamestown and began directing Virginia's affairs. Governor Berkeley came to Jamestown carrying yet another charge, to build

> *...at ye public charge of ye country a convenient house to be built where you and the council may meet and sitt for dispatching of public affairs and hearing causes.*[36]

By February 1645, Governor Berkeley's "house" in town was well underway.[37] Even though this was not built *"at ye public charge"* (with public funds), this house appears to have been Berkeley's version of a *"convenient house where you and the council may meet and sitt."* The cellar units of the governor's new hosue had been completed before the builder ran into a shortage of materials (brick?). In a letter to Governor Berkeley, Secretary Richard Kemp, wrote: *"...that at Towne for want of materials* [your building] *is yet not higher than ye first storye above ye cellar."* [38] Based upon a number of descriptions of this building when it sold in later years, it is clear that once completed (1645?), it was a three-part brick row house (so described in 1655).

Before 1655, certain units of the governor's new house at Jamestown hosted the General Assembly and served as the town residence of Berkeley himself. Berkeley left the governorship in 1652 when he surrendered to the Commonwealth troops at Jamestown's door. Berkeley then retired to his country home, Green Spring, five miles from Jamestown. Thereafter he sought to get rid of his three-unit Jamestown building, hereafter referred to as Berkeley Row.[39]

Changes in ownership of Berkeley Row over time led to the building being invariably referred to as a three-part building at first called "*the late State house*" and then the "*old State house.*" It is useful here to recount the post-Statehouse history of Berkeley Row because this background may eliminate confusion between references to Berkeley Row and the Statehouse Complex.[40]

Two real estate references begin to indicate that Berkeley Row was "*the State house*" before 1655:

> *March 24, 1655. Ordered that Collo. Francis Morrison [former Berkeley Councilor] take assurance of Sr. Wm. Berkeley, Knt., of the middle brick house in James Citty bought of him the said Sr. Willm Berkeley, as also that he give Mr. Tho. Woodhouse Livery & Seizen of the late State house.*

On March 30, 1655, William Berkeley for 27,000 pounds of tobacco sold to "*Richard Bennett, Esq., Governour of Virginia…my house in James Cittie, lately in the tenure of William Whittby being the westernmost of the three brickhouses which I there built.*"[41]

So these documents establish that during the last few months of his governorship, Governor Richard Bennett bought the westernmost unit of the "late State house" which had been so designated, perhaps, because it was the former governor's house, it was likely the meeting place of the council, and it was possibly the meeting place of the burgesses. It is tempting to assign the governor's residence, the council chamber, and the burgess assembly room to each of the three units. The middle unit and/or the middle and easternmost units seem to be called the "*late State house*" and therefore must have once been known as, or functioned as, the Statehouse.

It is equally tempting to conclude that the said westernmost unit of the row became Governor Bennett's house because it had already served as a governor's house (Governor Berkeley's), and so was conveniently designed for the residence of a governor and was possibly somewhat furnished as such. It also makes sense that Thomas Woodhouse, who was given the "*late State house*" by the March 30, 1655 Berkeley grant, would be interested in the units formerly used for the Statehouse because Woodhouse was a tavern-keeper. A building built for gatherings of some size would appear to be easily adaptable for use as the public rooms of a tavern.

It is puzzling, however, why the Jamestown colony itself did not buy "*the late State house*" building from Berkeley. Perhaps this was the sign of an ailing public treasury. Instead, at General Assembly time, the colony's government occasionally opted to rent the space, a fact lamented by the burgesses in 1656 and 1660.[42]

Figure 73. A Chain of owners/occupants of Berkeley's Row,
1655-1671.

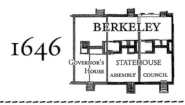

1646

APRIL, 1655

1661- 1667
(MISSING TRANSACTION)

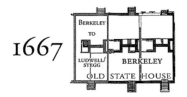

1667

1667 - 1670
(MISSING TRANSACTION)

1670

1671

It is clear from subsequent transfers of this property that the building was once the "*State house*" and then became the "*late State house*" until after 1665, when the building became the "*old State house*" and the final and most substantial "new" Statehouse existed at the western end of town.

The next Berkeley Row transaction was a January 1, 1667 grant to two men, Thomas Ludwell, Secretary of the colony, and Thomas Stegg, Councilor and Auditor General of the colony. The 1667 grant gave half an acre of land: "...*adjoyneing to the westernmost of those three houses all wch jointly we formerly called by the name of old State house...*"to Ludwell and Stegg, provided they build another house on the property.[43] Apparently they never occupied the "*old State house*" unit, nor did they follow through with another "house" construction. The property description gives useful details of the building's history, plan and location: the building now had become the "*old State house*" and had three units running 34 degrees south of east, 67 feet from the James River shore.[44] These details are critical to identifying the building site at Jamestown today (see Cotter map, page 88).

Then sometime between the 1667 Ludwell/Stegg acquisition and 1670, Berkeley regained all three units of his row house, and the western unit burned. Today we know about the re-acquisition and fire because in April 1670, for £25 sterling, Berkeley sold the western unit to Henry Randolph, Clerk of the

House of Burgesses.[45] Since Bennett is named in the 1670 transaction as the former and therefore probably last occupant, then Ludwell/Stegg apparently never occupied this unit. It may be that the burning of the westernmost unit quelled their plans for occupation and additional construction. Thus, the land reverted back to the now re-appointed Governor Berkeley .

From 1671 sales records, it is clear that after Henry Randolph, Clerk of the House of Burgesses, acquired the burned western unit, that Henry Randolph briefly owned or soon would own the entire three-part Berkeley Row. On April 7, 1671, there are clear records that show Randolph sold off all three units, one by one, to Council members or former Council members.[46] Here again it is shown by the sales records that since Bennett was the last occupant of the westernmost unit mentioned in the title chain, then not only did Ludwell/Stegg apparently never occupy their 1667 property, neither did Henry Randolph. It appears, however, that Randolph did repair the western unit because it is no longer called a ruin. Or, it could have been that the unit was still in ruins, but not listed as such, and perhaps it was Ludwell who actually rebuilt it. In fact, the price of the parcel had jumped from £25 to £150 by the time Berkeley bought it back, suggesting that Ludwell did rebuild it.[47] This is all to say that even though there was a rather complex chain of ownership of Berkeley Row, these records of change of ownerhip and all the noted conditions of various parts of the building begin to form a list of details about the building that appear to pinpoint the exact location of "*the State house.*"

So where on the town site did Berkeley's three-part, brick "*State house*" which eventually became known as the "*late State house*" and finally the "*old State house*" actually stand?[48] In fact, there is a three-part brick building foundation with the Berkeley Row dimensions, and compass alignment on the river bank, known as Structure 17.

Structure 17 is in all likelihood the Statehouse dating from ca.1646 when Berkeley returned to the colony and could oversee the building's completion, until 1652 when he surrendered to the English Commonwealth and temporarily retired to Green Spring. Just as there is a compelling chain of documentary proof, so too there is compelling archaeological/architectural evidence that dovetails with the story of ownership of Structure 17, beginning with Berkeley's original construction ca.1646 and ending in 1671, the last time the "*Old State house*" is on a record of sale.

The chain of evidence is compelling. First is the fact that Structure 17 is the **only** brick building found on the town site that was built as three equal-sized attached units. The compass orientation of its walls, 34 degrees east of north, matches perfectly the axis recorded for the "*old State house*" in 1667. No other building yet found at Jamestown was built in three-parts and on the 34-degree axis. This is not to say that all of the

Figure 74. Structure 17 during National Park Service excavations.

town has been completely excavated. But total excavation is not necessary because it is a known fact that the "*old State house*" of the sales record of 1667 was 67 feet from the river bank. Beginning in 1901, the various Jamestown excavations have together revealed any sizable brick foundation that has ever been built that close to the shore.[49] This can be said because of the way archaeologists have approached the process of digging, and because of the subsequent use of the town site itself.

As the town evolved into a plantation and its buildings disappeared in the 18th and 19th centuries, the land reverted to agriculture. Practically all of the 17th-century Jamestown site went under the plow. Consequently, with the exception of the Civil War earthworks area, all that archaeologists have had to do in order to reveal surviving 17th-century foundations is to remove the upper foot or so of blended soil. That means that **everything** that was left intact from as early as 1607 to the end of any construction at the site, shows up in excavations at the same relatively shallow depth. In other words, nothing can be missed by not digging deep enough. Also, and almost certainly, both the wider area excavations and the spaced cross-trenching during the extensive National Park Service excavations exposed all the substantial brick construction there was to see in a given area or trench. The "odd" compass axis recorded for the Statehouse in the 1667 sale, makes it all the more likely that the National Park Service's extensive north-south trenches would intersect every sizable brick foundation built on that angle in their path, even given the unexplored space between each trench.[50] Also the *Jamestown Rediscovery* excavations have revealed all buildings along the river from its property line 250' northwest. So by default, Structure 17 is indeed the prime candidate for Berkeley Row.

Actually, National Park Service excavations lead by Dr. John Cotter uncovered the three-part brick Structure 17 foundation for the third time.[51] What did remain of the building for Cotter consisted of three identical 20' x 40' (inside measurements) attached units with identical central H-shaped chimneys. Each chimney unit had closets attached between the north and south rooms, and each unit had a curious "dead" space between the chimney and their east walls. These plans are, in fact, **unusual** and **identically** so. It is reasonable, then, to suppose they were all designed and constructed by the same builder and therefore probably built close in time to each other. Each room of each unit also had identically placed entrances on the north and south. The building was likely all brick, the outer walls being built thick enough to support a one and one-half story, triple-gabled building above a half-below-ground English basement. The fact that the long axis walls are one-half course thicker than the end walls indicates the triple gable construction; that is to say, the long walls had to support two stories above the basement, while the end walls supported a single story to the roof. All four walls of the westernmost section were built at once and apparently first, but not long before the middle and eastern sections were added at one time.

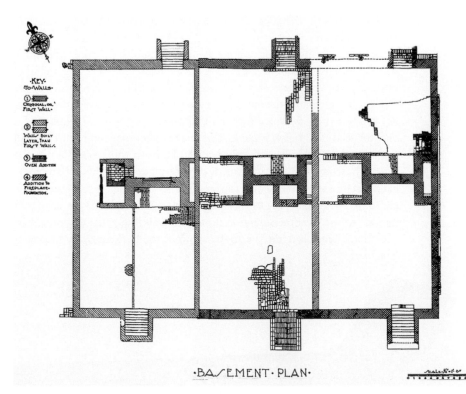

·BA/EMENT·PLAN·

Figure 75. Plan of Structure 17 foundations.

The identical plans and yet the flimsy original partition wall of the western unit may suggest that this was indeed Berkeley Row, including the unit Kemp reported having trouble getting completed for lack of bricks during Berkeley's absence in 1645.[52] An apparently projected shortfall of bricks by the builders may have resulted in less substantial construction. The subsequent halt in construction for want of bricks might explain a puzzling wall joint as well. The flimsy partition wall in the western unit cellar bonded into an outside wall which ordinarily suggests a two-phase building campaign, quite separate in time. But a single-course thick wall could not ever support an exterior wall of a building of Structure 17's proportions. In other words, builders may well have built what they could with the dwindling brick supply, assuming the supply ship would eventually come in so they could eventually complete the original three-part design. There is also evidence that after the three-part building stood, someone dug another cellar hole of equal unit size and began laying bricks for the cellar of a fourth unit on the west. Again the Ludwell and Stegg grant of 1667 required them to build or forfeit, which they apparently began to honor but then aborted. This physical evidence then seems to account for how Berkeley may have come back into ownership: forfeiture. So Berkeley could sell the same property to Henry Randolph in 1670.[53]

There remains the question of the age of Structure 17. Unfortunately what could be recorded archaeologically and what was recorded is meager owing to the number of different people digging into the ruins over three decades and the not so precise state-of-the-archaeological-art at the time of excavation. That is to say, the recovery of artifacts found in deposits that could have dated the building's construction, largely went unheeded. All of the dating evidence from all this digging appears to amount to a clay tobacco pipe bowl, some locally-made clay pipe stems, and a small fragment of bottle glass all found sealed beneath the brick floor in the central basement floor.[54] The most datable piece from this archaeological collection is a molded clay tobaco pipe bowl shaped into a style made ca. 1630-1640. This suggests a construction date for Structure 17 in that period of time, or sometime soon thereafter. It is likely that this pipe style could have been used into the 1640s, which is the Berkeley Row construction period.[55]

Figure 76. Molded local clay tobacco pipe of 1630-40 style found beneath the floor of Structure 17.

Berkeley Row, the "*old State house*" and Structure 17 are one and the same. By sorting through the various Statehouse references—"*country's house*" / "*State house*" / "*late State house*" / "*old State house*"—throughout the 17ᵗʰ century **which do not** pertain to the five-part Statehouse Ridge Complex on the western end of the town site, one can clearly see which references actually **do** pertain to the five-part Statehouse Complex on the western end of the town site

King Charles II charged the restored Governor Berkeley with a renewed and more serious effort to develop Jamestown into the prototypical "Cittie" it was supposed to be. Berkeley himself decided the details, which included a number of brick houses of standard size built at a scale that would command respect for the Crown as well as prominence and permanence for the colony.

On December 14, 1662, the burgesses specify,

> *Whereas his sacred majestie by his instructions hath enjoyned us to build a town...at James Citty as being the most convenient place in James River...the towne...shall consist of thirty-two houses...brick, forty foot long, twenty foot wide, within the walls, to be eighteen foot high above the ground, the walls to be two foot thick to the water table, and a brick and a halfe thick above the water table to the roof, the roof to be fifteen foote pitch and to be covered with slate or tile...That the houses be all regularly placed one by another in a square or such forme as the honorable Sir William Berkeley shall appoint most convenient.*[56]

In all likelihood, this legislation resulted in construction of the earliest of the four westernmost units of the Statehouse Ridge Complex. These four units were completed in just ten months. One of these would become a massive Statehouse, (Building 5) built specifically for the meeting place of the colonial government and completed in 1665:

> *April, 1665. [Virginians have] ...begun a town of brick & have already built enough to accommodate both ye public affairs of ye country & begin a factory for merchants.*[57]

Next, one of the statute brick houses belonging to the Colony, i.e. "*Countrie house*" was converted into a prison. It is possible that the first addition to the earliest unit, Building 1, served that purpose.

In 1672, the threat of an invasion by the Dutch prompted the Colony to construct a fort to protect the new Statehouse nearby. It apparently was a substantial structure being built of brick and some 250 feet in breadth. However, according to Reverend John Clayton, who was rector

1663

1665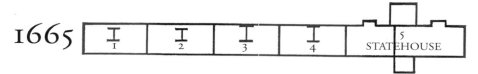

of James City Parish in the 1680s, it was a "*silly fort*" in that it was built in the "*vale*" which was at the head of a branch of the pitch and tar swamp that once extended out onto the longtime eroded-away Church Point.[58] Being on the southern slope of that valley appeared to render the fort ineffective. Artillerymen would not be able to train their guns on attacking ships coming up river until the ships cleared the high ground of Church Point that stood in the line of fire. By that time, the ships would be too close and could fire away point blank at the Fort and Statehouse. Apparently this critic did not know that the so-called "*silly fort*" had in fact succeeded at least once under fire. In 1673, the fort was apparently effective enough to protect the Statehouse as well as the Virginia tobacco fleet. In that year, Virginia ships escaped the Dutch by retreating up river and, by managing to get "…*above the Fort at James Towne* [and] *were safe.*"[59]

1668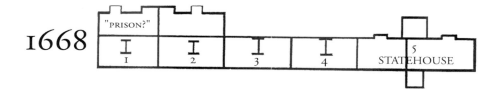

By the 1670s, the line of houses west of the Statehouse had been leased primarily to various men with political connections, a tradition apparently begun at the "*old State house*" of Structure 17. There, Building 1 was the "*country's house*" which was Berkeleys town "*apartment*" at the other end of the State House of Governor Berkeley,…. "*a coits toss…*" from the front of the Statehouse.[60]

Next to the "country's house" in Building 2 lived Major Theophilus Hone, Burgess for James City County and one of the builders of the Brick Fort. After the rebel, Nathaniel Bacon, destroyed the entire Statehouse Complex in 1676, Hone successfully petitioned the Assembly for a 50-year lease for the ruins of brick Buildings 3 and 4 formerly occupied by Arnold Cassinett, and Richard Aubourne, Clerk of the Council and later the House.[61] It is not known whether or not Cassinett played any role in

1673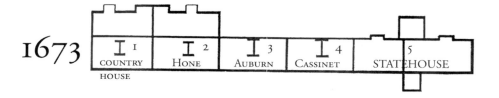

1677

the colonial government, which seems to be a common trait among most of the other 17th-century men who, in some way, occupied Jamestown's public buildings. Aubourne on the other hand was certainly at home among the political leadership of the time as a staunch supporter of Governor Berkeley, especially during Bacon's Rebellion. Aubourne eventually served the Colony as a Clerk of the House in 1680.[62]

Major Hone obviously never lived up to the lease requirement that he rebuild Auborne and Cassinett's house. The ruins went up for lease to Colonel Nathaniel Bacon (cousin of Nathaniel Bacon, Jr., the rebel). Colonel Bacon, a longtime Berkeley councilor, won out over another lease petition by a George Lee. At the same time, Colonel Philip Ludwell petitioned for a lease for Buildings 1 and 2, the jail and the land belonging to this complex. That this transaction and the other adjoining leases pertain to the Statehouse Complex is clear from the fact that the land of Ludwell's Building 1 and 2 shows up as a northern boundary of a 1683

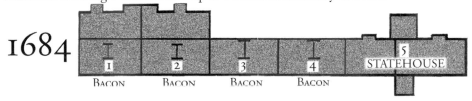

1684

land grant south of the Statehouse Complex, to Edward Chilton. Chilton was another politico serving as Assembly Clerk and ultimately Attorney General. Chilton's grant also mentions the Brick Fort as a reference point on the northwest corner of the property.

Meanwhile, the Statehouse lay in ruins and nothing seems to have been put in motion to rebuild it until a contract was let to Colonel Philip Ludwell for that purpose. The building was in all likelihood finished by Henry Hartwell by 1685.[63] Ludwell apparently did not rebuild it. Nor were Buildings 1 and 2 rebuilt, so they then reverted to Nathaniel Bacon. This made Bacon the sole leasee of the entire complex except for the Statehouse.[64]

Oct. 5, 1685 *"...in order to hold a General Assembly...they [Burgesses] repair to the ye state house*[65] and *"Ordered that Mr. Auditor Bacon pay to Col. Phillip Ludwell fouer hundred pounds sterl ...for and in consideration of rebuilding ye state house."* [66]

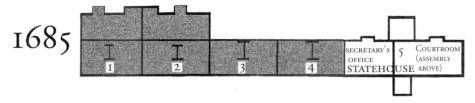

1685

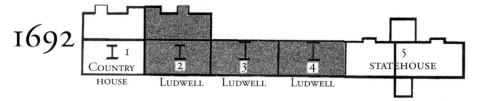

Records show that the new or rebuilt Statehouse sat on the same site as the 1665 building, and there are references as to which rooms were used for various governmental functions, such as the Secretary's office, the courtroom, and Assembly room.

After Ludwell/Hartwell rebuilt the Statehouse in 1685, legislation directed the construction of a prison. Records of the fire that ended the life of the Statehouse and Jamestown as capital in 1698 mention that the jail was part of the Statehouse Complex. If that is the same prison as that mentioned in 1685, then it follows that just like the Statehouse itself, the prison may well have been another Statehouse Complex ruin conversion.

Col. Nathaniel Bacon died in 1692, leaving Buildings 2, 3 and 4 to his niece, Abigail Smith, the wife of Lewis Burwell II, but she died that same

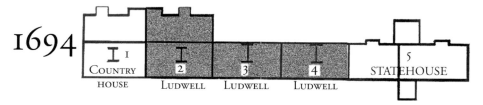

year. It is likely that Bacon's lease of the "country's house" terminated with his death, and that the Colony reclaimed ownership. Following the death of Col. Bacon's neice, also in 1692 ownership of Buildings 2, 3 and 4 passed along to her brother-in-law, Philip Ludwell II.

In the spring of 1694, Philip Ludwell II received a grant for an acre of land to adjoin his Statehouse Complex holdings, Buildings 2, 3 and 4. The metes and bounds leave no doubt that this is a detailed description of the Statehouse Complex Buildings 2, 3 and 4. It cites the Jamestown pitch and tar swamp as the northern boundary, and its parcel is exactly as wide, 124', as the east-west width of the foundations of Buildings 2, 3 and 4. This grant also confirms that Building 1 did revert back to the "country's house" after Nathaniel Burwell died, and that the 1685 Statehouse (which was a rebuild of the 1665 Statehouse) and Building 5 of the Statehouse Complex are one in the same.

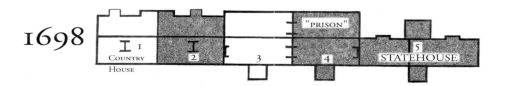

April 20, 1694. *"Edward Andros, Governour ... give and grant unto Phillip Ludwell Esqr. One acre and halfe of Land adjoying to the ruins of his three Brick houses* **between the State house and Country house** *in James City which land is bounded Vizt beginning Near Pitch and Tarr swamp Eight Cheyes [N] of the Eastrmost End of the said houses and running by the said End south two degrees westerly sixteen Cheynes thence North Eighty Eight degrees westerly three and three quarter Cheynes thence North two degrees Easterly sixteen Cheynes by the other End of the said houses and thence south Eighty Eight degrees Easterly three and three quarteres Cheynes to the place it began...*"[67]

It seems logical that since Ludwell owned Buildings 2, 3 and 4 and the one acre of land adjoining it, Ludwell would have been the person who rebuilt, doubled in size and modernized the ruins of Buildings 3 and 4. This effort would have resulted in moving the kitchen to the north addition, replacing the old fashioned central H-shaped fireplaces with end chimneys, and adding porch tower entrances to replace the old fashioned lobby entrance.

Finally the fire of 1698 that sealed the fate of the Statehouse and led to the removal of the Capital to Williamsburg began in an adjoining building which had to be Building 4, and/or its addition, which seems to have become the prison. It may be that one Arthur Jarvis, sentenced to death for *"...Burglary & Felony..."* took revenge on the Colony for his sentence by setting fire to the jail, but in such a way that the authorities could not prove it. October 20, 1698. *"...fire broke out in a house adjoining the Statehouse, which in a very short time was wholly burnt, and also the prison."* [68]

The evolution of representative self-government at Jamestown in the 17th century, as reflected in the buildings which can be associated with it, is one of the most significant of Jamestown's stories. Symbolically, the 1665-1698 State House complex in its day was the largest secular public building in 17th-century America. With its two stories and garrets, additions, porch chambers, cellars and a stair tower, the complex totaled 23,000 square feet under one roof. No other governmental/public building in Colonial America was even close to that scale. And it can be argued that what happened there of significance was equally beyond the scope of the government in the other colonies in the 17th century. *"It was the place where the habits of self-rule and legislative politics were sorted out."*[69]

Within the walls of the Jamestown Statehouse Complex, the legacy of the 1619 first representative assembly in North America evolved into the form of self-government that later day native sons, such as Thomas Jefferson and George Washington, would consider a birthright worth dying to preserve. It is also true that the public good of the Jamestown self-government legacy is mixed. Within the walls of the Jamestown Capitol buildings the enslavement of Africans in the 1660s evolved toward rigid law. And only a landed few in the beginning had the right to have their voices heard. But at the same time, the legislative mechanism to outlaw slavery and enfranchise a diverse and vibrant country of the future grew from a process born in the statehouses at Jamestown. Such is the precious value of these Jamestown places of America's political beginnings.

Chapter IV
Signs Of Life

When paramedics first arrive on an accident scene today, they immediately search for signs of life. They look for the vital signs. If they are not there, or not there for long, the job is essentially over. But in a way, "life" is not over. The remains of the body become the responsibility of forensic science; there is the legal requirement to identify the body, if unknown, and determine cause of death. To do that, forensic scientists look for other "signs of life." Physical inspection of the remains and biological tests can reconstruct much of a person's life story. The dead inform the living.

The same process can lead to knowing more about the lives of long-deceased people when the "paramedics" are archaeologists who recover skeletal remains, even centuries after death. Burial study on Jamestown Island has done precisely that. We can come to know 17th-century Jamestown from written fact and artifacts, but we can come face-to-face with Jamestown people of the past and get to know them more or less personally from signs of their lives still held in their skeletal remains.

Statehouse Burials

Fort Burials

Figure 77. Jamestown Island showing two major fort period burial sites with superimposed site map.

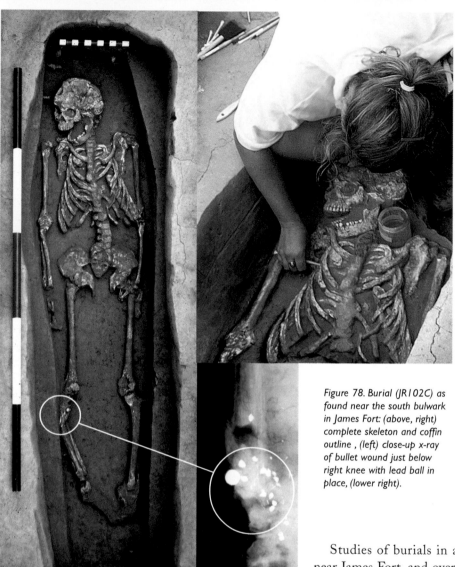

Figure 78. Burial (JR102C) as found near the south bulwark in James Fort: (above, right) complete skeleton and coffin outline , (left) close-up x-ray of bullet wound just below right knee with lead ball in place, (lower right).

Studies of burials in and near James Fort, and over 70 other burials from an unmarked burial ground at the Statehouse Complex, introduce us to some of the otherwise obscure early Jamestown population.

Excavations near James Fort's south wall, intended to more clearly define Structure 160 and its yard, unexpectedly exposed a burial, the first found during the course of the *Jamestown Rediscovery* excavations. Even though this grave lay beneath a once well-traveled gravel road, traces of a decayed coffin and a fairly well-preserved skeleton were eventually exposed. The greatest surprise of all, however, was the discovery that the remains included a lead bullet embedded in a severed lower leg.

The burial was possibly as old as the first months of James Fort. It was not only located within the archaeological traces of the wooden palisade, but it was also aligned with it. The few fragments of pottery found in the soil that originally covered the coffin all dated to either the years just before English settlement or to 1607-1610. Indeed this was apparently a grave put into ground that had only been trod by prehistoric Indians or briefly by Europeans sometime very soon after they arrived at Jamestown Island on May 13, 1607.

This was a grave of a European male, according to forensic anthropological study conducted on site and then later at the Smithsonian Institution.[1] The fact that this man was buried in an hexagonal coffin, as indicated by some surviving nails and the shape of the dark soil left by the decayed wood, meant that he was someone of some social standing. During that time, this meant that he was likely one of the 54 "gentlemen" listed by Captain John Smith in his series of monographs on the early years at Jamestown.[2] This was also the remains of a person who died when he was in his late teens to age 20. This was determined primarily by the stage of development of the wisdom teeth and the lack of complete fusion of the bone near certain joints. This young man also suffered from decayed teeth, one painfully abscessed. Judging from the bone formation where major muscles attach, this individual was moderately muscular but not used to performing hard labor, perhaps indeed someone living the life of a 17th-century gentleman. At a height of 5'9" he was slightly taller than the average Englishman of the period. It is almost certain that this young man died from a massive gunshot wound to the lower right leg, caused by the side entry of a .60 caliber lead ball and 21 smaller misshapen lead shot, all of which caused a severe compound fracture of the tibia and fibula.

Forensic reconstruction of the area damaged by the gunshot showed a trajectory that started with an impact to the outside surface of the right knee by the lead musket ball, which proceeded to break completely through the leg bone just below the joint, and finally came to rest beneath the skin on the inside of the lower knee. The smaller shot penetrated and shattered bone across a five-inch area centered on the knee. The angle of the trajectory of the ball indicated that the individual likely was in a position about level with the gun that fired the shot. There is no sign of medical treatment to the wound, nor of any healing; the force and magnitude of the impact of the lead musket ball and shot likely severed an artery. Massive blood loss from such a wound would have caused this person to bleed out, resulting in death in a matter of minutes. There were no other signs of trauma before death. The fractures in the skull were apparently caused when the coffin eventually collapsed.

On the young man's skull on the left temple there was found a copper straight pin, and a copper stain presumably from another pin was found near the leg wound, suggesting that the victim was either buried wrapped in a shroud held together with pins or possibly had bandages on the leg wound and on his head. The position of the legs, spread apart at the knees,

Figure 79. Burial analysis at Jamestown requires field archaeologists, historians and scientific specialists: left to right, Jamie May, APVA staff archaeologist, Dr. Douglas Owsley, forensic anthropologist, Dr. Ashley KcKeown, skeletal biologist, and the author examine resin casting of JR102C.

seems to indicate that if the corpse had been wrapped in a shroud, then it may have come undone as the body shifted in the coffin as it went into the grave.

The burial was basically oriented east-west with the head to the west, apparently positioned according to traditional Christian beliefs and practices of the time. And significantly, the degree that the burial was actually oriented south of east is the same orientation as the nearby fort building and palisade, which helps to establish the early date of this burial. A test of the state of the carbon decay in the bone indicated that this person could have died as early as 1607. Found in the third layer of the 102nd excavation unit dug since the *Jamestown Rediscovery* archaeological project began, this young man became thereafter known by his field record number: JR102C. JR for short.

Science may offer clues to the identity of JR, including tests that can determine his diet. Some of the chemical composition of people's bones can be determined by what they ate during their lives. Of particular interest to the analysis of the remains of early American settlers is the relative presence of two types of stable carbon isotopes: the C^3 isotope, found in the bones of people who primarily ate wheat, and the C^4 isotope, found in the bones of those who primarily ate corn. The bones of fairly recent

English immigrants in America, so the theory goes, would show a wheat diet, while the bones of American Indians, and seasoned English immigrants at Jamestown, would show a corn diet. JR's diet tested out to be somewhat different than either the English or the Indians, but he was certainly closer to corn-eaters.

JR's chemical readings seem to show a diet considerably short of the readings for wheat and even slightly below the readings for corn.[3] If that test is valid, and if therefore the numbers tend to say that something is suspect in JR's case, then this person may not have come from Europe, or may not have died in the early years of Jamestown settlement. In other words, if JR were European and died in 1607, his profile would be that of a recent immigrant, a wheat eater. JR would not have lived long enough in Virginia to build up the carbon signs of a corn diet. Or perhaps this man had never eaten wheat, so he likely did not come from England or Europe. Nonetheless, while the tests of a great number of skeletons buried in the Chesapeake region present a very standard pattern suggesting that this procedure is reliable, JR's strange numbers demand other explanation before this evidence can cancel out the documentary and archaeological story.

Other evidence about JR was produced by another isotope test that can detect isotopic signs of the regional differences in the water individuals drank during their younger years. Tests of one of JR's teeth for lead, strontium and oxygen isotopes seem to indicate that during his childhood, JR once resided in the southwest of England or Wales.[4]

Of course, there is no way to know for sure who JR102C actually was, and there is no grave stone to mark his burial. Nearly four centuries after his death, learning JR's true identity is unlikely. That being said, there are still more archaeological and written facts to go on than one might suppose. Like a modern death investigation, one can string together enough circumstantial evidence to suggest at least the identity of the victim, a possible scenario for the shooting, and a weapon.

The facts are that, in or around James Fort, a young "gentleman" in his late teens to age 20 or so, died of a gunshot wound to the right side of his right leg, the injury occurring possibly during the first months or possibly the first years of settlement.[5] George Percy, during an apparent period of eye-witnessing and accurate reporting, names some of the colonists who died during the summer months of 1607.

According to Percy, 24 men, mostly gentlemen, died by September 1607, after which he himself apparently became too weak to keep up with the death record. According to John Smith, a total of 66 out of the original 104 settlers died by the fall of 1607. One entry listed Jerome Alicock, an "*ancient*" (meaning ensign, junior officer) as dying from a "*wound*" on August 14, 1607.[6] Of course the word "wound" could mean any number of injuries, including one caused by an arrow. But it may be significant that in a preceding paragraph, Percy points out that on August 10, only four days before Alicock's death, William Bruster (or Brewster) died from a wound *"given by the savages."* This seems to be saying that an arrow killed Brewster. Judging from that earlier entry, it seems likely that Percy would also name the cause of Alicock's wound if it were inflicted by the Indians. So why would Percy use the unqualified word, "wound"?

Perhaps Percy knew that the wound was a gunshot wound, but hesitated to admit that colonists were shooting each other. Percy may not have been keen to admit a death by "friendly fire" either. There is no doubt that August 1607 was a time of great stress among the settlers, with heat, disease and starvation magnifying their plight. In fact, after September 5, Percy may have felt that he had covered all the previous unattributed deaths by stating that:

> *...they were destroyed with cruel diseases as swellings, fluxes, burning fevers, and by wars, and some departed suddenly but for the most part they died of mere famine.*[7]

Under the extreme conditions which Percy describes, it stands to reason that civil unrest could easily break out among the struggling colonists, perhaps resulting in the shooting of one of their own, either accidently or on purpose. In any case, death caused in this way would hardly be good news to send home to England, especially by or to someone who was particularly interested in promoting the expansion of the Virginia Company venture and might be urging other Englishmen to emigrate.

Along with Alicock and Bruster, there are a number of other candidates for the identity of JR, by reason of their status as gentlemen and age at death and perhaps their political leanings, although Percy gives no cause of their deaths.[8] They are:

John Martin, Jr., gentleman, died Aug.18, 1607, approx. age 19
Richard Simmons, gentleman, died Sept. 18, 1607, age 17
Robert Pennington, gentleman, died Aug. 18, 1607, age 20
Stephen Calthrop, gentleman, died Aug. 15 1607, age 22

John Martin, Jr. and his father Captain John Martin, Sr., along with Anthony Gosnold and his son Anthony, were the two father-and-son teams that came to Virginia on the first voyage. John Martin, Jr. seems to have had a well-traveled past even before he took his last and fatal trip to Jamestown. His father, Captain Martin, was a mariner and a gold refiner who may have apprenticed John Jr. in his youth to his grandfather's ironworks on the Welsh border by 1596. The Martin family was connected in Italy, and John Martin, Jr. may have spent time studying at the University in Padua, a fashionable place for young gentlemen to study abroad at the time. So John Jr.'s death as early as 1607 and the possibility of his spending his early years in or near Wales and Italy seem to make him a strong candidate for the identity of JR. He could have acquired the isotopic signature found in JR's tooth during early years at the ironworks and the corn signature may actually be a result of eating millet (another C4 isotope producing plant) in Italy.

Richard Simmons also fits the gentleman and age-at-death criteria. There is some evidence that he was from Wales as well, presenting the possibility that he would have the stable isotopic signature found in JR's tooth.

Besides his death date at Jamestown, nothing more is known of Robert Pennington except that he grew up in Lancashire, England, which would not give him the same isotopic reading as JR's. Nor would the isotopic test on Stephen Calthrop match JR's, because Calthrop was from Norwich, England. He was also 22 years old when he died, which would put Calthrop a few years older than JR's estimated date of death. But more can be known about young Calthrop than the others, and there is some reason to believe that he would have been a likely target during a time of civil unrest at Jamestown.

Percy wrote that Calthrop (or Galthrop) died the day after Alicock (August 15) with no cause of death specified. This offers the possibilities that Percy perhaps did not know what killed Calthrop, or perhaps that Percy had ceased to specifically list causes, or perhaps Percy wanted to hide the details. Church records show that a Stephen Calthrop was a resident of Norwich, Norfolk who was christened in the church of St. Peter Mancroft in 1585 in England, which would make Calthrop's age 22 at a death date of 1607.[9]

Calthrop also had the typical young gentleman's incentive to risk the Virginia adventure—he had two older brothers. As third born, according to English law he would have been totally left out of any chance of inheriting family property in England. Perhaps more significant to our search for the identity of JR, is the historical fact that Calthrop was in some way allied with Captain John Smith. Smith, Calthrop, and one other man named Robinson, led or conspired to lead a "*mutinie*" against Captain Christopher Newport and his friends, one being Edward Maria Wingfield, probably in the Canary Islands where the original ships stopped to re-supply.[10] The unsuccessful mutiny could have served to spawn or intensify the distrust that Wingfield and his friends had for the commoner and soldier-of-fortune, John Smith. Calthrop, being of the gentleman class and also related to Wingfield, may have gotten off scot-free. Wingfield could have spoken on Calthrop's behalf to Wingfield's friend, Captain Newport, and perhaps also to the English settler with the highest social rank aboard, George Percy. Consequently, as historical accounts indicate, Captain Newport took out his wrath only on John Smith who for the rest of the voyage to Jamestown was placed "*in restraint*."

While this aborted mutiny ultimately led to Smith's near execution and exclusion (for the first two months) from the Virginia governing council, nothing seems to have been done to punish Calthrop. Nevertheless, young Calthrop's part (or perhaps even leadership) in the mutiny attempt against Newport, and indirectly against Wingfield who would eventually be elected as the Virginia colony's first president, certainly must have fostered permanent distrust between Wingfield/Newport and Calthrop, and almost certainly between the rest of the governing council and Calthrop.

Living conditions in the colony may have further magnified personal distrust and political differences. Men were dropping like flies that first August in Jamestown, as disease, bad water, native arrows, and lack of food took their toll. Percy's report sums up the situation clearly: "*There was never Englishmen left in a foreign country in such misery as we were in this newly discovered Virginia.*"[11] Power struggles, for those strong enough to stand, may have become inevitable.

Stephen Calthrop and his friends could have become marked men, perhaps suspected of plotting against the governing council. Either a preventative shot or a return shot from a military round fired in Calthrop's direction, may have been an inevitable result of struggle and suspicion in the early years at Jamestown. Although there is no written record of this, news of political infighting and the death of Alicock or Calthrop as a result, would hardly be a topic to report back to England, especially if Percy himself were in the middle of it. So like death by friendly fire, it is little wonder then that Percy might under-report the cause of Calthrop's death.

Finally, it may be significant to consider the record of a death, probably at Jamestown, from a gunshot wound in the knee, although it happened long after that first settlement summer. In 1624, Jamestown's first landowner on record and Governor's Councilor, Richard Stephens, fought a duel with a George Harrison who later died from complications from a slight wound in the knee.[12] Stephens himself apparently left the dueling field unharmed. Could JR be Harrison? Probably not. Stephens' age at death is unknown, and JR's wound could hardly be considered slight. Also there was no sign of healing of JR's shattered leg bone, so there is no reason to conclude that JR suffered a lingering death. It is also difficult to explain how a shot from the side could be inflicted during a duel.

Another question to consider about JR102C's demise is that, if JR really was the victim of political intrigue, then why was no one brought to justice when his ally, Captain John Smith, came to power in 1608-09? There is no record of a trial or an execution for such a crime against JR. One execution that is on record is that of Captain George Kendall who was tried and eventually shot as an alleged spy, just after John Ratcliffe, John Smith and John Martin, led by Gabriel Archer, deposed Wingfield from the presidency. Ratcliffe then became President of the Council.[13] The so-called Kendall crime is not clearly explained, but there is no reason to believe that Kendall supported Wingfield or any other possible faction (except perhaps the Spanish) that put him in harm's way.

There is some other "archaeological" evidence of a gunshot death at early Jamestown that might suggest an execution. In 1896, just after grading was done to stabilize the river shoreline 200' west of the church tower, wave action exposed several human skeletons "*lying in regular order.*"[14] At that time the grading engineer, Colonel Samuel Yonge, thought these skeletons had been originally buried in the early churchyard. Yonge went on to report that "*one of the skulls had been perforated by a musket ball and several bits of lead shot, which it still held, suggesting a military execution.*" Was this the skeleton of George Kendall? Or was it the remains of the man who shot "JR," finally brought to justice?

Unfortunately for historians, Yonge further states that "*soon after being exposed to the air the skeletons crumbled.*" Without the crucial dating evidence of artifacts from the burial shaft, and without the skeleton itself to test for other revealing forensic evidence, there is no chance of learning any more about the circumstances surrounding this death. Therefore, to suggest that "*the 1896 skull*" holding the lead shot belonged to the killer of JR is pure speculation. In fact, it is also only fair to point out that there are great numbers of capital offenses recorded in early 17th-century Jamestown when martial law ruled the colony after the "Starving Time" and until the late teens of the 1600s. For example, picking flowers from your neighbor's garden carried the death penalty during the period of martial law at Jamestown.

So who was JR? Was he Alicock, Martin, Pennington, Calthrop or even Harrison? We, of course, cannot know in any definitive sense. The most logical choice would seem to be Jerome Alicock, based on his status, age and the wound. But the study can never be over, as there appears to be no bounds to the development of scientific forensic techniques. Biogenetics will likely prove as effective for identifying people of the distant past as it has been in freeing long-jailed but innocent people today. There is no reason to doubt that eventually JR will have his proper gravestone.

While it is clearly impossible today to establish precisely who JR is, who shot JR, or why he was shot, it *is* possible to determine *what* shot him. During the course of the *Jamestown Rediscovery* excavations, a number of gun parts were found in deposits that can be dated to the period 1607-1610, all types of weapons capable of shooting the lead ball and shot found in JR102C's leg wound. The .60 caliber ball, middle-sized shot, and scrap lead found in the bone could have come from a range of weapons, anything from a pistol to a full-sized musket.

The firing mechanisms from four types of firearms were found archaeologically. These include military-issue matchlocks of both the standard-trigger and lever-trigger types. Also among the recovered parts were

Figure 80. Jamestown Settlement Museum musketeer test-firing, at the James Fort site, a caliver with load similar to that recovered from JR102C.

a lever-fired matchlock of a smaller and more ornate "civilian"-style caliver, and a Scottish pistol with a snaphaunce (flint-and-steel) firing mechanism. The most common firearm in the collection is the matchlock, a type that required the musketeer to light and continuously burn a fibrous wick in order to ignite the powder pan and discharge the piece. This type of weapon would have obvious drawbacks in combat, the most serious being accidental, premature explosions during the loading process and the revealing light given off by the match during night battle. A humid and rainy climate, as in a typical Virginia summer, would hardly be matchlock-friendly either. The muskets may have been loaded from the two types of bandoliers (single-shot powder containers) found with the gun parts or found in deposits dating to the same 1607-1610 period. These bandoliers were leather-covered tin or copper cylinders that soldiers carried, in groups of twelve, from belts draped across their chests.

The five-inch spread of the lead in JR102C's leg can be a clue to the distance between him and the gun that shot him. Testing of a caliver and pistol, two of the weapons that could have fired the .60 caliber ball and shot, determined that at point blank range (three feet from weapon to target), there is essentially no spread of the projectiles in a load similar to the makeup of lead in JR's wound. This fact tends to eliminate the possibility that JR was the victim of an accidental, self-inflicted wound from a dropped pistol. *Someone* fired a gun at JR. The pistol fired eight feet from the target produced a five-inch spread pattern as did the caliver at 15 feet. These distances and the trajectory of the bullet and shot in JR's leg suggest a number of scenarios to explain JR's death: a case of "friendly fire" occasioned by mistaken identity; a freak, accidental discharge in camp; a hunting accident whereby the lead hunter (JR) got shot by a stumbling follower; a gunshot wound inflicted in a close-range battle; feuding among the desperate settlers; or an accident in battle ranks.

All of the above scenarios are certainly possible, but other facts seem to suggest that some are *more* possible than others. JR's possible death in August might eliminate the Indians as suspects, who likely had not acquired any English guns that soon. Fighting among the settlers is certainly possible, but if murder were intended, then only a shot to the leg seems an overly poor attempt or poor marksmanship. A hunting accident is certainly possible, yet the military load combining small shot and a lead ball might be a bit of overkill for hunting. More likely is an accident in rank.

In the 17th century, military procedure for musketeers was very structured, requiring constant practice. There is clear record of exercise at arms at Jamestown which took place in an open area on the western side of the fort known as Smithfield.[15] Here the musketeers would form "ranks" of multiple rows of men with their weapons in various stages of readiness. As soon as each front row would fire, the row of men would file to the right, allowing the row behind them to step forward with their fully primed piece

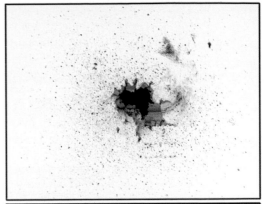
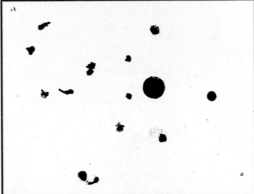

Figure 81. Target shot patterns from modern ballistic test: point blank from a pistol (top), 15 feet from a caliver (center) compared with the shot pattern of JR102C's wound (from x-ray, bottom).

to volley, then file right, and so on. In a full rank, there would be enough rows to allow the musketeers an opportunity to advance through the laborious number of steps required to load and prime the weapons. It would not be unusual, in the heat of the action, for someone in the almost-ready row behind to fire accidentally, which could well bring down one of their own in front. A hit to the outside of the right leg of a retiring front-line man could have been common. So friendly fire in the heat of battle, or even during the "exercise in arms" held in Smithfield, may be the most logical scenario to explain JR's demise.

A way to identify a modern crime victim from skeletal remains is by reconstructing the face, hoping to find surviving images that match or to find living relatives and friends who could identify the reconstruction. Of course, for a 400-year-old skeleton, identification by friends, living contemporary relatives, or photographs are out of the question. In addition, there are only two known likenesses of any of the original settlers: an engraving by Simon de Passe of Captain John Smith, and an anonymous portrait of George Percy. Ironically, these likenesses may represent the two quarreling political "parties" at James Fort, who therefore may have played some role in JR's death. Nonetheless, by combining science and art to reconstruct the facial features of JR, it is possible to know what JR102C looked like, in spite of the fact that the skull was seriously damaged in the grave.[16]

The first step was to reconstruct the skull by piecing together the 102 fragments left of it. That required days of experienced mending. Still the skull offered unusual challenges, in that the pressure of the collapsed coffin and soil resting on it caused the skull to warp. The fact that JR's grave lay below what would become a much-traveled automobile road made matters even worse.

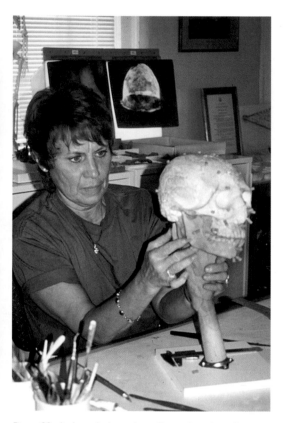

Figure 82. Anthropologist sculptor Sharon Long in early stages of reconstructing the face of JR102C.

Add to that the centuries of decay that caused some of the bone to either disappear or become so brittle that it could not be used in the mending process. To overcome this, gaps in the skull were reconstructed through computer manipulation, electronically "lifting" the unmendable pieces from a photograph of the crushed skull, as it was first found in the grave, and placing them on a digital photograph of the mended skull. Then parts of the skull that could not be put back physically or digitally were created by copying what did survive on the opposite side, then reversing it, and "pasting" it into the gaps. With this mirror imaging, the skull could begin to approach its exact pre-death shape.

No matter how accurate the skull reconstruction, it still is, of course, not a perfect likeness of the flesh and blood face. However, the shape and characteristics of a human skull primarily determine what people do "look like" more than most people imagine. Scientifically and artistically rebuilt muscle and tissue thicknesses on a repaired skull can practically bring a face back to life. Guided by sci-entifically-generated thickness markers on a plaster mold of the skull, an experienced forensic sculptor skillfully applied modeling clay to reconstruct JR's face within an estimated 85 percent of its true former appearance. Eye and hair color, facial hair, and hair style were based on examination of 17th-century portraits and engravings. It is interesting to note that the final rendering of JR could be a distant

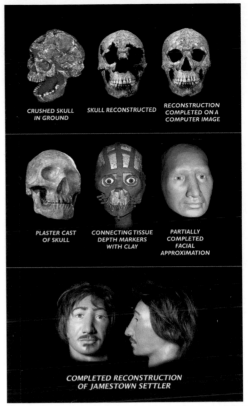

CRUSHED SKULL IN GROUND   SKULL RECONSTRUCTED   RECONSTRUCTION COMPLETED ON A COMPUTER IMAGE

PLASTER CAST OF SKULL   CONNECTING TISSUE DEPTH MARKERS WITH CLAY   PARTIALLY COMPLETED FACIAL APPROXIMATION

COMPLETED RECONSTRUCTION OF JAMESTOWN SETTLER

Figure 83. Steps in the reconstruction of the face of JR102C.

cousin to George Percy whose sharply sloping forehead, and rather gen-erous nose, match the skeletal evidence of JR102C. In fact, Ensign Jerome Alicock could be a relative of Percy, as they come from the same town in England.[17]

While archaeology deals with the remnants of dead people and their broken things, archaeology also tries to picture living people using intact things. Educated speculation about the identity, motive, weapon, and scene of the death of JR is an intriguing exercise, but trying to know who he was, why he was shot, and what shot him is really not why the discovery of this burial is so significant. Rather, going through this exercise brings into clearer focus a number of things about these "*able men*" in "*miserable distress*" at early 17th-century Jamestown. As that first summer at Jamestown came to an end, Percy poignantly assesses the desperate state of the James Fort outpost:

> *There were never Englishmen left in a foreign country in such misery as we were in this new discovered Virginia. We watched every three nights, lying on the bare, cold ground...which brought our men to be most feeble wretches. Our food was but a small can of barley, sod in water, to five men a day, our drink, cold water taken out of the river, which was at flood very salt at a low tide full of*

Figure 84. JR102C, a composite of a 1606 Dutch engraving, artifacts from James Fort deposits and facial reconstruction.

slime and filth.... Thus we lived for the space of five months in this miserable distress, not having five able men to man our bulwarks upon any occasion. If it had not pleased God to have put a terror in the savages' hearts, we had all perished by those wild and cruel pagans, being in that weak estate as we were, our men night and day groaning in every corner of the fort most pitiful to hear.[18]

In some ways JR may represent a typical settler, a young gentleman with some military experience, risking life and limb on the chance that he could better his circumstances in Virginia when his future had become "hopeless" back home. It is also instructive to realize that civil unrest must have run rampant at Jamestown, as there was less and less possibility of getting rich quick, and more and more possibility of dying young. It is little wonder that the colony only picked up momentum because Smith instituted military discipline and a "food for work" program.

Eventually the Virginia Company started giving land to those who paid their own transport and, even better, a new commercial crop emerged that could be grown on the rich Virginia land and practically transform anyone with even the slightest ounce of ambition into an instant millionaire. The attendant tragedy was that some of the native Powhatan and some of the English settlers (some of whom grew tobacco on native land) mostly saw each other as "savages,"[19] but the young gentleman, JR, like the majority of Jamestown's first settlers, never lived to share in this tobacco boom.

JR did not lie alone for long in the southeast corner of the Jamestown Fort. Excavations in 1997 uncovered a second burial three feet north of JR's grave, that of a 40- to 55-year-old Caucasian woman (field number: JR156C) who died of unknown causes.[20]

Only five teeth were in place at the time of the woman's death. Some of her teeth had been missing so long that the tooth sockets had completely closed. There was evidence that she had spent a lifetime of fairly strenuous physical work. Her grave was slightly out of line with JR's grave, but was basically positioned in the east-west Christian manner. That nonalignment and the greater amount of European artifacts in the backfilling indicate that some period of time had passed between the two interments. Nonetheless, the fragmented pottery in the grave shaft still indicated that death occurred probably in the period 1607-10. The woman was buried in a relatively well-preserved yellow pine coffin.[21] Ironically, while portions of the coffin did survive, the eggshell thin skull was practically the only recoverable bone. Coffin nails survived, and their positions and a ridge of coffin wood down the center of the burial indicated that it had a gabled lid, a common style for the period.

So who is JR156C? The fact that this burial turns out to be that of an older European woman may narrow the possibilities. Women did not come to Jamestown until the second supply, September 1608, when Mistress Forest and her maid, Anne Burras arrived. Anne Burras went on to marry John Laydon, a laborer who came to Virginia with the first 104 adventurers in 1607; their first child, named Virginia, became the first Anglo-American born at Jamestown.[22]

The Laydons were still alive in 1625, when a census lists John and his wife Anne, then aged 30, and their four children as living at Elizabeth City (today's city of Hampton, Virginia) in 1625, but records do not mention Mistress Forest again, which may mean that she did not live long. With so few women in the colony in the first two years, there are good odds that a female buried in a coffin in precious ground inside the fort could well be the wife of a gentleman, perhaps Thomas Forest. Being the wife of a gentleman and having a 13-or 14-year-old maidservant in 1608 might also indicate that Mistress Forest was at least in her 30s when she arrived in the colony. But the wife of a gentleman with a maidservant

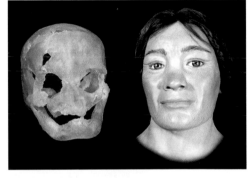

Figure 85. The reconstruction of the face of the female buried near "JR" required a CT scan generated stereolithographic reconstruction of the fragile skull before creation of this likeness, perhaps one of the earliest women living at Jamestown.

would hardly develop signs of hard labor. JR156C is more likely to be one of the females who came from England to Jamestown after the arrival of Mistress Forest. Radio-carbon testing indicates a burial date of ca. 1620/40 for JR156C. But again, with no names and dates on a gravestone, a positive identification of JR156C is even more guesswork than JR himself.

Like JR102C, our woman JR156C deserved a facial reconstruction. The delicate skull, too fragile to use for molding, made the effort more challenging. But in this case, a computer-generated process known as stereolithography was able to produce the mold even more accurately than plaster, without as much as touching the original fragile skull. The process begins with a Computed Tomography scan (CT) that produces a three-dimensional file. That information then is transferred to a stereo-lithography apparatus that guides a laser beam to exactly recreate the skull in a light-sensitive epoxy material.[23] At that point, a forensic sculptor produced a face through the same casting and reconstructive processes used to recapture JR's appearance. The physical condition of JR156C at the time of her death did not result in an especially pretty face, but rather an image that is perhaps more reflective of the reality of rugged early Jamestown than most want to imagine. Regardless, the 1617 engraving of Pocahontas is now no longer the only existing image of an early Jamestown woman.

While the interplay of archaeological/scientific facts and documentary reference surrounding these two burials can, at best, offer *possible* identification, the burial discovery, circumstances, and written references of another Jamestown colonist can reach the level of *probability*. Excavations within the Civil War earthwork in search of the western 1607 fort wall not only turned up a well (see Chapter II) but also another unmarked grave.[24]

Even the circumstances of the discolored-soil outline of an unexcavated burial shaft immediately brought great attention to it. The burial was aligned with the predicted west wall of the fort, a compass direction that only made sense in light of and associated with a triangular plan, i.e. the fort. But part of the discolored soil in the shaft seemed to be underneath a circular, well-like feature jammed with 17th-century brickbats. If this were a well, then it, of course, post-dated the burial, suggesting an early 17th-century interment.

Removal of the brickbats and about a foot of fill containing domestic trash dispelled the well theory. That digging quickly reached the bottom of what was in reality a shallow pit. Significantly, the mixed clay in the burial fill was still visible at the bottom of the pit along with an outline of a posthole, which slightly penetrated the shaft. Artifacts from the pit fill, notably tobacco pipes including a local coarse-ceramic type probably first made at Jamestown after 1630, indicated the date of deposit. This fact in itself was cause for greater expectations for an early date for the burial beneath. Clearly enough time had passed for the burial to be forgotten. Unlike JR and other burials found at Jamestown, here literally was a time "lid" on the age of interment. The fact that undisturbed strata, from at least as old as the 1630s, had inadvertently sealed the burial in time, presented for the first time a date before which the burial could have taken place, ca. 1630. And the grave's location in and aligned with the fort began to point to the possible discovery of the most important of lost burials at Jamestown, that of ship's Captain Bartholomew Gosnold.

When a decorative, iron captain's leading staff appeared at the excavation level of the coffin lid, expectations of finding Gosnold below seemed inevitable. Then the superbly preserved skeleton lying within the coffin

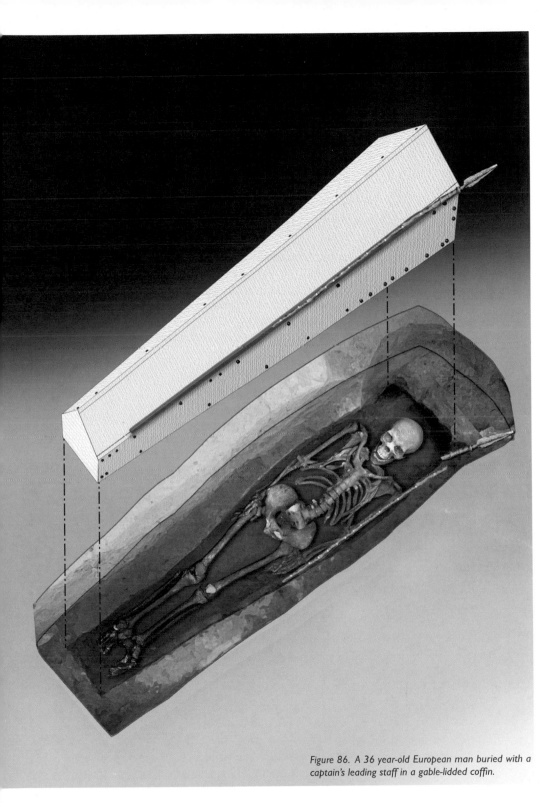

Figure 86. A 36 year-old European man buried with a captain's leading staff in a gable-lidded coffin.

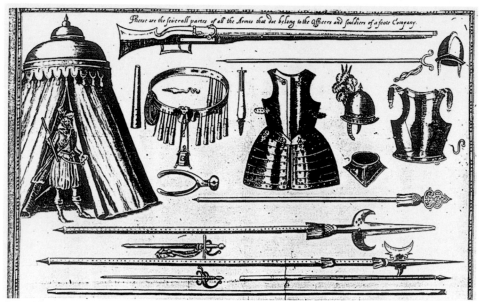

Figure 87. "Drill Postures" a detail from an engraving by T. Cockson, English 1615-1620 showing a leading staff identical to the Jamestown burial staff (arrow).

outline offered an even more telling link in the chain of evidence leading to Gosnold. The well-preserved pelvis allowed our steadfast forensic anthropologist, Dr. Douglas Owsley, to determine that this 5'5" European man died in his mid- to late-thirties. It is a known fact that Gosnold was 36 years of age at his passing on August 22, 1607, the day when George Percy reported that after a three-week illness:

> *...there died Captain Bartholomew Gosnold, one of our council; he was honorably buried, having all the ordinance in the fort shot off with many volleys of small shot.*[25]

Finding Gosnold was a goal for the *Jamestown Rediscovery* project from the beginning. Why? For one thing his vital importance to both the planning and reality of the Jamestown adventure is unquestionable but generally unknown. The discovery of his death begs the question of his life, requiring a careful reading of the record of initial English colonization.

Gosnold's success as mariner and privateer led him to briefly colonize one of the Elizabeth Isles and explore and name Cape Cod and Martha's Vineyard.[26] This previous exploration seems a preface to Gosnold later being the prime energy behind the planning, fundraising, recruiting, transporting and settling of the Virginia Colony of Jamestown. Even the self-promoting Captain John Smith and his archenemy, Edward Maria Wingfield, the colony's first Council President, agreed on Gosnold's value upon his passing. Smith named Gosnold: the *"prime mover"* of the planting of Jamestown. Wingfield, in an apologia after his removal from office lamented:

...divers of our men fell sick...amongst whom was the worthy and religious gentleman, Captain Bartholomew Gosnold, upon whose life stood a great part of the good success and fortune of our government and colony.[27]

Wingfield predicted then that, in the absence of Gosnold's support, he would be deposed as council president. This is clearly a strong statement about Gosnold's great value to the colony. Obviously Gosnold's death so early in Jamestown's history robbed him of a chance to produce his own memoirs. And his eventually lost grave site also helped relegate him to historical obscurity. But just as the discovery that James Fort itself was not lost to posterity, so too the discovery of the probable lost Gosnold grave revisits and revitalizes those first very understated Gosnold accolades.

The most telling piece that establishes the high status of his burial was the captain's leading staff or half pike found in it.[28] Only the metal parts, the decorative point fashioned into a cruciform, and two metal fastening straps (lanquets) survived. However, the decay of the pike's wooden shaft left enough of a dark stain in the ground to reveal its original five-and-one half feet in length. During excavation, the corrosion on the metal point disguised its true shape, but laboratory x-rays left no doubt that it was a ceremonial piece. To further identify it, a search led by experts in the collections of European military staff weapons and period illustrations produced early 17th-century examples of officers' half pikes.[29] A 1626 woodcut shows an identical pike, describing it as a type of captain's half pike intended to be used by a captain when deployed in combat.[30] This means that the more decorative ceremonial captains' staffs stayed in England, while the more weapon-like half pikes went to the Jamestown frontier.

The presence of the wartime staff at Jamestown is interesting in that the colonists were instructed by the Virginia Company not to appear menacing to the Virginia Indians when they first met. At first, for this reason Gosnold and the rest of the council even de-

Figure 88. Dutch officers with leading staffs, early-17th century.

123

Figure 89. Theodore de Bry engraving of the landing of Bartholomew Gosnold in New England in 1602.

layed constructing the fort. It is apparent that Gosnold (or whoever the buried captain may be) had a more realistic understanding than the London-based Virginia Company of the situation they would face at Jamestown. He seems to have known that no matter how peaceful the settlers tried to appear, sooner or later relations with the natives would indeed require the combat version of his leading staff. There was, in fact, combat upon first contact at Cape Henry, and it only took a few days of incoming arrows at Jamestown before Gosnold and the rest of the council "*contrived*" and directed construction of James Fort.[31]

Whether or not this burial is Gosnold might be further determined by comparison of its skeletal DNA with a known relative, dead or alive. The challenge would be to find the right relative, which means only a maternal descendant. Why? Cells contain two kinds of DNA: nuclear and mitochondrial. Mitochondrial DNA is contained in the mitochondria of the cell.[32] This type of DNA preserves well in bones, is relatively stable, and can be compared across several generations. Mitochondrial DNA is only passed along the maternal family line, so in order to compare a sample from the bones of a deceased individual, a sample from the mother or any of the female siblings who share the same sequence of mitochondrial DNA as the mother of the deceased, would have to be found.

Documentation of about 16 generations of maiden names going back to Gosnold's mother, aunts or sisters would need to be researched. Such research has proven to be impossible, so far. The other possibility is to find the burial of a female relative of Gosnold, and sample it for comparison. She can be found, at least theoretically. In 1646, Elizabeth Gosnold Tilney, Bartholomew's sister, left instructions in her will to be buried beneath the chancel of Shelley Church, next to her husband, Thomas Tilney, who died in 1619 near the Tilney family estate, Shelley Manor near Ipswich. [33] That church still stands with its chancel intact. But there is a major problem: the chancel is now paved over with tiles, obscuring any tombstones beneath. At any rate, even without the DNA, the age at death of the European captain, buried ceremoniously, are reason enough to likely identify the remains as those of the leading Jamestown pioneer, Captain Bartholomew Gosnold. The *Jamestown Rediscovery* burial studies have not been the first at Jamestown.

In the early 20th century, Mary Jeffrey Galt, one of the original 19th-century founders of the Association for the Preservation of Virginia Antiquities (APVA), personally directed extensive excavations near the church tower. Galt traced the brick church foundation, another earlier church inside it, and at the same time, opened some 50 graves.[34] She and others reported some details of many of the 50 burials, including one buried deep with an "*Indian arrowhea*d" embedded in it.

Mary Galt and her team found the stone of what they concluded was a memorial for a Reverend John Clough, and another stone commemo-

Figure 90. Shelley Church, Suffolk, England where Bartholomew Gosnold's sister, Elizabeth, was buried in the chancel, in 1646.

rating a "knight" with a brass inlay. Found between two sets of ten burials from separate areas in the chancel, this latter stone seems to commemorate Governor Sir George Yeardley, who died at Jamestown in 1627. Silver thread was recovered from just above the skeleton, but it is not recorded whether or not any bones were actually removed. It seems likely that some of the bones were generally left undisturbed, and the shafts were backfilled, where they rest today, beneath a reconstructed brick floor in the 1907 church.

Other burial were recovered in the mid-1950s during the National Park Service excavations at the Statehouse Complex. The clearing of the topsoil around the foundations uncovered the soil stains of approximately 70 grave shafts. National Park Service archaeologists uncovered skeletons in ten of the 70 graves, and were able to recover bones from six of the 70 grave shafts. The extremely fragmentary remains then became part of the collections at the Colonial National Historical Park, Jamestown. Recent analysis using modern forensic science indicates that of the six skeletons that could be reliably studied, there were three males and three females, the women ranging in age from 15-34 years old, and the men from 15-29 years old.[35]

While too little of the Statehouse Complex skeletal remains survived to establish the cause of death, the vast number of burials (archaeologists at the time estimated that there may be as many as 300) and their haphazard alignment strongly suggested to the archaeologists that this was literally a "potter's field," that is to say, likely the final resting place of the estimated 155 of the 215 settlers who died during the "Starving Time" winter of 1609-1610.[36] The reasoning was that there were so many deaths during that winter that the few left alive were not strong and healthy enough to bury the bodies properly.[37]

Another reason for so many deaths during the "Starving Time" winter of 1609-1610 was unknown to the National Park Service archaeologists of the time: drought. A recent study of the growth rings of local cypress trees old enough to have been alive in the late-16th and early-17th centuries indicates that by 1609, Tidewater Virginia was in the midst of its greatest drought in 500 years (see Chapter II).[38] In fact, the pattern of narrow cypress growth rings indicating natural stress (from drought) can be dated to the period 1606-1613. Therefore, it is little wonder that the colonists could not grow enough food to feed themselves, and that at times the Virginia Indians stopped trading with the settlers. The Powhatan were in the midst of hard times themselves. It also may not be just coincidence that the colony begins to succeed only after 1613, which was apparently the year the drought ended. Of course, that is the same year that John Rolfe successfully introduced the growing of Caribbean tobacco in Virginia soil. There is no doubt that the cash crop saved the colony, but wetter weather may have given a boost as well.

Figure 91. Record of the Statehouse Complex burial ground excavation 2001.

In any event, such consideration among others prompted the *Rediscovery* team to study the apparently early unmarked burial ground below the foundations of the Statehouse Complex. For one thing that study was predicated on the assumption that because the burial ground lay beneath the 1660s Statehouse, it would likely date to the early years of Jamestown settlement. Therefore systematic recovery and preservation of at least 50 burials would make it possible to reconstruct an early Jamestown population profile, of which there is little, or no other, record.[39] This profile of the early Jamestown population would include details on the ratio of females to males, ancestry, social and economic status, life expectancy, foreign-to-native birth ratios, general health, disease, causes of death, burial customs and possibly dates of death. This data also could be compared to other broader studies of 17th-century burials in the Chesapeake region and provide researchers with the earliest evidence of the Anglo-American population, in order to measure physiological and cultural change over time and across the region.

Figure 92. The unmarked burials excavated 2000-2001 that lay beneath and near foundations of the 1660-1698 Statehouse Complex.

Over an 18-month period, excavation of 63 graves resulted in the recovery of the skeletal remains of 72 individuals.[40] While there were many deep graves containing carefully positioned individuals, a number of graves were rather shallow and haphazardly aligned. Some individuals appeared to have been placed in the shaft in a careless manner, and there were a number of cases of multiple burials in the same shaft: ten graves held two burials, and one shaft held three. This may have been due to a desire to minimize contact with the bodies of the deceased by throwing them into hastily dug graves.

In-situ buttons, pins, and other artifacts were found with the remains of three skeletons, two men and one woman, indicating that they were buried wearing clothing. This was an extremely unusual custom for the time, as clothing was in extremely short supply and considered part of a person's estate.[41] It is likely that these individuals were buried in their clothes because the survivors knew the deceased had died from a contagious disease that could infect the survivors. One clothed man had gone to his grave with a tobacco pipe and spoon in his pocket or purse. This pipe stylistically dates to ca. 1610-1630, suggesting the years when the burial ground was active.[42] A number of grave shafts appear to have been purposefully reused for second burials, and several burials actually cut through earlier burials, suggesting that there was a significant time difference between the early and later burials and/or that no grave markers were used to identify individual graves.

The clothing, multiple burials, misalignment, careless disposal, shallowness of some graves, and the possible 1610 beginning date for the cemetery suggest that some burials indeed could date as early as the "Starving

128

Time" winter of 1609-1610. According to Smith, only 60 of 215 settlers survived that tumultuous winter.[43]   But disease was apparently not the sole sign of trauma among the burials. Lead pistol balls were found in the skeletal levels of three graves, but none of the bullets were embedded in surviving bone in such a way as to prove death by gunshot. Certainly there is an outside chance that gravediggers dropped the bullets accidentally as they filled the shafts. If that were the case, however, one would expect to find the occasional dropped lead ball at different levels in the fill as well. None were found. So it is more likely that these three people were indeed shot, probably causing or leading to their deaths.

The age at death varies considerably. Most appear to be adult males, but the sample also includes infants, adolescents, young adults and middle-aged adults. There is some evidence for childhood malnutrition and disease, and the development of muscle attachment sites on many of the skeletons indicates that they were regularly engaging in strenuous, physical activity. Initial impressions, therefore, suggest a mostly male, not so healthy, working-class population. But this was not strictly a "potter's field." Seven people were buried in coffins, which were expensive to acquire, and typically purchased only by wealthy families for funerals.

One of the seven coffins may not point to high status, however. A woman was found "wedged" in a narrow re-used wooden shipping crate. Yet she wore copper hair styling or cap wires. The rest of the people were unceremoniously buried in wrapping shrouds only, or were completely uncovered. Taken all together, initial analysis of the burials beneath the Statehouse Complex confirms that this burial ground held a true cross-section of the Jamestown population. Buried there until about 1630 were people from all walks of life who lived and died at early Jamestown – some likely from the winter of the "Starving Time" and others during times of rampant disease, while still others died during times of conflict. Before these skeletal remains are reburied at Jamestown, future and ever-improving forensic scientific analysis (however slow and expensive, and including chemical and DNA testing) promises to more precisely establish the time of burial, the ages, the causes of death, the ratio of male to female,

Figure 93. One of the Statehouse Complex individuals buried in clothing, with a pocket or purse containing a clay tobacco pipe of the 1610-1630 style. This is likely the time period when the burial ground was active.

other trauma that may have been suffered, the ratio of immigrants to native-born, and perhaps even family relationships, among the "signs of life" still being held in the graves at Jamestown.

The clear archaeological indications of death all over Jamestown's Old Town site underscores the fact that it took enormous courage to come to Jamestown from England during those first few years. There was danger from every quarter—salt in drinking water from the river, contaminated well water, disease from insects, empty food stores, accidents, warfare with the Virginia Indians, and, of course, jealousy and political battles within ranks. After the first few months of settlement, it is unlikely that the great risk for an "adventuring person" who wanted to join the Virginia colony was totally unknown back in England. One can only conclude that even the slim chance for a better life for some in Virginia simply outweighted the prospects of sudden death in the process.

Chapter V
A faire Well of fresh water…

Hopes were high that a well found during the search for the western palisade wall was the first well that the colonists had dug at James Fort (see Chapter II). Finding the first well has always been on the archaeological "wish list" because of the type of evidence it should contain. The very nature of the wet, contained environment of a well means that artifacts, which accidentally fall or are thrown into it, survive in very good condition. Further, as the water in a well becomes unusable through contamination or other means– which appears to have happened after only a few years at Jamestown – the shaft becomes a convenient receptacle for trash. Wells, therefore, can provide a wonderful snapshot of the time in which they were built, used, and abandoned.

But while the well, designated Well 27, was the first 17th-century well completely excavated during the *Jamestown Rediscovery* project, it was not the *first* well that John Smith documents digging within the fort in 1609. Not only did the artifacts in the well date firmly within the second and third decades of the 17th century, but also locating the western palisade in the summer of 2003 placed the well outside the fort's perimeter and not **in** the fort as Smith had stated. This fact does nothing to diminish Well 27's importance, however, for its contents encapsulate an important period of Jamestown's history – a time when the settlement's problems are escalating, the returns to investors are diminishing, and the Virginia Company's charter will be revoked.

There are no freshwater springs on Jamestown Island, so potable water was always an issue for the colonists. For the first year and a half, it appears that they had no well but were drawing water from the James River. According to colonist George Percy, "*our drinke [was] cold water taken out of the River, which was at floud, verie salt, at a low tide full of slime and filth.*"[1] As Percy observes by this statement, the James River is tidal and

Figure 94. Structure 170 was the first 17th-century well to be completely excavated by Jamestown Rediscovery archaeologists.

131

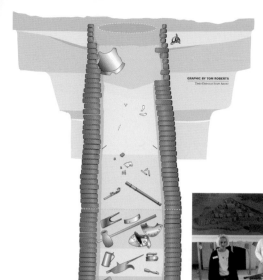

Figure 95. The brick-lined shaft of the well was filled with almost 1,400 objects dating to the early years of the 17th century.

Jamestown Island is located in the estuary's freshwater-saltwater zone. Not only is the river saltier at high tide, but the level of salinity is particularly high during the summer and fall when freshwater inflows from the tributaries diminish. Historian Carville Earle estimates that "*at flood tide the colonists drank water containing salinity concentrations of over five parts per thousand — far above the recommended standard for constant daily usage of one part per thousand.*" Much of the sickness, factious behavior, and perceived "laziness" of the colonists may be a result of salt poisoning from drinking James River water.[2]

The first well on Jamestown Island appears to have been dug at the beginning of 1609. John Smith reports, "*we digged a faire Well of fresh water in the Fort of excellent, sweet water which till then was wanting.*"[3] His qualification, *which till then was wanting*, seems to suggest that up until that point they had no source of fresh water and had been relying on the brackish river for their water supply.

William Strachey, who arrived at Jamestown in May 1610 after having been shipwrecked for one year in Bermuda, noted that the colonists are "*weakened and endangered ... by drinking of the brackish water of James Fort.*"[4] After only a year, the "*faire Well*" of John Smith appeared to be turning foul. Strachey commented that there were "*no fresh-water springs serving the town, but what wee drew from a well six or seven fathom deep, fed by the brackish river oozing into it.*"[5]

Arriving with Strachey was Sir Thomas Gates, the new governor of the settlement. Soon after his arrival, Gates drafted a code of conduct for the colony in which he also appears to mention the well described by Strachey. The code not only provided martial and moral laws, but also addressed matters of hygiene in the settlement. Among other things, Gates was concerned that careless cleansing of cookware could contaminate their well, and enacted a law that the colonists could not rinse or "*make cleane, any kettle, pot, or pan, or such like vessel within twenty foote of the **olde well**,* *or new Pumpe.*"[6] The reference to the new pump is interesting and suggests that the colonists from Bermuda had installed an apparatus for raising water from the well. It is very possible that the pump was a bilge pump (either ready-made or made up of spare parts) from one of the ships.[7] Perhaps the pump was installed out of necessity, as there were now 100 more individuals in the fort needing access to the single source of fresh water.

Figure 96. A cooking pot dries upside down after having been washed at the wooden pump in this mid-17th-century painting. The pump at Jamestown probably looked a lot like this.

The second well to be built at Jamestown was apparently a full year later in May 1611. Among the improvements made to the fort with the arrival of the new deputy governor of Virginia, Thomas Dale, was *"a new well for the amending of the most unholsome water which the old afforded."*[8] Dale appears to be referencing the old well full of brackish water noted by Strachey and Gates. Dale also mentions the making of brick by the brickmakers that had been specially brought for that purpose. Since Well 27 is brick-lined, as opposed to being lined with barrels or just an earthen shaft, it is tempting to consider that it may be this second well.

It is certainly evident from the low-fired bricks that they were made on site. Some even contain the impressions of paw prints caused by dogs running over the wet bricks that had been laid out to dry and harden. But, if the recently-found well is the one that was built under Dale's tenure as deputy governor, then the artifacts within it would date no later than 1617 when the acting governor, Samuel Argall, arrives to find the *"well of fresh water spoiled."*[9] If, as implied by Argall, the well were open but no longer functioning as a source of water, its shaft would then serve as a convenient repository for food remains and other trash. The evidence from Well 27 shows that it was filled quickly after its abandonment; but it contains artifacts that appear to date the fill to the mid-1620s rather than to 1617.

Along with the fouled well, Argall discovers that the palisades are broken and the interior of the fort is planted in tobacco – the big money crop of the colony. Although it is not specifically mentioned, it can be inferred that a new well is constructed as part of what Argall describes as *"the repairing those defects which did exceedingly trouble us."*[10] That the well was built outside the palisade is not surprising, for the fort interior

Figure 97. Two bricks with three paw print impressions from dogs running over the drying bricks.

133

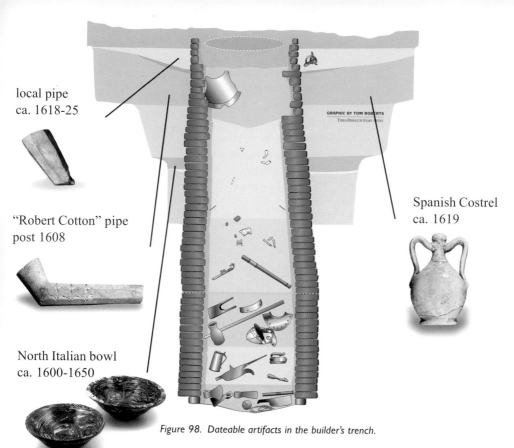

local pipe
ca. 1618-25

"Robert Cotton" pipe
post 1608

North Italian bowl
ca. 1600-1650

Spanish Costrel
ca. 1619

GRAPHIC BY TOM ROBERTS
Times-Dispatch Staff Artist

Figure 98. Dateable artifacts in the builder's trench.

appears to remain in use for agriculture, primarily for the company's tobacco.[11] Additionally, as will be shown below, the well appears to have been located near the workshop of a smith. The hot fires required by this craftsman, with all the risks involved, would not be conducive to the nurturing of crops and so would be kept on the other side of the wall.

In each of these historical references to wells, it is always to THE well, so it does not appear as though there were more than one functioning well at any one time. If this is true, then Argall's well, the third to be built in ten years, seems to be the best fit with Well 27. This is substantiated by the artifacts associated with the well's construction, which date after Argall's arrival in 1617.

Whereas the artifacts in a well reveal when the well was no longer being used as a water source and was filled with debris, the artifacts in the builder's trench surrounding the shaft establish when a well was built. Dateable artifacts in the builder's trench of Well 27 include: a locally made pipe bowl with octagonal facets that was also found at the Maine, a site near Jamestown occupied ca. 1618-1625;[12] a pipe that is known as the "Robert Cotton type" that is likely the handiwork of clay tobacco-pipe-maker Robert Cotton who arrived in Virginia in the fall of 1608;[13] sherds of a North Italian marbled slipware bowl that was produced during the first half of the 17th century;[14] and, fragments of a Spanish standing costrel. The earliest verifiable date for the appearance of these Spanish wares in the English colonies is 1619, on the Bermuda shipwreck, the *Warwick*.[15]

Even though there is an object dating ca. 1608 in the builder's trench, the date for the context must be established by the earliest manufacture date of the latest dated object. This is known as the *terminus post quem* or TPQ and is the basis for dating contexts in historical archaeology. The Spanish standing costrel with a ca. 1619 date, therefore, provides the TPQ for Well 27's builder's trench.

Most of the artifacts within the well appear to consist of objects that were purposely thrown in, either while the well was still in use or after it had been abandoned. If things such as shoe leather and food scraps were customarily dumped in wells while they were still being used, it can be easily understood why colonists through the years complained about the "unwholesomeness" of their water – especially considering the apparent practice of washing up pots and pans near wells. A few of the objects, including an earthenware pitcher, two German stoneware jugs, and two pewter vessels, could have been accidentally lost while colonists were retrieving water.

The earthenware pitcher was found broken into 166 sherds in a bottom layer of the well, but could be mended into its complete form with very few pieces missing. Red and micaceous, the pitcher's exterior is finished with

Figure 99. Merida-type jug from the well after mending.

a distinctive vertical burnishing, all characteristic of the ware known as Merida-type. While Merida is located in Spain, these wares have been shown by chemical analyses of the clays to most likely be Portuguese, rather than Spanish as originally thought. But, since the ware has been known as "Merida" since the 1960s, ceramic scholars have maintained the term with the addition of the "type" qualifier.[16] Merida-type olive jars, costrels, and bowls are found in small numbers on Virginia sites dating to the second quarter of the 17th century, although. Merida-type wares are found on Armada shipwrecks (1588) and in European port cities from ca. 1550-1650. They are considered to be low-status utilitarian wares commonly

Figure 100. A jug and bowl sit on the top of a well in this 17th-century painting. Brought to collect water or to rinse out, they are now prime candidates to become "pots down the well" for archaeologists to find centuries later.

carried by sailors and other travelers, rather than vessels that were highly prized and widely traded.

One can easily imagine the Merida-type pitcher sitting on the brick wellhead, prior to being filled with water from the well bucket, when it is accidentally knocked into the shaft. While perhaps also at the well to collect water, the two German vessels appear to have been broken outside the well before being tossed down the well shaft as trash. This is because, unlike the pitcher that mended into a complete vessel, there are substantial parts of the German jugs missing. These sherds probably never made it into the well shaft proper, and may possibly be found in the area surrounding the well as excavation continues in those contexts.

One of the stoneware jugs was made in the Westerwald region of Germany near Cologne. It is a form known as a baluster jug and is decorated with sprig-molded friezes derived from pattern books of the period. Reflecting the biblical themes that were popular in the early 17th-century Westerwald, the seven panels around the middle of the jug depict the New Testament story of the Prodigal Son. It is a close parallel to another Westerwald jug that bears the date 1618, and was probably made around the same date.

The other stoneware vessel was made in Frechen, Germany, and is a type known as a Bartmann jug. Bartmann means "bearded man" in German and refers to the bewhiskered face that adorns the necks of these jugs. Unfortunately, the mask is missing on the Well 27 jug. Bartmann jugs also usually have one or more medallions applied to their bellies. These medallions are often armorial, reflecting the coat of arms of affluent patrons, European cities and royal houses, ecclesiastical offices, or even the potter's own *Hausmarke* or symbol.

Figure 101. The Prodigal Son jug from the well (above) and a parallel jug dated 1618 (right).

The medallion on the Bartmann found in the Jamestown well bears the arms of the German duchies of Jülich, Cleve, and Berg. From 1521 to 1609, these three territories were united under a single ruler who also held the title of Count of Mark and Count of Ravensberg. It was a *"multifarious agglomerate of many little countries, gathered by marriage, heritage and luck, in the course of centuries."*[17]

When the last Duke of Jülich-Cleve-Berg, Johann Wilhelm, died in 1609, his territorial possessions were parceled out to the houses of Orange-Nassau and Saxony. Logic would suggest that any Bartmann produced after this time, unless the potter is using old sprig molds, should incorporate elements of either the Orange-Nassau or Saxony arms with

Figure 102. A soldier has just filled his glass with beer from the Bartmann jug that is sitting on the floor at his feet.

137

those of Jülich-Cleve-Berg. Unfortunately it is not that simple. Many variants of the Jülich-Cleve-Berg medallion have been recorded that have so far not been explained in relation to political history.[18] Medallions very similar to that on the Jamestown Bartmann have been recorded as late as 1629 on the Dutch shipwreck, *Batavia*.[19] To further complicate dating evidence on the *Batavia*, however, is a German stoneware jug bearing the date 1595. Since the vessel has no signs of wear, and there are fragments of at least five identical jugs, it appears it was decorated with old sprig molds, and therefore the date does not reflect when the vessel was made.[20]

Crowned Lion = Berg

Charbocle = Cleve

Lion = Julich

Fess Checky = Mark

Chevrons = Ravens

Figure 103. The Bartmann medallion with the arms of Jülich-Cleve-Berg. The oval medallion consists of a crowned shield with two rampant lions as supporters. The crowned lion on the left represents Berg whereas the lion on the right symbolizes Jülich. The triparted shield consists of a charbocle (Cleve), a fess checky (Mark), and three chevrons (Ravensburg).

Two pewter vessels found at the bottom of the Jamestown well probably ended up there in much the same way as the ceramic vessels just discussed. It is very unlikely that any pewter object would be purposely discarded, because pewter maintained value even if it were damaged or out of style. The high demand for the metal and its low melting point meant that old pewter objects could easily be sold for scrap to be recycled.

Figure 104. Pewter baluster measure for a gallon of liquid.

By the late-16th century, people were trading in their wooden spoons and platters for pewter as their finances allowed. Pewter was produced in forms mirroring silver prototypes and was a cheap alternative to the precious metal. Its popular use for a wide range of household goods can be explained by the metal's *"bright appearance, easy and safe transport, and durability."*[21] Even so, early 17th-century Virginia inventories reveal that pewter ware in any quantity was confined to the wealthier households with increasing usage by those of average means only during the second quarter of the century.[22]

Figure 105. Two pewter measures with different capacities are shown being used as decanters in this 17th-century Dutch tavern scene.

Figure 106. Pewter flagon and close up of initials stamped under the thumbpiece.

One of the pewter vessels from Well 27 is a common form known as a baluster measure. *"Pewter measures in standard sizes of verified capacities have been used in England in the commerce of alcoholic beverages since at least the 15ᵗʰ century."*[23] But, while measures were commonly used to transport alcoholic beverages from tavern cellars to the table, inventories show that pewter measures were also used in private households.[24] Missing its handle and lid, the measure from the well could contain a gallon of liquid and is of a slender shape seen on measures dating to the second half of the 16ᵗʰ century. Even in its incomplete condition it would be a useful container in which to gather water.

The other pewter vessel is a lidded vessel for transporting and serving liquids, known as a flagon. Probably made in England, its simple lines indicate a pre-1620 date.[25] Flagons were used both domestically and by the church in the communion service although prior to the reign of King James I, pewter was decreed unworthy to contain the Holy Eucharist.[26] The flagon from the well was probably owned by a private individual as indicated by the underside of the thumb piece, which is marked with the three initials of the vessel's owners – P R E – arranged in a triangle with the P above the other two letters. For individuals who were not entitled to coats of arms, the stamping of their initials was an acceptable way to mark valuable metal objects. There appears to be no standard convention for arranging initials, but the most commonly used would make the upper letter "P" the surname, while "R" is the man's Christian name and the wife's Christian name begins with "E." The identity of this couple will probably never be positively known, because there is not a record of everyone who resided at Jamestown. Additionally, while there are many matches to men in the colony with the initials "RP," there is no mention of wives for these individuals. One tantalizing match, however, is Richard and Elizabeth Pierce who arrived from England on the *Neptune* in August of 1618.[27] The Pierces were *"relatively successful planters"* and so would be expected to own some pewter.[28]

Figure 107. According to a 17th-century description, the bill is "an Instrument used both in warre, and also in domestick affaires, by Labourers and husbandmen."

In the February 1624 census of the colony, a Richard Perse (Pierce),[29] his wife and "*his man Allen*," are listed as living at Neck of Land,[30] which is an area adjacent to Jamestown and only separated from the island by the Back River and its marshlands. In the muster dated January/February 1625 — but possibly incorporating data as late as December 1625[31] — the Pierces are still listed at Neck of Land but with no servant. They own a house and a pig and have two firearms with accouterments, one pound of powder, the only suit of armor at Neck of Land, three and one-half barrels of corn and two bushels of meal. The servant, whose full name is Allen Keniston, is recorded with one armor and 10 bushels of corn at the James City suburb of Pasbehay.[32] He is no longer part of the Pierce household because he has been freed from his indenture, and he is living on the Governor's Land. This property, consisting of 3,000 acres of land, was set aside by Governor George Yeardley in 1618 to be worked by tenants. The tenants were entitled to half of the profits of their labor, with the other half divided between the governor and the Virginia Company.

A March 1625 court case records that at about the time of the census, Pierce promised to release Keniston from "*the Time he had to serve*" in return for a payment of a barrel of ears (corn) by April of the following year.[33] The court ruled that not only was Keniston freed from his debt, but also that Pierce had to pay him freedom dues of a bushel of corn and "*a hundred pound waight of good merchantable Tobacco.*"[34]

But how do we explain the presence of the Pierce's flagon in a well on Jamestown Island? It is possible that the Pierces lived on Jamestown Island upon their arrival in 1618 and before the unknown date of their settling at Neck of Land. Or, their stay at Jamestown could be related to the Indian uprising of March 22, 1622. With more than a third of the colonists killed in one day, Governor Wyatt ordered the survivors from all the outlying areas to move into one of eight fortified settlements for safety.[35] Jamestown was one of those settlements and the closest safe haven to Neck of Land. It will probably never be known for certain, but if the flagon does belong to Richard and Elizabeth Pierce, then it was most likely lost sometime between August 1618 and February 1624, the window of time during which they could have been living on Jamestown Island.

Another artifact in the well that may point to the time right after the 1622 uprising is a weapon known as a bill. Derived from an agricultural tool known as a billhook that was used to prune trees and slash brush, the bill is a staff weapon.

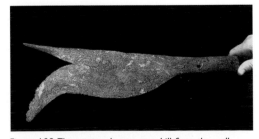

Figure 108. The weapon known as a bill from the well.

141

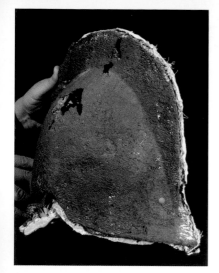

Figure 109. Burgonet helmet found in the well. This is light headgear with cheek protection that was worn by both infantry and cavalry.

Its heavy scythe-shaped blade has a short dorsal spike and a longer terminal spike. Believed to have originated in Italy in the 13th century, it was not commonly issued to large organized armies in Europe even though it required no specialized training to use it effectively. Instead, the bill was relegated to small local fighting forces and contingents of *"common countrie men who were unschooled in the use of the more efficacious halberd."*[36] The increased reliance of armies on protective armor coupled with the development of firearms resulted in the bill falling into disuse by the time the colonists first set foot on Jamestown Island.[37] While there is documented use of bills by royalist forces as late as the English Civil Wars, it is believed that this resurgence is primarily the result of the short supply of more conventional staff weapons.[38] This may also account for the bills at Jamestown.

After the massacre of 1622, one thousand bills were released from the King's armory in England as part of the obsolete weaponry made available for the colony's defense. While the documentary record shows that Bermuda requested half of them for its own use, it appears that a substantial number of bills came into the Virginia colony at this time.[39] It is indeed possible that all the archaeologically recovered bills from Jamestown area sites are a result of this 1622 shipment.[40]

Only nine bills have been excavated on Jamestown Island, and none were found in the early ca. 1610 contexts. Four of them are from contexts relating to the last statehouse on the island (Structure 144), which burned in 1698. The appearance of this number of bills in such a late context can be explained by the changing role of bills through the 17th century. Although no longer used as a weapon, the bill still functioned as a ceremonial arm. In this role the bill became *"what it had never been able to become in its heyday: a proper regulation-issue military weapon, even if only symbolically."*[41] The Jamestown bills were probably mounted on an interior wall of the statehouse as part of a panoply of arms representing strength and power in the government building.

Figure 110. Partially conserved breastplate from the well.

Figure 111. Exterior and interior close-ups of right shoulder modification to the breastplate.

Besides the bill, there were other elements of arms and armor associated with the well. These include a pistol barrel, a musket barrel, a matchlock lockplate, a sword blade, a rapier hilt, and, seemingly, one man's suit of armor. The latter comprises the breastplate, front and back gorgets to protect the neck, a burgonet helmet, and tasset lames to protect the thigh. The most interesting object in this assemblage is the breastplate because it provides a very definite TPQ for the filling of the well.

The breastplate is the typical peascod type made and used in the early 17th century. It has the pronounced central ridge and elongated V-shaped front that reflect the male civilian doublet then in vogue. But the breastplate has a modification that is also seen on breastplates from the New Towne area of Jamestown and from Jordan's Point in Prince George County (ca. 1620-35). On the right shoulder a separate plate has been riveted onto the armor through a carefully cut slot in the underarm edge area. All indications are that this modification was made in James Fort sometime after June 22, 1611. This is the date that Sir Thomas Dale gives his "*exemplified and enlarged*" version of Gates' "*Lawes Divine, Morall and Martiall*" and the reason for the alteration.

To understand the significance of the breastplate modifications, it is necessary to examine the organization of the English army in the early 17th century. Patterned after Dutch military reforms implemented around 1590, there were three components to the army: the pikemen (who car-

Pikeman

Shot

Musketeer

Figure 112. Jacob DeGehyn's illustrations of the arms and armor required by the pikeman, the shot, and the musketeer, from his Exercise of Arms *that was published in 1607.*

144

ried a pike and wore armor), the musketeers, and shot,[42] who were unarmored but carried firearms.

Dale implemented many plans to strengthen the colony. In an attempt to cut down on the deaths of his men from Indian arrows, he made it a law that *"every shot shall either be furnished with a quilted coate of Canvas, a headpeece, and a sword, or else with a* **light Armor** *and Bases quilted."* The Governor, moreover, had to ensure the *"dayly wearing of these Armors, least in the field, the souldier do finde them the more uncouth strange and troublesome."*[43] These laws must have worked, for one colonist remarked that the *"Indians not being acquainted nor accustomed to encounter with men in Armor, much wondered thereat especially that they did not see any of our men fall as they had done in other conflicts."*[44]

In light of the implementation of this new order for all to wear armor, the modification to the breastplate provided the men with firearms a way to steady the butt of their weapons against the slippery surface of the breastplate.[45] In other words, the added plate functions as a stop. Thus the altered breastplates are a direct response to the 1611 law, but this doesn't necessarily provide the date when the breastplate went into the well. The Jordan's Point breastplate from a context of ca. 1620-35 suggests that they were still in use from ten to fifteen years later.

Unlike the ceramic and pewter containers, it is not so clear why the elements of arms and armor are in the well. The same question surrounds a number of tools, many in useable condition, which were also found at the bottom of the well shaft. Lost and stolen tools were enough of an issue in 1610 to warrant mention in Gates' code for the colony, which states:

> *"No man shall imbezell, lose, or willingly breake, or fraudulently make away, either Spade, Shouell, Hatchet, Axe, Mattocke, or other toole or instrument vppon paine of whipping."*[46]

Why would colonists "willingly break" tools? Possibly so they would have an excuse for not working? Human nature being what it is, a "workers' revolt" is also a possible explanation for the two dozen perfectly good hoe blades found in the bottom of an 18th-century well on one of the nearby Kingsmill plantations.[47] Another explanation proposed for the miscellany of iron objects found in well bottoms is that they had served as makeshift bucket weights,

Figure 113. Apart from a helmet, soldiers bearing firearms would not normally wear armor. But this depiction of "JR," wearing a breastplate while wielding a matchlock gun, accurately reflects the laws implemented by Sir Thomas Dale in 1611.

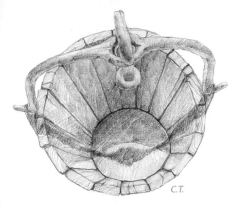

Figure 114. The heavy iron swivel on the handle of the wooden bucket acted as a weight to force the bucket to tip on its side once it hit the water.

C.T.

tipping the well bucket once it hit the water. Over time, these objects would come loose from the bucket, falling to the bottom of the well, and would need to be replaced. This idea is supported by a bucket found in another 18th-century well at Kingsmill that had two worn horseshoes attached to the bucket chain.[48]

But based upon the design of the well bucket handle that was recovered from the well shaft, this bucket would not have required the extra weights. The U-shaped, round-sectioned iron handle attachment for the bucket was attached to the bucket through loops at the top of a rectangular iron strap mounted on each side of the bucket. The handle swung from the well rope by a loop at the end of a large and heavy swivel, which would serve to tip the bucket on its side as it was lowered into the water.[49] One arm of the bucket handle was broken, but it is not known if this happened before or after the well was no longer being used.

Another argument against the bucket-weight theory is the fact that similar collections of seemingly useful iron objects have been recovered from trash pits that are totally unassociated with wells. It has been conjectured that these objects may represent the stock of scrap metal accumulated by a blacksmith.[50] This seems even more likely in the case of the iron tools and tool fragments found in Well 27 because evidence of a smith's workshop was found nearby during National Park Service excavations in the 1950s. Archaeologists uncovered lots of clinker, nail rod (the raw material for making nails), hot cut iron scrap, and indications of gun repair.[51] The same clinker from iron working was found in the top layers of the well, along with a bar of wrought iron with a chisel hot cut, suggesting that it may be a piece of the smith's square stock.

Three agricultural hoes were recovered from the bottom of the well. Two of the hoes are very similar and bear maker's marks in a rectangular stamp on the blade. The mark is only decipherable on one, however, and consists of the initials "IH" or "HI." Very little research has been done in reference to maker's marks on ironwork either in England or America, so it is impossible at the moment

Figure 115. A 17th-century painting depicting a pile of damaged or obsolete iron objects to be recycled by the blacksmith.

146

to trace an object to an individual craftsman. At the very least, it would be important to know all the 17th-century sites near Jamestown with marked pieces to trace distribution. It is believed that all marked iron of this early period was produced in Europe, as were most of the tools. Production in Virginia was not substantive enough for the blacksmiths to warrant personalized

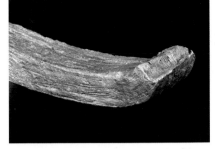

Figure 116. Wrought iron bar with a chisel hot cut.

stamps, which are believed to have served as marks of assurance from craftsmen who were selling their products in quantity. The role of the Virginia blacksmith at this time was primarily in repairing damaged objects and in making small tools. Mass-produced tools from Europe were easily attained throughout the colonial period, providing little economic incentive for local production.[52]

The hoes found in Well 27 are all of narrow heavy type known as grubbing hoes used to chop out roots in tobacco cultivation. Tobacco quickly became the colony's principle money crop after 1613 with the introduction of John Rolfe's successful blend of West Indian and Virginia tobacco. By 1616, most (32 of the 50) of the inhabitants on Jamestown Island were farmers.[53] This is a totally different emphasis than is seen with the initial years of settlement at James Fort. The low priority that farming held for the first settlers is exemplified by the fact that only two agricultural

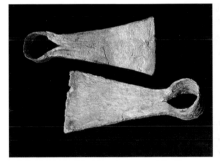

Figure 117. Two early 17th-century agricultural hoes from the well.

hoes were recovered from over 130,000 artifacts in the contexts within the fort dating ca. 1610.

The first colonists "*were not permitted to manure or till any ground*" but were directed by the Virginia Company to engage in activities that would "*make return of present profit.*"[54] The colony's food was to be obtained through trade of inexpensive items with the Indians. Not only would this free up the colonists to work at making money for the London investors, but it would help frame a friendly rapport with the native inhabitants whose information on the local resources was needed.

Six spades, represented by the straight square-ended nosings or shoes that fit onto the end of wooden blades, were also found in the well. Used as early as the 14th century in England, iron-shod wooden spades are common on Virginia sites dating to the first half of the 17th century.[55] Spades with solid iron blades are known to have been contemporary with the iron-shod wooden spades,

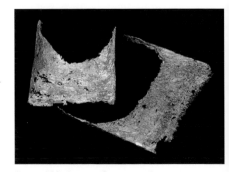

Figure 118. Iron reinforcements known as nosings for the ends of wooden spades.

Figure 119. Spades were among the most useful tools brought by the colonists. They were needed for husbandry, constructing houses and fortifications, and digging up commodities such as sassafras roots and, the ever-elusive, gold!

but the latter are a lighter and less expensive alternative. In addition, as the edge is worn down, which would happen quite rapidly in the Virginia clay, the nosing could be replaced without having to discard the entire spade.[56]

Two of the spade nosings – one complete and one fragmentary – have maker's marks in the form of an open left hand. This same mark is on a spade from Ditch 7, which was filled in the 1620s, and on a spade from the Maine on the Governor's Land.[57]

Like the complete well spade, the marked spade nosing from the Maine has a sharp cutting edge that does not look as though it has been used. Since the Maine does not appear to have been occupied post-1625, the marked spade provides a similar contextual date of ca. 1618-1625 for the spades in the well. It is very possible that all these spades may represent Virginia Company property that arrived in the colony with Yeardley and was distributed under his governorship.

There were also seven axes in the well, although some are represented by no more than the eye, presenting good evidence of scrap from a smithy. Three of the splitting axes have tubular shaped eyes for attaching the handle. This is a feature of early axes that Europeans traded to the Indians, as indicated by their appearance in Native American contexts from New York to Florida.[58] Even though axe types tend to have a long chronology, the tubular-eyed axe type has been excavated on other sites in the Virginia colony primarily dating to the second quarter of the 17th century.[59]

Another small splitting axe from the well has an eared eye and a maker's mark of "RC." Its

Figure 120. Detail of a maker's mark found on two of the well's spades. A spade with the same mark was found at the Maine, a site near Jamestown occupied ca. 1618-1625.

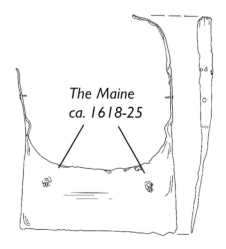

The Maine
ca. 1618-25

cutting edge is in mint condition and does not appear to have been used. Splitting axes are common on early Virginia sites and reflect the colonists' reliance on log splitting to derive useable wood from their timber. Whereas sawmills had largely taken the place of hand splitting in England, the colonists had *"revitalized a technology well suited to their labor-scarce, timber-rich environment."*[60]

Figure 121. A broad axe, a felling axe, and two splitting axes from the well.

There is one broad axe, which also appears as though it has never been used as it still maintains its sharp, steeled edge. Since the blade is double-beveled, it could have been utilized for both dressing and chopping wood. The broad axe bears a maker's mark of a twice-stamped raised dot in a diamond cartouche.

Two of the well axes are felling axes for cutting down trees. They exhibit eared eyes and no poll. One is complete and appears by its still sharp double-beveled cutting edge as if it had never been used. It also has a maker's mark of "RB" in a square stamp. Two additional eared eye fragments, probably from felling axes, were found in the builder's trench of the well. Unlike the complete felling axe, one of these eyes exhibits signs of use in that it still contains two small wedges that had been added to tighten up a loose handle.

A heavy tanged chisel, in excellent condition, was also recovered from Well 27. *"Tanged chisels were used for the light-to-moderate work of shaping and cleaning up wood joints for close fitting."*[61] A wooden handle would fit over the tapering tang, but unlike most 17th-century chisels recorded on Virginia sites, it has no bolster to hold the end of the handle.[62] Instead, the thick square-sectioned blade is shouldered at its join with the tang. The blade, which is beveled on one side of the bottom edge, was constructed with a layer of steel along its entire length so as to provide a continually strong sharp edge despite any resharpening necessitated by wear.

A couple of objects considered structural ironwork were also found at the bottom of the well. One is a looped spike consisting of a tapering wedge-shaped shank with a large eye. Unlike the shank, which is very squared on the edges, the eye has been rounded and shows signs of wear. Perhaps the spike

Figure 122. The chisel, missing only its wooden handle, from the well.

149

Figure 123. Two objects of structural ironwork, a holdfast and a looped spike, were found in the well.

was used as part of the rigging for the well bucket. The spike would be driven through a structural post and the bucket rope would pass through the eye.

The other object is a tanged spike known as a holdfast. It has a rectangular sectioned and tapering tang with a flattened laterally set triangular head. The head has a single nail hole, although some holdfasts have two. The holdfast is used architecturally to secure wooden elements to masonry, brickwork or other timbers. They are commonly used to secure mantles to brick chimneys and doors or window frames in masonry construction. At nine-and-a-half-inches long, the holdfast would be used for the more robust construction required for doors and windows. The holdfast doesn't appear as though it had ever used, but it was obviously intended for a substantial and important building at Jamestown. [63]

The iron artifacts in the well consisted of not only tools and hardware, but also a few domestic objects. One of these was a cleaver used for cutting up mammals and large fish. It is in excellent condition with a sharp blade and a solid iron handle, making it hard to understand why such a useful tool would have been discarded. Perhaps it had slipped into the well while being used by a butcher nearby, although the faunal remains that have been excavated from the site are not substantive enough to indicate that this activity was going on near the well.

In not as good condition is a gridiron with two legs missing. Unchanged over hundreds of years, the gridiron is a platform used to support a pot heating in a fire or in front of it. This simple piece of equipment allowed for the fire to remain unattended while cooking pottages and stews, thereby leaving the colonists more time for other important subsistence activities such as hunting, fishing, and harvesting tobacco.

Figure 124. It is hard to understand why this cleaver, in seemingly mint condition, was thrown down the well.

They haue set men & women on hot Grideorns to make them Confesse whe re there money was

Also damaged is a flat iron that is depicted in the 17th century as a *"Taylors pressing iron."*[64] A precursor of the box iron, which is heated by a separate piece of iron that is placed inside it, the flat iron would have been heated directly over the fire. The disadvantage of this type of iron is that the solid iron handle would also heat up and would require a cloth or some other protection to pick it up.

Figure 125. Gridirons are iron platforms for heating pots of food over, or in front of, a fire. This 17th-century English engraving depicts a rather unconventional use for the "Grideorn" as an instrument of torture.

In the first few years of the colony, it is likely that a pressing iron would only be associated with the gentlemen who could afford tailors and other servants to keep their clothing in order. By 1610, however, it appears that even the common man can use the services of persons in the settlement whose sole task in return for their share out of the company store is *"to wash the foule linnen of any one labourer or souldier."*[65] Not all clothing was laundered in the early 17th century, but the undergarments and clothing that touched the skin were typically made of linen, which could be washed and bleached.[66] Perhaps the *"Laundrer or Laundresse"* also had the responsibility of pressing the *"foule linen"* shirts once they had been cleaned.

The pressing iron has a maker's mark of "IP" in a circular stamp and does not appear to have been used although it is in two pieces. The handle had snapped off where it bends up from the heavy rectangular-shaped iron, which may explain why it had been discarded.

Figure 126. Damaged gridiron from the well.

Also incomplete and representative of high status is a fireplace shovel handle with decorative cast brass elements. Fireplace tongs with the same brass ornamentation and thus either part of the same set of fireplace equipment (which would have included a poker, tongs and andirons) or part of another set from the same workshop was found at Martin's Hundred. The context there is associated with Governor William Harwood who arrived in 1620.[67] These same cast brass elements, although detached from the tool, were found at Jordan's Journey, near Hopewell (ca. 1620-35) along with matching heavy finials to firedogs or andirons. This was the fortified settlement headed first by Ancient Planter Samuel Jordan and then William Farrar. A study that ranked the 28 settlements listed in the 1625 Muster by quantifiable attributes determined that only three

Figure 127. Pressing iron with broken handle from the well.

rated higher than Jordan's Journey.[68] These were individuals in the upper echelons of Virginia society who could afford the more expensive household goods to furnish their homes.

As hoped, Well 27 yielded a number of organics preserved in the wet mud at the bottom. These included pieces of rope – still smelling of pitch and probably used to haul up the well bucket – wooden staves from the well bucket, beans and seeds, and fragments of two leather shoes. There was enough of one shoe to determine that it was a high-quality youth's latchet shoe, English size 8 ½. It has a very narrow arch that is typical of shoes dating to around 1610 although it also shows a repair to the heel, so the shoe was not new when it was discarded.[69]

Figure 128. A woman uses a pressing iron to press linen in this 17ᵗʰ-century Dutch painting.

In conclusion, an examination of the dateable objects in the well seems to indicate that the well was filled sometime at the end of the first quarter of the 17ᵗʰ century. If, as we are theorizing, the discarded iron objects comprised a smith's stock of damaged objects, what caused them to be thrown away? Archaeological deposits often result from a change of the status quo, precipitated by events such as a death, a new spouse, or a property transfer. Perhaps the well deposit had something to do with the major changes at Jamestown that were put into action on May 24, 1624, when the Virginia Company's charter was revoked by King James. At that time, Virginia Company lands and servants, including smiths, were reassigned to several gentlemen in the colony, forcing many individuals to leave the island. It is not inconceivable that a Company smith who had been compelled to relocate from Jamestown would discard the Company-owned supply of scrap iron.

The historical records reveal that there were a number of smiths working in the Jamestown colony in the 1620s. Three of them, all Virginia Company servants, arrived together on the *Bona Nova* in 1619. George Beale was a 22-year-old blacksmith from Staffordshire, John Blisse was a 19-year-old smith from Sussex, and John Jefferson was a gunsmith. In 1623, Blisse is recorded as being a servant of the governor, Francis Wyatt. Jefferson is documented as being assigned to Captain Francis West in 1627

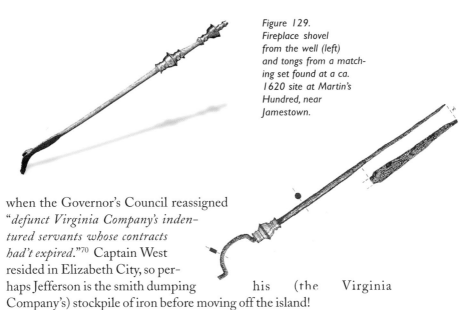

Figure 129. Fireplace shovel from the well (left) and tongs from a matching set found at a ca. 1620 site at Martin's Hundred, near Jamestown.

when the Governor's Council reassigned *"defunct Virginia Company's indentured servants whose contracts had't expired."*[70] Captain West resided in Elizabeth City, so perhaps Jefferson is the smith dumping his (the Virginia Company's) stockpile of iron before moving off the island!

As the area around the well is investigated, perhaps the answers to these questions will become clearer. All indications are that Well 27 was built no earlier than 1618/19 – the TPQ of the builder's trench – and was filled before 1630 when pottery production began on the island and the "Jamestown potter's" wares become ubiquitous. There were no fragments of this pottery found in the well, which would be almost a certainty if the well shaft had been open this late. The filling date appears to fit with the mid-1620s, but it will require further archaeological excavation in the areas surrounding the well to reach a more definitive conclusion. To truly understand the collection of iron artifacts in the well, the smith's refuse

Figure 130. The youth's latchet shoe found in the well is very similar to this ca.1605-1613 child's shoe and to the footwear worn by the boy being disciplined in this Dutch painting.

arca that was uncovered in the 1950s should be re-excavated and the actual site of the forge defined. In addition, there are already indications of other wells and foundations within and near the palisade walls that could be excavated in the near future. Analyzing the contents of these features may make the sequence of events on the site clearer and help uncover the deeper secrets of our "*faire Well*."

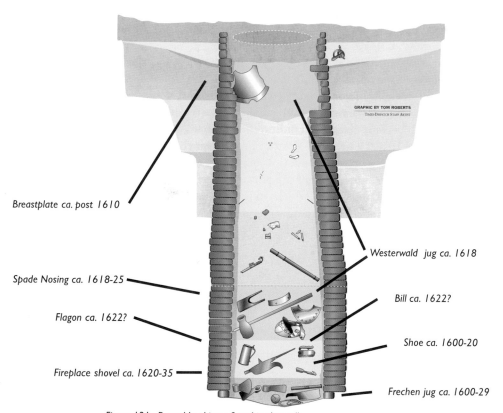

GRAPHIC BY TOM ROBERTS
Times-Dispatch Staff Artist

Breastplate ca. post 1610

Westerwald jug ca. 1618

Spade Nosing ca. 1618-25

Bill ca. 1622?

Flagon ca. 1622?

Shoe ca. 1600-20

Fireplace shovel ca. 1620-35

Frechen jug ca. 1600-29

Figure 131. Dateable objects found in the well.

154

Chapter VI
Tinker, tailor, soldier, sailor ...

Of all the surviving documents relating to the early English colonizing effort at Jamestown, it appears that the backward-looking lens of history has crystallized around a single remark. In 1615, colonist Ralph
Hamor relates that when Thomas Dale arrived in May 1611 at Jamestown,
"where the most company were," he found the men at *"their daily and usuall
works bowling in the streets."*[1] The picture engendered by this statement,
of men engaged in idle entertainment while their dilapidated houses were
ready to fall upon their heads, has come down through history to epito-
mize the colonizing efforts at Jamestown. The perception has been that
the first individuals sent to Jamestown were a bunch of bumbling idiots
who didn't know what they were doing, avoided work, and chose the worst
possible place to settle: low, swampy, unhealthy ground that almost spelled
the demise of the colony.

Jamestown as a joke, a settlement that nearly failed, is not a very noble
representation for the beginnings of America, as we know it today. Perhaps this is why historians have largely ignored Jamestown and when
patriotism stirs Americans to remember their roots, thoughts are of Plymouth, a later but more successful colony built on respectable religious
principles, and not that scruffy (but earlier) military-commercial settlement in Virginia.

The *Jamestown Rediscovery* excavations on the site of James Fort are
uncovering information that contradicts this characterization of early
Jamestown. While it is probably true that many of the colonists who participated in the Virginia adventure in the first few years were *"poore Gentlemen, Tradsmen, Serving-men, [and] libertines"*[2] who did not contribute
much to sustaining the fledgling colony, archaeology is revealing another
compelling story. Artifacts, including tools, equipment, and industrial
byproducts, indicate that many of the craftsmen were actively working at
what they had been sent to do: to make money for the investors back home
in England.

During the first 1-½ years of colonization at Jamestown almost 300
individuals arrived for the purpose of turning a profit for the Virginia
Company, the London-based group of entrepreneurs who were bankrolling
the enterprise. The colonists were not sent with the idea of establishing a
new country. Instead, their instructions were to set up a *center of exploita-
tion* whereby they could venture out from a secured home base and ex-
tract any marketable resources the land had to offer. According to the *"instructions by way of advice"* that the colonists were given by the governing
council of the Virginia Company, they were even expected to pull the

Virginia Indians into this system of resource extraction as the primary suppliers of "*corn and all other lasting victuals.*"[3]

The colonists were supposed to establish a symbiotic relationship with "*the naturals*" whereby European trade beads and copper jewelry would be exchanged for foodstuffs to sustain the settlement. "*This,*" instructs the Council for Virginia, "*you must do before…they perceive you mean to plant among them.*"[4] Opening up large areas of land in cultivation right away would send a signal of permanency that might alarm, and possibly alien-ate, the Indians. Reliance on the "*country corn*" made sense, not only because it was not known how well the planted English seed would prosper but also because, ideally, it would help frame a friendly rapport with the native inhab-itants whose information on the local resources was needed. Most importantly, it freed the colonists to focus on their principal goal, which was gen-erating commercial profit for the London investors. The men "*were not permitted to manure or till any ground*" but were directed by the Virginia Company to engage in activi-ties that would "*make return of present profit.*"[5] The low prior-ity that farming held for the Jamestown settlers is exempli-fied by the fact that only two agricultural hoes have been recovered by archaeologists from over 130,000 artifacts in the pre-1610 contexts in James Fort.

Figure 132. Bowling was a popular leisure-time activity for men and women in all levels of English society, as it required little more than a grassy area or alley and the bowls (balls). Gambling was usually associ-ated with the game, as was rowdy behavior, which often led to prohibi-tions against bowling on the Sabbath. The men in this Dutch painting are playing skittles, a type of bowling game using nine wooden pins as the target. Skittles is the precursor of the modern bowling game of ten pins.

Luckily for us, John Smith recorded the names of many of the colonizers —common craftsmen as well as men of position — with the arrival of every supply from England and at the outset of each expedi-tion. As cape merchant for the colony, he was the officer in charge of sup-ply and would have had lists of all the individuals who had arrived at Jamestown and whom he was responsible to provision.[6] Smith identifies the majority of the men as gentlemen, many of whom were veterans of wars in the Low Countries and/or Ireland, and largely comprised the military component of James Fort. Others are described generally as laborers or tradesmen, but some are labeled with their specific crafts, many of which seem superfluous to the survival of the colony.

Smith bemoans the Virginia Company's drive for profit at the expense of the settlement's welfare that he claims "*most plainly appeared by sending…so many Refiners, Gold-smiths, Jewellers, Lapidaries, Stone-cutter, Tabacco-pipe-makers, Imbroderers, Perfumers, Silkemen with all their appurtenances.*"[7] None of the colonists on Smith's surviving lists are identified specifically as lapidaries, embroiderers, or silkmen but the refiners, goldsmiths, a jeweller, a stone-cutter (or mason), a tobacco pipe maker, and a perfumer are named. In addition, several other craftsmen are identified in the records with trades not on Smith's "worthless" list, such as blacksmiths, bricklayers, and carpenters.

What do we know about these identified craftsmen, and what objects have been unearthed that may relate to the practice of their crafts at Jamestown? Most importantly, why were these particular individuals chosen to be among the first to exploit Virginia's resources?

Refiners and Goldsmiths

Based upon the Spanish experience in the New World, the English also hoped to find riches – particularly gold and silver – in the Virginia soil. The search began almost immediately upon the first landing at Jamestown in May 1607; so, when Christopher Newport returned to London in June, he was able to carry what he believed to be samples of gold ore. Unfortunately, when London assayers tested the "gold," the sample "*turned to vapore.*"[8] But this did not dissuade the effort, especially since Newport claimed that he must have mistakenly brought the wrong sample. The Virginia Company continued to believe in the accuracy of Newport's assessment that Virginia was "*very rich in gold and copper.*"[9] So, on the next ship to the colony, which arrived in January 1608, they sent two refiners (William Dawson and Abram Ransack) and two goldsmiths (William Johnson and Richard Belfield).

Goldsmiths were craftsmen who, as their name suggests, worked with precious metals to fabricate jewelry, drinking and eating vessels, as well as decorative objects. They comprised the wealthiest and most powerful metalworkers in London up to the middle of the 18th century.[10] Since, as history shows, gold was never found by the colonists in

Figure 133. Goldsmiths were of high status in early 17th-century English society. They not only worked with precious metals and stones but also were merchants dealing in these expensive materials.

157

Figure 134. A still, composed of elements in the same shape and of the same materials as the James Fort still, can be seen sitting by the alchemist's right knee.

Virginia, it is not surprising that John Smith writes that the goldsmiths never had an opportunity to exercise their craft.

The refiners are a different story. Smith had little respect for the "*guilded refiners with their golden promises.*" Dawson and Ransack not only recruited most of the colonists in a frantic search for gold along the muddy banks of the James River, but also detained a shipload of mariners from returning to London in order to do the same. For fourteen weeks "*there was no talke, no hope, no worke, but dig gold, wash gold, refine gold, loade gold.*"[11] The outcome was a depleted store of provisions from the extra burden of supporting the mariners for this length of time. There was also no progress on the colony's essential duties, but a shipload of "*guilded durt*" was sent back to London.[12]

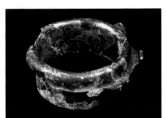

alembic

cucurbit

receiver

Figure 135. Drawing showing the three major parts of a still: the cucurbit, the alembic, and the receiver.

Another refiner, William Callicut (Caldicot), probably arrived with the Second Supply in September 1608. He is "*fitted*" for the purpose of refining, as he accompanies Newport west on an expedition into the territory of the Monacan Indians in October 1608. Smith relates that "*from that crust of earth we digged he perswaded us to beleeve he extracted some small quantitie of silver.*"[13] The assays appeared to confirm the presence of silver ore, but, as Smith reveals, the quality was "*so poore it was not regarded.*"[14] This test did not dissuade others from believing Callicut's assessment that "*not unlikely better stuffe might be had for the digging.*"[15]

William Henrick Faldoe (Volday), "*a Zwitzar by birth,*"[16] returned to Virginia in June 1610, after a few months in London during which he convinced the Virginia Company to fund a one-and-one-half-year contract for him to explore the same area as Callicut. Faldoe, who was a gentleman Adventurer and member of the Fishmongers Company,[17] had first arrived in the colony in 1608. It is possible that he had attained his "*intelligence*" about the silver mines from being part of Callicut's earlier exploratory party. He kept this information "close to the chest" however, for when he died in the latter half of 1610 of "*a burning-Fever*"[18] the mines still had not been located

The matter does not die with Faldoe, however. In 1628, a letter to the king from the General Assembly at Jamestown refers to Callicut's silver mine discovered "*nineteen years ago, at a place about four days' journey from the falls of the James river.*" The letter goes on to explain that the reason this resource has not been exploited is that there is "*not the means of transporting the ore.*"[19]

Refiners were specialist goldsmiths who refined or separated precious metals. The processes of distillation and cupellation were involved in the refiner's work and materials relating to each have been recovered from the site. Cupellation was used in the process of assaying or testing the purity of metals. The sample to be refined was melted with lead, which oxidized forming lead oxide. The lead

Figure 136. Bottom collar section of a glass alembic found in the pre-1610 cellar of Structure 165 (top), and a London earthenware distillation flask from the same context (bottom).

159

oxide also oxidized any base metals present in the sample, leaving a residue of silver or gold.

A shallow vessel known as a cupel, which was used in small-scale cupellation, was excavated from the fort site. It is made of bone ash, which was preferred by refiners because this material would absorb the lead oxide leaving a purer residue.[20] The James Fort cupel has some residues indicating that it had been used.

Vessels associated with distillation have also been uncovered. Distillation was used in the production of nitric acid, which was required for the parting or separation of gold from silver. Metallurgists produced nitric acid, using a method known since the 14th century, by distilling sulfuric acid with sodium or potassium nitrate.

A distilling unit consists of two main parts: the lower vessel or cucurbit, and the upper vessel with a spout and domed head known as an alembic. The liquid was boiled in the cucurbit, the resulting vapor condensed within the head of the alembic, and the condensate was channeled out through the spout into a receiver. The receiver did not have to be a specialized vessel. Domestic bottles and flasks were also used to catch the distilled liquid.[21]

A bottle-shaped cucurbit, or distillation flask, with a long tubular neck was recovered from the cellar of Structure 165. It is unglazed and is made of the London red earthenware fabric. Several of these vessels have been recovered from London metalworking contexts dating c.1580-1650.[22] These London vessels exhibit residues of hematite, which is a by-product of the distillation of ferrous sulfate to produce sulfuric acid.[23] The Jamestown flask has no such residue and therefore was either never used or was used in another distillation process, such as the production of alcohol or perfumes.

Both a glass alembic section, incorporating the complete bottom rim with part of the collection channel, and a fragment of its spout have been found in the same fort context as the flask. Alembics were also made of earthenware fabrics[24] but it would not be unusual to mix the two materials in the distilling unit. A glass alembic is depicted in use over a distilling flask made of earthenware in Cornelis Bega's painting *The Alchemist.*

Figure 137. Distilling equipment recovered from the excavations include a distilling dish (front left), an earthenware dipper (center), and Hessian crucibles.

Other recovered objects that possibly relate to the distilling efforts of the refiners are distilling dishes, an earthenware dipper, and refractory clay crucibles. The dishes and the dipper are also made of the London redware clay and have been found in association with metalworking in England.[25] The crucibles are of the triangular Hessian type, which were preferred by metalworkers for the fine pouring stream it provided. One crucible contains interior deposits of copper, which could be the result of heating hydrated sulfates of copper to produce sulfuric acid.[26] As previously mentioned, this acid is required to make the nitric acid needed for refining.

Figure 138. A collection of semiprecious stones found within the pre-1610 fill of Structure 165.

Jeweler

A jeweler by the name of Daniel Stallings arrived with the first supply in January 1608. Jewelers in England were variously retailers and appraisers of gemstones and rarely were the craftsmen who actually set the stones.[27] Stallings was probably sent by the Virginia Company to survey the landscape for its potential as a source of gems. At the time, foreign merchants had control of the importation of precious and semi-precious stones into England. Most of the favored stones came from far-away places. Garnets, for instance, came from Bohemia and Sri Lanka.[28]

Stallings may be responsible for the collection of garnets, amethysts, and quartz crystals that have been recovered from the pre-1610 fill of Structure 165. These lithics are not rare in the Jamestown area. He could have found these materials washing out of the cliffs on the James River beaches or during expeditions up Virginia's waterways.

Bricklayers

Three bricklayers arrived with the first colonists in 1607, but only two – John Herd and William Garrett – are identified as such by Smith.[29] There is no further mention of Herd in the records, but the name William Garrett appears in colonial court documents twenty years later. In 1627, a William Garrett, identified as a servant of Abraham Peirsey, is being accused of lewd behavior with a fellow (female) servant.[30] If this is the same William Garrett, he has not only survived in the colony for twenty years, but he has also not risen above his status as servant in all that time.

The third bricklayer is identified when Edward Maria Wingfield, the first president of the Virginia council, refers to *"ould short, the Bricklayer."*[31] This is probably the same individual, of apparently advanced age, that Smith records in the 1607 manifest as *"Old Edward, laborer."*[32] There is no more mention of "old" Edward Short, but he may be the *"poore old man"* that Wingfield claims to have fed *"halfe a pinte of pease ... sodden, with a peese of porke"* before the individual died of an illness.[33]

Even though the Virginia clay is very suitable for making bricks, the presence of bricklayers rather than brickmakers seems to imply that the first colonists were not intending to make brick, but had brought the bricks they would need from England. Indeed, some of the excavated brick appears high-fired and atypical of the local products, which are soft and, at times, very friable. Future clay analysis of the bricks recovered from Jamestown will help to determine how much of the brick is locally produced.

The archaeological evidence indicates that the brickwork in the first few years of the colony was confined to hearths of buildings. The first documented use of brick for building foundations occurs in 1611, but it is not at Jamestown. Brickmakers arriving from England with Sir Thomas Gates were quickly dispatched to Dale's settlement of Henrico near Richmond. There, *"the Brick men burnt their bricks"* to build *"competent and decent houses (the first storey all of bricks)."*[34]

By the 1620s, the use of brick on Jamestown Island appears to have extended to wells (see Chapter IV),[35] and to chimneys by the 1640s (See Chapter II). The first brick building on Jamestown Island is believed to be that of Secretary Kemp, built in 1638 and described as *"the fairest that ever was knowen in this countrye for substance and uniformitye."*[36]

Mason

A mason by the name of Edward Brinton (Brinto/Brynton) arrived at Jamestown with the initial group of colonists in May 1607. He is probably the *"stone-cutter"* to whom Smith refers because masons were specialized craftsmen qualified to cut and carve stone for major building projects, as well as to do the initial quarrying. No tools relating to masonry have thus far been excavated from James Fort, but there is other information in the historical records about Brinton's activities at Jamestown.

Despite John Smith's disparaging remarks about the usefulness of Brinton's craft, Smith must have respected Brinton because he was selected to be a *"soldier"* on Smith's December 1608 food-gathering expedition to Powhatan's home at Werowocomoco. Brinton also must have been skilled in the use of firearms since he was left *"to kill...foule"* for Powhatan while the rest of the expedition continued their mission.[37] Smith would not have chosen an inexperienced marksman to hunt for the powerful leader of the Algonquian Indian chiefdom. Firearms, with their fiery retorts and occasionally deadly consequences, gave the colonists an advantage in their dealings with the Virginia Indians who respected the power of these weapons. It would not be wise, as the Council for Virginia advised, to allow *"your learners miss what they aim at"* in front of the Indians, for *"they will think the weapon not so terrible, and thereby will be bold to assault you."*[38]

Most Englishmen at this time were not well trained in the use of firearms. Guns were expensive and hunting preserves were in the domain of the wealthy so that the common man in England would have had nowhere to practice, even if he owned a weapon. Expertise in hunting on the part of a tradesman such as Brinton indicates a certain level of wealth and is reflective, in Brinton's case, of the high status of masons in English society.

Since masons at the time were also stone merchants,[39] Brinton's inclusion with the first group of colonists is totally understandable from a monetary perspective. He was not in the colony to construct masonry buildings. More likely, he was expected to survey the landscape for known and unknown lithic materials that could be successfully marketed in London.

Figure 140. Masons were buyers and sellers of stone as well as the craftsmen who shaped the stone and built the walls of masonry buildings. They were typically the most highly paid workers on a construction site.

Tobacco Pipemaker

The inclusion of a tobacco pipemaker in the first groups of craftsmen is as enigmatic to researchers today as it apparently was to John Smith when Robert Cotton, *"tobacco-pipe-maker,"* arrived on the *Phoenix* in January 1608.[40] No other mention is made of Cotton, so it is not known how long he remained at Jamestown; he is not listed in the muster of 1624-25, so presumably Cotton had either perished or returned to England by then. With archival information lacking, the material evidence of very accomplished mold-made clay tobacco pipes, fabricated from the Virginia red clay and decorated on the stem with European stamps, provides the sole documentation for this early craftsman's work. These distinctive pipes only occur in the early James Fort features that date around 1610 and have not

Figure 141. Tobacco pipe with distinctive markings (shown in detail), thought to be the product of Robert Cotton, "tobacco-pipe-maker," who arrived at Jamestown in January 1608.

Figure 142. Fragments of a clay saggar probably made by Cotton to fire his clay pipes.

yet been recorded on any other early Virginia sites.

The design of the stamp on the pipe stems consists of four fleur-de-lis forming a cross within a diamond. The sides of the diamond are incurving as on the 1580-1610 pipes documented in England and thought to be the product of London pipemaker, William Batchelor.[41] Robert Cotton must also have been a London pipemaker because pipemaking was almost entirely restricted to that city by monopoly, until the second decade of the 17th century.[42] Other aspects of Cotton's stamp reflect decorative motifs of late 16th-and early 17th-century London pipes, which most often include incuse *"diamond patterns enclosing initials, crosses or fleur-de-lis on the stems."*[43]

Along with the many fragments of *Robert Cotton* pipes, there have been pieces of what appear to be pipemaking saggars. A saggar is a portable clay container in which the pipes would have been fired to keep them out of direct contact with the flames. This piece of kiln furniture would be particularly necessary if the pipemaker were sharing his furnace with another craftsman. The early craftsmen working within the confines of James Fort probably had to share one source of heat for the production of their wares.

By the late 16th century, tobacco smoking was a very popular pastime in England among the upper classes. It had been introduced into the country by English explorers returning from the Americas, such as Sir John Hawkins and Sir Francis Drake, and was first adapted as a medical treatment. As early as 1573, the English are curing ailments by *"the taking-in of the smoke of the Indian herbe called 'Tobaco' by an instrument formed like a little ladell."*[44] It is not known of what material the *"ladell"* was made, but, by 1598, tobacco was being smoked in clay pipes. A German traveler noted in that year, *"the English are constantly smoking Tobacco … they have pipes on purpose made of clay, into the farther end of which they put the herb."*[45]

Figure 143. A young soldier uses a candle to light a white ball clay pipe. These small-bowled pipes were made in both England and the Netherlands in the early-17th century.

The white ball clay from Poole, Dorset, on the southern coast of England, was the preferred clay for 17th-century tobacco pipes, and remained so through the 19th century. It fired up white and hard

Figure 144. By the late-16th century, smoking had become tremendously popular in English society. English soldiers who were in the Low Countries to fight the Spanish introduced the Dutch to tobacco's pleasures. In this painting by Adrian Brouwer, the artist depicted himself as a mercenary soldier sharing tobacco and a mug of beer with acquaintances in a Dutch tavern.

and is called white ball clay after the practice of forming the mined clay into large balls that could be easily rolled onto wagons for shipment.[46] Lots of English pipe clay was also exported to the Netherlands for the Dutch pipemaking industry, reportedly established after 1608 by political refugees from England.[47] Some of these early pipemakers may indeed have been English veterans of the Dutch war of independence from Spain, as were many of the first Virginia colonists.

Figure 145. A brick which has been modified for use as a tobacco pipe, probably using a reed for the stem.

Pipemaking was a lower class trade requiring minimal investment in tools, materials, and training. Pipes were inexpensive but, luckily for the pipemaker, also easily breakable so that pipes were produced and sold in great quantities.

Why was Robert Cotton at Jamestown? The presence of this craftsman at early Jamestown and the fact that he practiced his craft could indicate how important smoking was to the early colonists, particularly to the gentlemen. They knew they were coming to a place where tobacco was readily available and they wanted to be assured of a means by which to smoke it. One colonist in the fort at this time was apparently so desperate for a pipe that he fashioned one out of brick!

More likely Cotton was sent by the Virginia Company to assay the clays for their potential in pipe making and pottery production. If the clays proved adequate, this could break the monopoly held by the Dorset clay merchants in the London pipemaking industry, and allow the London investors in the Virginia Company to participate in the lucrative pipe clay export to the Netherlands.

Perfumer

One perfumer, identified as Robert Alberton, was on the First Supply that reached Jamestown in January 1608. Perfume was relied upon heavily in 16th and 17th-century Europe to help dispel the unsavory odors of unwashed bodies and refuse-laden streets. Scent was worn by both sexes, whether it was an herb or spice, such as the sweet marjoram favored by Queen Elizabeth, or waters distilled from aromatic plants.[2] Perfumers produced a variety of scented preparations, in liquid, dry, or salve form, from the plants, or 'simples,' that grew wild or that were cultivated in herbal gardens. Like apothecaries, perfumers must have had the skills and equipment for filtering, distilling, powdering and blending various substances. The 1590 inventory of a perfumer in Ipswich, England, for instance, includes waters, oils, and ointments made of roses and chamomile as well as the funnels, scales, and mortars needed to prepare them.[48 2]

The word *perfume* comes from the French *par fumer* or "by smoke" which hints at the original use of perfume as a burning substance, like incense, that would scent the air.[49] Aromatic substances would be dropped over smoldering coals contained in a specialized vessel known as a fuming pot. One section of an earthenware fuming pot has been un-

Figure 146. A complete Border ware fuming pot from the Museum of London collections.

166

covered during the excavations. Also known as a stink pot or perfume jar, this form is a cylindrical container on a pedestal with a narrow neck and pierced sides. The holes allow for the escape of the smoke or perfume of the substance, which has been placed on burning charcoal in the pot. A triangular opening in the pedestal base aids in the airflow to the burning coals. The fuming pot from James Fort is Red Border ware, produced in the potteries along the border of Hampshire and Surrey counties in England. While fuming

Figure 147. A section of a Red Border ware fuming pot from the James Fort excavations.

pots are encountered in redware and silver, they are rare in Border ware.[50]

Stale air was thought to be unhealthy and perfumers were employed to correct offensive environments. Shakespeare's character Borachio in *Much Ado About Nothing* refers to this role of perfumers when he says that he was "*entertained* [taken] *for a perfumer, as I was smoking a musty room.*"[51] Because of the association of perfume with health, there was an overlap in the roles played by the apothecary and the perfumer. The royal apothecary, for example, was personally responsible for perfuming and fumigating the monarch's clothes and bedding.[52]

Fumigating the sick with herbs had been practiced since ancient times in England and was especially popular during the

Figure 148. The smoking chafing dish seen in the lower left corner of this painting is being used as a fuming pot to burn curative essences in the sick room.

167

Figure 149. Gloves were popular dress accessories for both men and women in the 17th century and were often heavily scented with perfume.

medieval and early post-medieval periods. A proscribed *"fume"* in 1592 against the London plague consisted of *"dried rosemary, juniper, bayleaves or frankincense burnt in a chafingdish and carried about from room to room."*[53] Chafing dishes are footed bowls containing hot embers that were normally used to heat or warm a plate of food. In the absence of a fuming pot, a chafing dish would work quite nicely to contain smoldering essences.

The illness need not only be of the body to warrant fumigation. The *Grete Herball* published in 1526, which was a guide to the medicinal properties of simples, advises using the herb mugwort to treat an anxious child by making a *"smoke therof under the chyldes's bedd."* Further, if a patient should suffer from *"weyknesse of the brayne,"* he should *"receye the smoke"* of rosemary *"at his nose."*[54]

By the time of Elizabeth, the practice of perfuming fabrics and dress accessories, particularly gloves and bags, had become popular. Both men

Figure 150. As depicted in this 17th-century Dutch painting, tailors customarily sat cross-legged upon a table while plying their craft.

168

and women wore leather gloves for almost every social occasion from dancing to fighting. Symbolic of trust and honor, gloves were often given as scented betrothal and wedding gifts.[55] This practice is reflected in Shakespeare's play *Much Ado about Nothing* when a courted female character states *"those gloves the Count sent me, they are an excellent perfume."*[56]

A seventeenth-century recipe for perfuming gloves consists of making a paste of gum-dragon, musk, civet, oil of cloves, cinnamon, and jasmine to be rubbed into the leather.[57] It is interesting to note that the pair of *"white lambe gloves"* provided to each of the women sent to Virginia in 1621 to become wives for the settlers was purchased from a perfumer.[58] This indicates that the perfumers were in the business of selling accessories that they had treated with their special potions.

Why did the Virginia Company send Alberton to Jamestown? Even with the medicinal applications of *"fumes,"* it is doubtful that Alberton was considered part of the medical team sent for the welfare of the colonists. It is much more likely that a perfumer was sent by the Virginia Company to search the woods for new simples that could be made into effective perfumes marketable in London.

Tailors

Seven tailors are identified as arriving at Jamestown in the first year of settlement.[59] Three are never mentioned in the records again. Three are further named when John Smith drafts them as soldiers for expeditions in the summer and winter of 1608.[60] One of these individuals, William Ward, even had a landform named after him during one of the exploratory expeditions in which he participated.[61] One tailor, Thomas Hope, accompanies Smith and Newport to Powhatan's home at Werowocomoco in February 1608. On this listing he is identified as a gentleman, and he is further identified as one of the authors of the Third Book of John Smith's *The Proceedings of the English Colonie in Virginia*, [1606-1612].[62]

Tailors were trained in *"the cutting up of a length of cloth and the shaping of it by cut and stitch to fit the contours of the human frame."*[63] Their trade in England was primarily with individuals of the privileged classes and rarely with the average person who, except for perhaps one special garment, would wear homemade clothing. Textiles were expensive and clothing so valuable that it was often mentioned in wills and appraised in inventories.

Tailors could also apply their craft to the repair and modification of old garments, but it is unlikely that they were included on the voyage for the benefit of the average colonist. Tailors were much more likely to have been in the employ of some of the gentlemen in the colony who were

Figure 151. Until the late-17th century, tailors were usually men who made clothing for both men and women. Women, known as seamstresses, were confined to sewing the accessories.

169

concerned that their social standing be correctly reflected in their wardrobes and in the servants they had to attend them. *"A person of importance proclaimed his status by his choice of dress and jewels and by the number of liveried servants who accompanied him in public – the assumption being that the greater the number of retainers, the more important the man."*[64]

Along with food, clothing was the most frequently requested commodity in the early years, starting in 1608 with Francis Perkins' pitiful plea for used clothing after a fire in the fort destroyed much of what the colonists had.[65] By the winter of 1613, the individuals at Jamestown state that it is no longer necessary to send food – now they need only clothing. In the same year, the Spanish spy Don Diego de Molina corroborates the *"wretched clothing"* that was worn by the individuals at Jamestown.[66]

Some tools traditionally used by tailors have been excavated from early contexts within James Fort and may relate to the presence of the first seven tailors. These include thimbles, needles, straight pins, pressing irons, and bodkins.

Fourteen thimbles have been recovered from the excavations within James Fort. They represent the two types depicted by the 17th-century chronicler of material culture, Randle Holme[67] – the ring or open-ended thimble and those with closed ends. The word *thimble* is derived from the medieval English word *thymel* or *thuma* meaning thumb or thick finger.[68] This reflects its purpose as a protection for the finger in pushing a needle through fabric or leather.

Eleven of the James Fort thimbles are made of brass and six of them were recovered from the same pre-1610 context in the cellar fill of Structure 165. These all appear to be of Nuremberg manufacture. By the middle of the 16th century, the city of Nuremberg in Germany prevailed in the production of small brass objects, particularly thimbles. This dominance is primarily attributable to the discovery of a high-quality brass, produced by alloying copper and zinc, *"which created a smooth bright brass of an even texture."*[69] Also, the Nuremberg craftsmen developed a technique by the end of the 16th century of making two-part thimbles. This simplified the process of decorating the thimbles, as it could be done while they were in flat sheets. The sides were then rolled into cylinders and soldered together, the cap similarly attached on the top edge. The prior technique had involved heating the brass and punching it into molds. Any decoration then had to be applied by hand to the molded thimble.

Figure 153. Brass Nuremberg thimble found in the bulwark trench of James Fort. There is a maker's mark in the symbol of a bell just above the decorative band of foliage.

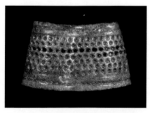

Figure 154. Brass ring thimble from Pit 3, ca. 1610, which has an undecipherable maker's mark.

Nuremberg thimbles typically are tall and narrow with a flat or only slightly rounded top. They are punched by hand around the sides in a spiral that continues over the top. Often, these thimbles bear decorative stamping around the border and/or maker's marks in the way of initials or symbols. So far, these marks have not been linked to individual makers.

Figure 155. Group of brass doublet buttons and an iron ring thimble that were found joined together in Pit 1.

Three of the ring thimbles found at James Fort are iron and one is of brass. This type of thimble is usually associated with working heavy, thick fabrics such as sailcloth, although one of the excavated iron ring thimbles was concreted to nine copper alloy doublet buttons. A doublet is a closely fitting man's jacket, which is fastened down the front, from neck to waist, by many closely spaced buttons. The buttons found with the thimble still contained remnants of the thread that had once strung them together, suggesting that these objects had been stored together, possibly in a pouch, as a small repair kit. Perhaps the kit had also once contained a needle, which, being thin iron may have rusted away.

Fifty-five iron needles ranging in size from 40 mm to 59 mm have been excavated from the site thus far. Half of them were recovered from the cellar-like pit found just north of Structure 165. They all exhibit a round-sectioned shank tapering to a point, but the eye on each of the examples is either broken out or lost. These needles would have been used for regular sewing of clothing. Larger needles would be used for repairing fishing nets.

Because of the metal's durability in the ground, brass straight pins are much more common on archaeological sites than needles. Over 500 pins and almost 200 pin fragments, without heads, have been recovered from James Fort. These range in length from 30 mm to 51 mm. Pins were used extensively in the 17th century, not only in the process of constructing garments, but also to hold some clothing, particularly accessories, together. They are also commonly found in Virginia's colonial-period burials where they were used to fasten the cloth shroud wrapping the body.

The technology for pin manufacture remained much the same from the mid-16th century to the 19th century. Drawn brass wire was used for the shaft, which was cut into short lengths and filed to a sharp point. A length of wire wound on the shaft in two complete turns made the globular head. In the late-18th century, heading wire was

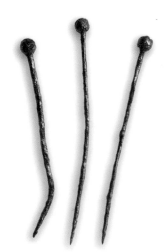

Figure 156. Three of the over 500 17th-century brass straight pins from James Fort.

171

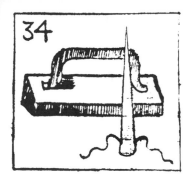

Figure 157. A tailor's pressing iron and a needle depicted by Randle Holme.

thinner than the shank and was usually wound five times to form a conical head. In the beginning of the 19th century, the modern form of pin was introduced whereby a solid head is fabricated using part of the shank.[70]

England imported most of its straight pins from the Netherlands in the medieval and early post-medieval periods.[71] Pins could be produced more cheaply there for two basic reasons: proximity to brass production areas along the river Meuse, and lower labor costs as the industry was not controlled by guilds as it was in England.[72]

Two types of irons have been found during the Jametown excavations. One consists of a flat heavy piece of iron with a handle that Randle Holme depicts as a "*Taylors pressing iron.*" This type would be heated over the fire before use and presumably picked up, using a cloth or some other protection wrapped around the handle. Another ironing device, known as a goffering iron, was used in England in the 17th and 18th centuries. To goffer means to crimp or frill, and these tools were necessary to maintain the large cartwheel neck ruff that was popular men's fashion from c.1580-1610. The goffered bands of linen were sometimes so large that they had to be supported by an inner wire frame known as a supportasse. The goffering iron, or *poking stick*, consisted of a tube that was heated by inserting a red-hot iron of a slightly smaller diameter. The material to be ironed would first have to be stiffened with white starch and then pressed over the heated tube to make a semi-circular fold.

The presence of a goffering iron within the confines of James Fort is yet another suggestion that the gentlemen continued to dress the same way they had at home. As mentioned earlier, it was very important in English society at the time to maintain distinctions of class, rank, and profession by the clothes one wore and the objects one possessed. These social customs, of conspicuous display of class rank, were continued in the isolated, military colony, far removed from the society that they would most impress.

The starch[73] that was so important to maintaining the fashionable ruffs, is known from the historic records to have been used at Jamestown although not always in the way that it was originally intended. George Percy, the "*highest*

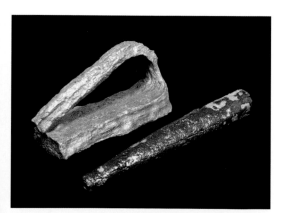

Figure 158. A goffering iron and pressing iron from the excavations.

172

born gentleman of the settlement" requested that his brother in London send him £4/6/0 worth of "*Starche*" in July 1608.[74] This is presumably for the treatment of the "*apparrell of diuerse sewts*" worth over £32 that was also a part of Percy's order. Perhaps this same starch helped Percy to survive the Starving Time winter of 1609-1610, for John Smith writes that food supplies were so low "*those that had starch for their ruffs made a gluey porridge of it.*"[75]

Holme depicts another tailoring tool known as a bodkin. He describes this object as "*a blade or round Pin of Iron fixed in a Halve, it is not very sharp at the end: by its help, is Eye lid (eyelet) holes and all other holes, (which are not very large) made.*"[76]

The tailor's bodkin is an awl-like tool used to make the holes in clothing through which the laces used to bind or secure a garment are threaded.

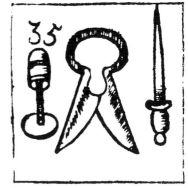

Figure 159. 17th-century portrait depicting the fashionable large ruffs which required frequent treatment with a goffering iron to maintain their shape.

One handle of a tailor's bodkin has been found within James Fort. It consists of half of a cast brass handle that would secure the tang of the bodkin. The handle is deeply molded with three figures: starting from the top is a demi-figure of a woman with her arms folded on her lap, a lion's head holding a ring through its mouth, and a crowned female figure in Elizabethan clothes.[77]

The "*eye lid*" or eyelet holes mentioned by Holme are also known as aglet holes. Aglets (also known as tags or points) are the metal tips folded on the ends of the laces. A modern corollary for this object is the plastic tip that is fitted on the ends of shoelaces and that serves to keep the lace ends from fraying. Laces were used to secure many parts of 17th-century clothing. The hose that men wore, for instance, were held up by an average of nine pair of laces, requiring two aglets each, which were threaded through holes at the waist of the doublet.[78]

Aglets, were, for the most part, functional and were constructed of unadorned copper alloy, as are most of the 1,600 aglets excavated from James Fort. But, they were also used for decorative effect and dangled from

Figure 160. A bodkin (right) is illustrated by Randle Holme with shears and another tailor's tool, known as a scorer, whereby the fabric is marked before cutting.

173

all parts of gentlemen's clothing. Some of the aglets excavated from James Fort are of the decorative type and are stamped with a waffle, stars in a scale pattern, or a dot and diaper motif. Two of these decorative aglets are constructed of silver.

Another class of artifact that has been found during the James Fort excavations also relates to tailors in its association with fabric. Small leaden devices known as cloth seals were part of the European textile industry's system of industrial regulation and quality control between the 14th and 19th centuries. Manufacturers and finishers of cloth as well as merchants and tax officials once crimped these diminutive objects onto textiles as they moved through the various processes from loom to consumer.[79]

The most common type of cloth seal is two-part, consisting of a disc with a tapered rivet (disc 1) connected by a thin strip to a similarly sized disc with a central hole (disc 2). The seal is folded at the connecting strip

Figure 161. Ornately cast bodkin handle from Pit 1.

Figure 162. Plain copper alloy aglets.

Figure 163. Aglets can be seen at this gentleman's waist. They are securing his trousers through holes in his jacket.

over the edge of fabric "*so that the rivet on one disc could be pushed through the fabric and the corresponding hole in the other disc.*"[80] The discs were sealed firmly over the cloth by being stamped with one, or between two, dies that impressed the discs with various numerals, letters, and/or decorative motifs.

Seventy-six cloth seals have been excavated from James Fort. The various impressions upon the seals can provide a great deal of information beyond that of simply identifying the types of material shipped to the colony. Status can be indicated as well as suggestions of trading patterns and practices. One of the seals (1216-JR), for instance, is an Elizabethan alnage seal impressed with the Tudor coat of arms. The alnager is the crown's official representative who insures that the proper taxes have been paid on the textile. This particular impression would not have been used beyond 1602, the year of Elizabeth's death, being at that time replaced by the symbols of James I. Since the Jamestown colony did not start until 1607, this means that the textile must have been produced at least five years before it reached Virginia. This is a surprisingly long time for the fabric to be languishing about unused, considering the high value of textiles in the 17th century. A lot of capital was tied up in the production and distribution of cloth; and all indications suggest that textiles were sold and subsequently used soon after production.[81]

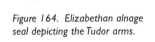

Figure 164. Elizabethan alnage seal depicting the Tudor arms.

Another Elizabethan seal (1112-JR) appears to be from the county of Kent, which was a major producer of kersey and broadcloth during the late-16th and early- 17th centuries. Broadcloth is a fine traditional woolen textile used primarily for men's clothing in England from the 12th century. The previously mentioned Jamestown gentleman, George Percy, ordered "*6 yardes of Broade Clothe for a Cloke a Jerkin and a paire of breeches.*"[82]

Eight alnage seals dating to the period of Elizabeth's reign have been excavated during the *Jamestown Rediscovery* project. One seal (520-JR) even bears a date in the 1590s (although the last digit is obscured). The frequency of these early seals (11%) indicates a pattern of textile supply to the colony consisting of old stores of material. These supplies had perhaps been assembled for previous voyages of the merchant adventurers that abounded during Elizabeth's reign and continued under James I. Possibly the goods not used during the journey were off-loaded at London on the return voyage to be stored for another venture.

Court minutes from the East India Company dated September 1607 appear to substantiate this practice. It records "*beads and cloth very much*

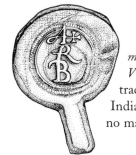

moth eaten, sold to the Governor Sir Thomas Smythe for £3.5s. for the Virginia Voyage."[83] The beads were clearly intended for the Indian trade, but was the cloth as well? Perhaps the English considered the Indians to be undiscriminating consumers who would accept fabric no matter what its condition. Or, was Smythe trying to save his undercapitalized Virginia Company some money by purchasing hole-ridden textiles for the colonists? Smythe, a

Figure 165. One of two privy seals that have been found in James Fort with the initials RB.

highly successful London merchant had controlling interests in both the East India Company, of which he was governor, and the Virginia Company, of which he was the treasurer and the first chief executive. He would be aiding both organizations by buying up the unused supplies from one group that would be needed by the other. The East India Company surplus may also be the source of the inadequate tents of which John Smith complains.[84] The Virginia Company pattern of supplying its colony with second-rate goods seems to endure throughout its tenure. As late as 1623, colonists are grumbling that they are being "victualed wth mustie bred the reliques of former Vioages."[85]

Other cloth seals found are known as privy seals. They were used by weavers, merchants, and dyers and usually include initials in conjunction with the stylized privy or *huismerk*. This mark consists of the number 4, sometimes depicted backwards, on the top of a vertical line that terminates in two side-by-side x's. Initials are usually ligatured or astride the mark.

The privy mark was a sort of commercial heraldry used quite commonly from the early 16th century.[86] They are believed to have begun as marks of property in northern and central Europe when most individuals were illiterate. Dutch and English merchants adapted privy marks as trademarks—an easily recognizable guarantee of quality.[87] Very few of these marks have been identified with English merchants, so the dating of these seals must be primarily by the style of the mark and letters.[88]

One dyers' guild seal (656-JR) contains the word *SEARCHED,* which indicates that the cloth had been inspected. Less visible are the large letters W—A D that probably stand for WOADED which is a blue colored dye.[89] An inspector of the guild certifying that the dye was up to standard would have applied this seal.

Figure 166. Dyers' seal from London stamped with SEARCHED indicating that the cloth had been officially inspected.

A number of the cloth seals from James Fort are associated with Continental fabrics that had been imported into England, probably through London, before being shipped to Virginia. Imported textiles are generally types that were not produced in England, but occasionally they are fabrics that could be obtained more cheaply abroad. From the lead seals that have been recorded in England, only one in forty is foreign, which indicates that Continental imports were not very prevalent there.[90] The percentage of non-English seals is much higher at Jamestown, with sixteen (21%) from fabrics imported from the Continent.

Figure 167. Cloth seal from Haarlem in the Netherlands.

One of these seals is from the Netherlands and bears the arms of Haarlem, as well as the legend "HAERLEM GOET," or "goods from Haarlem. The other side has the number "1" representing the length of the fabric, or one Dutch ell (27 inches). Haarlem was a finishing center where fine linen cloth, woven in many different areas, was bleached. The Dutch city was well known in England for its fine linen, where the Haarlem fabrics became known as 'holland." [91] Linen was used for accessories such as aprons and handkerchiefs, and it was the preferred material for undergarments by both the rich and the poor. "*The idea was that everything that touched your skin was made of linen, which could be washed.*"[92]

Fourteen of the cloth seals bear the letter "*A*" and the pinecone heraldic badge of the southern German city of Augsburg. This type, known in over a dozen English counties, is the most common of the Continental cloth seals recovered in England, comprising one-third of the identified assemblage.[93] Augsburg seals have also been recovered at Martin's Hundred, the neighboring settlement to Jamestown. There, eight seals were excavated from c.1620–1622 contexts and represent the most closely dated Augsburg seals prior to the Jamestown finds.[94] In Britain they are generally dated between the late-16th and mid-17th century by which time "*the import of German fabrics was seriously curtailed.*"[95]

Augsburg was known for its production of fustian, which is a mixed linen-warp/cotton-weft fabric. Fustian could be made with a silky finish and was often used as a substitute for velvet.[96] In 1610, Virginia colonist George Percy ordered from England "*3 yardes 1 quarter of fustian for a dublett and Joanes fustian to lyn…4 suites & a dublett and a paire of clothe breeches.*"[97] Percy was a gentleman who at the time of this request had been newly elected president of the colony. His doublets and breeches would necessarily be made of a fabric reflective of his rank in society. There is a reference in Shakespeare's *Taming of the Shrew*, written sometime between 1594 and 1606, to the "*serving men in their new fustian.*"[98] In this case, the servants are clothed in this textile as an indication of the household's status.

Figure 168. Cloth seal exhibiting the pinecone and letter A, representing Augsburg, Germany.

Figure 169. Cloth seal from Gdansk.

Another Continental cloth seal from the site comes from the Baltic city of Gdansk, which was part of Germany in the 17th century but is now within Poland. Disc one of the two-part seal consists of the number "56" over an "E" on a garnished shield. This most likely represents the length of the cloth in ells.[99] Disc two bears the arms of Gdansk consisting of a crown over two crosses potent on a shield. This cloth seal was probably attached to sailcloth. "*In the late-16th century and the early-17th century some 5 percent by value of England's imports from the Baltic were canvasses for sailmaking, mainly brought from Gdansk to London.*"[100] The Jamestown colonists would have need of sailcloth to repair the sails on their shallops and other boats rigged for sailing. They also evidently had need of sailcloth for shelter as illustrated by John Smith's description of the first church at Jamestown.

"*When I went first to Virginia, I well remember, wee did hang an awning (which is an old saile) to three or foure trees to shadow us from the Sunne . . . this was our Church.*"[101]

Fishmonger and Fisher

A fishmonger, Richard Keale, and a fisher, Jonas Profit, were included in both of John Smith's exploratory trips up the Chesapeake Bay that took place in June and July of 1608. Even though Smith subsequently refers to them as soldiers, the skills of these individuals would be useful to have along on such adventures, if only for the sustenance of the group. The fishmonger, who is a fish merchant, would presumably be familiar with many different varieties of edible fish, and the fisherman would be skilled in catching them. Profit, who was also identified as a sailor when he arrived at Jamestown in 1607, must have been especially appreciated on the first expedition. A severe storm flooded the men's small boat and blew away the "*mast and sayle.*"[102] Perhaps it was Profit's idea of repairing the foresail "*with our shirts*" that enabled the men to continue.[103] Profit was obviously a very capable sailor, for by Smith's next expedition in December, he was listed as Master of the pinnace.[104]

Figure 170. The colonists found the Virginia waterways full of fish, and those who "would take paines" caught plenty to sustain them.

Despite the presence of these two men with knowledge of fish and fishing, the Smith party carried no fishing nets. So, when they encountered a wealth of fish during the course of the trip, the men had to resort to some fairly unconventional fishing methods. They first attempted to

Figure 171. Sturgeon is an anadromous fish, spending most of its life in salt water but migrating into freshwater rivers to spawn. The colonists remark that sturgeon were plentiful in the James River from May to October.

catch "*the abundance of fish lying so thick with their heads above water*" with a frying pan, but "*found it a bad instrument to catch fish with.*" Then they tried spearing fish with their swords, which worked quite well, and they "*tooke more in an houre then (they) all would eat,*" until Smith accidentally impaled a stingray and received a nasty wound.

The Fishmongers Company was one of the more prestigious livery companies in London. Many of its members were subscribers to the English companies of exploration and their contributions to the Virginia Company totaled over £1,000.[105] Only one of these gentlemen is known to have actually ventured to Virginia. He is William Faldoe, the Helvetian, who was involved in the search for silver mines.[106] Even though Smith identifies Richard Keale as a fishmonger, he is probably only an apprentice and not a member of the company, as he is not listed with the rest of the gentlemen.[107] It is interesting to note that until the mid-17th century, "*40% of the apprentices recruited by the Carpenters' and Fishmongers' companies were from the Highlands of Scotland.*"[108] That Keale may indeed be from the Scottish highlands is further suggested by the fact that Smith named "*the highest land*" on the Eastern Shore "*Keales hill*" after him. Perhaps because the landmark was nowhere near as high as the landscape Keale would be familiar with, Smith apologetically added, "*yet it was but low.*"[109] Future archival research may be able to identify the origins of Richard Keale.

When the colonists arrived in 1607, they found the Virginia waters teeming with fish. Early descriptions claimed that the James River was full of "*sturgeon, very large and excellent good; having also at the mouth of every brook and in every creek both store and exceeding good fish of divers kinds.*"[110] Besides sturgeon, Smith describes the most commonly encountered fish as "*Grampus, Porpus, Seales, Sting-graies . . . Bretts, Mullets, White Salmonds, Trowts, Soles, Plaice, Herrings, Conyfish, Rockfish, Eeles, Lampreys, Catfish, Shades, Pearch of three sorts, Crabs, Shrimps, Crevises, Oysters, Cocles, and Muscles.*"[111] Despite the abundance of this accessible food source, it has been assumed that the colonists did not

Figure 172. Large fish like sturgeon were caught with nets rather than hooks.

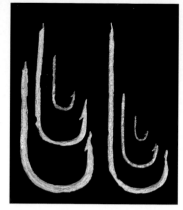

Figure 173. Over 160 fishhooks of varying sizes have been excavated at James Fort.

arrive in Virginia equipped to fish, since there is little mention of fishing gear in the early accounts.[112] Strachey's complaint in 1610 that "*nor was there at the Fort any meanes to take fish, neither sufficient Seine, nor other convenient Net*"[113] has been extended to encompass the entire early fort period. The archaeological evidence, however, paints another picture. A large quantity of bone representing 17 different species of fish has been found in trash pits associated with James Fort,[114] demonstrating the colonists' heavy reliance on fish for sustenance. In addition, over 160 fishhooks have been recovered from the site, and most are coming from two cellars that represent the earliest contexts in the fort. The fishhooks range in size between 2 cm and 13 cm in length and would be used to catch the variety of fish mentioned by Smith. In fact Smith claimed that "*in the small rivers all the yeare there is good plenty of small fish, so that with hookes those that would take paines had sufficient.*"[115]

Besides hooks, a fisherman would require a rod, some lines, and lead weights to plumb the line. Lines were made of twisted or braided horsehair, "*the longest and strongest yee can get,*" with the number of hairs depending on whether you were angling for minnows (1 hair) or pike (12 hairs).[116] The fishing weights would also vary in size depending on the type of fish you were going after. The first English book on fishing, *Treatise of Fishing with an Angle*, written by Dame Juliana Berners in 1496 cautions to "*make your plumbes round and smothe, yt they stick not on stones or weedes.*"[117] Leonard Mascall repeats this description of weights in 1590 with his book, *The Booke of Fishing With Hooke & Line*. By the mid-17th century, books on fishing suggest using a large pistol, carbine or musket bullet with a hole through it for the weight. Several of these round "bullet weights" have been excavated from the fort. There are also

flattened sheets of lead that appear to have been fashioned around the fishing line. These reflect Mascall's description of lead weights which are "*finely & thin beate, and lapt close about your line next your hooke.*"[118]

For the large fish, such as the sturgeon it was necessary to use nets and seines. Smith claimed that seven or eight sturgeon could be caught "*with one Net*" and four or five hours work. On one occasion, Smith bragged that 68 sturgeon were taken with just one throw of the net![119] Since the sturgeon

Figure 174. Lead fishing weights for fishing with a hook and line and heavy tubes of lead for weighting fishing nets.

ranged in size between two and nine feet in length and could weigh several hundred pounds, there is no wonder the colonists *"had more Sturgeon, then could be devoured by Dog or Man."*[120]

Four large tubular lead weights for weighing down the seines used to net the sturgeon have been recovered during the *Jamestown Rediscovery* excavations. They are all 6 cm in length and were cast in a two-part mold. Parallel weights have been found in a ca. 1619-22 context at the settlement downriver from Jamestown known as Martin's Hundred.[121] While lead weights would be fairly easy to fashion out of scrap lead in the fort, acquiring the material for the seines and nets seemed to be more problematic for the colonists. Hemp from the stems of the Cannabis sativa plant was the preferred fiber for ropes, sails, and fishing nets. The colonists appear to have arrived with hemp because net making was one of their first activities in 1607, along with designing James Fort and clearing the land for their tents.[122] Again, early in 1609, the colonists are noted to be making nets.[123] But by 1610, the date of Strachey's comment about no nets or seines to catch fish, seines and netmakers were being requested from England. Perhaps the necessity of relying on inadequate supplies of hemp from England is what necessitated Dale's implementation of *"common gardens for hemp and flax"* when he arrived in 1611.[124]

Cooper

One cooper identified as John Lewes was included in the First Supply of 1608. Cooperage was important to the colony for producing the containers needed to store and transport goods. Wooden barrels or casks would have provided the most satisfactory storage for the colony's provisions although they could not prevent spoilage in the extremes of the Virginia climate. Without the modern convenience of refrigeration, storing a surplus of foodstuffs for later consumption was nearly impossible for the colonists. As John Smith disappointingly relates in one instance, *"in searching our casked corn wee found it halfe rotten."*[125]

Figure 175. The cooper was essential to the colony for producing the containers by which goods could be shipped back to England.

Lewes would have been busy from the very beginning trying to keep up with the need for barrels to contain the immediately available commodities such as *"Sasafrix roots,"*[126] which members of the council described as being their *"easiest and richest comodity."*[127] It was so easy to acquire that the sailors returning to England in June 1607 had gathered up two tons of it as contraband. Not only did they break some of the colony's tools in the process of digging the sassafras roots, but they also upset Jamestown's future trade of the commodity by flooding the London market!

Figure 176. Randle Holme's depiction of a croze with the iron in place.

Containers were also needed to hold the substances the colonists would eventually produce to ship back to England. In a three-month period, for example, John Smith records the production of "*3 or 4 last of pitch and tar.*" A *last* is a commercial capacity, which for *pitch* would amount to between 12 and 14 barrels.[128]

The critical wood shortage in England resulting from shipbuilding, and the massive use of wood as industrial fuel for the production of iron, made Virginia's forests look very attractive to the colony's investors. The colonists noted that the Jamestown area was "*generally replenish'd with wood of all kinds and that the fairest, yea, and best that ever any of us (traveler or workman) ever saw, being fit for any use whatsoever, as ships, house, planks, pales, boards, masts, wainscot, clapboard – for pikes or elsewhat.*"[129]

Among the first commodities sent back to England and one that would continue to be exported for some time was "*a taste of Clapboard.*"[130] Clapboard refers to the short, split oak staves used to make barrels. In the production of a barrel, the clapboard or staves are curved by heating and are bound together by hoops of wood or iron, which are forced down over them. The top and bottom of the barrel sits securely in a groove known as a croze that is produced near the interior ends of the staves. The tool used to produce the groove is also called a croze, the iron element of which has been recovered from the fort.

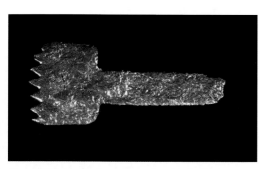

Figure 177. A cooper's croze iron found in Pit 1.

Besides the croze, a kit of cooper's tools would also include a broad axe for dressing the cut wood, and a small adze to cut the beveled ends of the barrel. Both of these tools have been found in the excavations and, along with the croze iron, may have belonged to Virginia's first cooper, John Lewes.

Carpenters

Although all the men, even the gentlemen, were engaged in felling trees and the making of wainscot and clapboard, there were four carpenters on the first ship. It is interesting that Smith made soldiers of all four and thereby kept them from exercising their craft. One, William Laxon, was even given

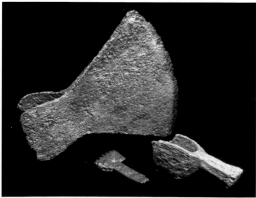

Figure 178. A broad axe and an adze along with the croze iron (center), which would have been required by the cooper in the process of his work.

182

the title *"Ensign,"* presumably taking over the duty of flag bearer from Ensign Jerome Alikock who *"died of a wound"* on August 14, 1607. Two others, Robert Small and Edward Pising, had points of land named after them to commemorate their participation with Smith on journeys of exploration. Small only went on one of these forays, but Pising accompanied Smith on two—in July and December of 1608—and thereby earned himself the title of sergeant by the second expedition. The fourth carpenter was not so lucky. Thomas Emery was slain by Indians while on a December 1607 excursion with Smith.

Figure 179. Wood was one of Virginia's greatest assets, and carpenters were needed by the colony to prepare it for export, as well as to build Jamestown's structures.

From all this military activity, it appears that the carpenters were not spending much time building structures. Personal dwellings apparently were not a priority in James Fort. By September 1607, a full four months after arrival, the president of the colony was still living in a tent.[131] Even in January 1608, the First Supply arrived to find the colonists *"utterly destitute of houses, not one as yet built, so that they lodged in cabins and holes within the ground."*[132]

The colonists appear to have followed one of the directives of the Virginia Company that stated, *"before any house be set up for any private person"* all *"carpenters and suchlike workmen"* should be put to work erecting public buildings such as the storehouse. The next bit of instruction is very interesting for the information it reveals about the relationship among the men in the colony. It states *"and though the workmen may belong to any private persons, yet let them all work together first for the company and then for private men."*[133] The craftsmen, then, were not necessarily Company men but were in the employ of some of the gentlemen in the group. They were part of the voyage to serve, provide comfort, and perhaps profit, for their masters and not to sustain or produce income for the Virginia Company.

Laxon, Pising, Small, and Emery may have been in the employ of one or more of the gentlemen who accompanied Smith on his expeditions, which would also explain their inclusion in the trips. It appears, at any rate, that three of them may have been no more than apprentices, for the historical records say that up until the Third Supply, there was *"but one Carpenter in the Countrey and three others that could doe little, but desired to be learners."*[134]

Woodworking tools such as felling axes, dividers, hatchets, chisels, gimlets, wedges, and files have been found in the excavations.

Figure 180. Collection of carpenters' tools recovered from James Fort, including dividers, a felling axe, a hatchet, a socket chisel, and two files.

Blacksmiths

One blacksmith is listed as arriving with the first group of settlers in 1607, although a second blacksmith and a gunsmith follow in the First Supply in January 1608. As workers of iron, both blacksmiths and the gunsmith would have had similar training and most likely worked together at Jamestown to repair firearms and other weaponry as well as tools. Only the first blacksmith, James Read, receives further mention after his arrival, and a colorful reference it is. In September 1607, Read is almost hanged. According to Edward Maria Wingfield, the newly deposed president of the Council, this punishment is for returning a blow from President John Ratcliffe.[135] John Smith says Read was sentenced for cursing at Ratcliffe and threatening *"to strike him with some of his tooles."*[136] In any case, Read literally saved his own neck by divulging that fellow colonist, Captain George Kendall, was planning a mutiny. Kendall was executed for his alleged conspiracies, but Read goes on to accompany John Smith on a couple of exploratory expeditions in June and December 1608. On one of those journeys with Smith to chart the landscape, he even had a point of land named after him.[137]

One has to wonder why a craftsman with an occupation so useful to the daily life of the colony goes off on risky trips with Smith. Is it possible that Read also came to Jamestown under the sponsorship of one of the gentlemen in the fort—one who had possibly died in the first few months, thereby leaving his servant as a free agent?

One likely gentleman is Dru Pickhouse (Piggase) who died in August 1607. Before coming to Virginia, Pickhouse owned and managed an iron forge on his family's Sussex County estate.[138] It is tempting, with both Pickhouse and Read arriving at the same time and with both men involved in iron working, to associate the two. With Pickhouse's early demise, Read would have been without a master and subject to the whims of the Council members who were leading the colony. Read would have been, thereby, available for soldiering.

Pickhouse appears to have had financial woes in England, which may explain why he left a wife and two children to go to Jamestown. He had been in debtor's prison in the 1590s for failing to pay for wood to fuel his forge, and by 1601 he was forced to sell the family manor.[139] Perhaps he participated in the first Jamestown venture with the hope that he could use the abundant forests in Virginia to reestablish a profitable iron forge – one, hopefully, in which he would not have to pay for the wood!

The production of iron in the colony was a driving interest of the Virginia Company investors. In December 1608, Smith, then president of the local council, sends *"two barrels of stones"* to London, which he believes *"to be good Iron ore."* The "stones" are coming from more than one source; Smith says that he has included notes describing where he found each sample.[140] Smith appears to have had faith in Virginia's potential for iron production. In his opinion, the colony's "*best commoditie was Yron*" which he says they "*made into little chissels.*"[141] This iron was probably the naturally occurring bog iron or limonite, a hydrated form of iron oxide, which is plentiful along the banks of the James River. The bog ore would have been treated in a small furnace known as a bloomery, which required little labor but could produce only modest amounts of iron.[142] In a bloomery, "*the ore was heated to form a semi-molten mass or bloom of wrought iron, which was refined by hammering on the anvil.*"[143]

The anvil is one of the most important components of a blacksmith's equipment. Comprising a heavy piece of metal that has maintained the same basic shape through the centuries, it is the surface upon which the iron is worked. A pointed element that projects from one or both sides of the anvil, known as a horn, has been excavated from a plowzone layer in James Fort. The horn is "*used to curve pieces of iron for shaping rings, links, shackles and other round or curving objects.*"[144] Since the anvil horn comes from the plowzone, which is a mixed context, it is not known if it is associated with the earliest blacksmiths in the colony.

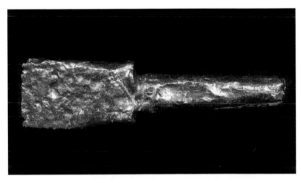

An element of an anvil, known as a hardy, was excavated in 1955 by National Park Service archaeologists from an area within the Confederate earthwork that lies under and

Figure 181. An anvil hardy that was excavated from the vicinity of James Fort by National Park Service archaeologists in 1955.

beside James Fort.[145] A hardy is a wedge-shaped tool with a square sectioned tang that fits in a hole in the anvil. The cutting edge of the hardy makes an "*impact on the underside of the work when the smith strikes it from above.*"[146] The hardy was found in association with forge refuse including slag, smithing scrap, and evidence of weapon repair that is believed to date to the first quarter of the 17th century.[147] It is not known how this feature relates to those of James Fort that have been excavated by the APVA, but this will be determined by excavations planned for the future.

The smiths in James Fort would be called upon for the repair of both military and non-military iron objects, the manufacture of tools, nails, and other small iron objects, as well as for the shoeing of the horses. By the summer of 1609, there were six mares and two horses,[148] but there have been no horseshoes found in the excavations to indicate that they had been shod. It would have been a needless exercise anyway as the colonists ate all the horses at Jamestown over the Starving Time winter of 1609-1610.

There is evidence of another activity that most logically would have been assigned to the smiths – recycling of the plate armor. For the body armor known as a cuirass, consisting of a backplate and breastplate, to be effective protection it had to be worn by the soldier whenever there was a threat of danger. In the early years of the colony, this meant all the time, which made it very uncomfortable for the colonists to perform such routine tasks as hunting or cutting wood. In addition, the heavy body protection was a detriment to quick maneuvers when involved in skirmishes with the Indians. John Smith revealed this handicap when he noted that *"the Salvages are so light and swift, though we see them (being so loaded with armour) they have much advantage of us though they be cowards."*[149]

Three intact breastplates have been recovered from the site.[150] A fourth breastplate had been reshaped into a container, perhaps a cooking pot or pail, reflecting new priorities for the colonists. Conversion of plate armor is also evident in the numerous pieces that have been cut to produce another type of body protection known as a coat of jacks. A coat of jacks would have resembled the tight-fitting man's jacket known as a doublet, but the material would have been strong and coarse like canvas or buckram. Sewn or quilted between the two layers of the coat would be over 1,000 small square or oblong metal plates known as jacks. The Spanish also had these garments which they called *escaupile* and which they found to be very effective against Indian arrows. Spaniard Gonzalo Mendez de Canzo tells the Spanish king in 1600 *"as for war with Indians no other armour except (the escaupile) is of any value."* He goes on to explain that arrows can pierce coats of mail, as they can leather buff coats. They can rebound dangerously from plate armor, perhaps injuring a colleague; but *"it is clear that the escupil is the best armour because the arrow is stopped by it and sticks."*[151]

Figure 182. A breastplate that has been cut up into jackplates, and a soldier wearing a coat of jacks (above).

Glassmakers

Glassmakers arrived at Jamestown on September 29, 1608 aboard the *Mary and Margaret*. Two months later, this ship returned to London freighted with Virginia commodities, among them a "*tryal of glasse.*" The glassmakers had been under pressure to produce proof to their English sponsors that the ingredients necessary to produce glass were available in the Jamestown area. Evidence of this two-month effort was abundant within the fort's pre-1610 features where crucibles were found —some still containing molten glass or sand—large melting pots with glass residues, and pounds of cullet, or waste glass. John Smith acknowledges the industriousness of these glass workers when he mentions that most of the "*labourers*" in the fort "*never did know what a dayes worke was, except the Dutch-men [Deutschmänner or German] and Poles, and some dozen other.*"[152]

The glassmakers have long been thought to be from Poland or individuals from both Poland and Germany.[153] Just as in the previous quote, the two ethnic groups are frequently mentioned in the same breath in the Jamestown records. This is possibly because both crews of men spoke little or no English, and this set them apart from the rest of the colonists. The linkage of the Poles and Germans starts with John Smith's list of the Second Supply, which records the arrival of "*eight Dutch men and Poles.*"[154] Another statement by John Smith criticizes the Virginia Company's search "*into Germany or Poleland for glasse-men and the rest.*"[155] What Smith means by "*the rest*" is revealed in another quote when he mentions "*the hyring of the Poles and Dutchmen to make Pitch, Tar...and Sope ashes*" as well as

Figure 183. Evidence of the glassmakers at work within the fort prior to 1610.

Figure 184. An 18th-century illustration showing how crown glass was spun into large rounds.

glass.[156]

Scholars now believe that the Germans were the glassmakers and the Poles were the producers of "*the rest*"— the pitch, tar, and soap ashes.[157] Of the eight Germans and Poles mentioned, we know that three were German and we know their first names—Adam, Samuel, and Francis. There were traditionally only two or three men in a glassmaking team[158] so the remaining five men were probably all Polish. At times the Germans and Poles would have had to work in tandem which may be another reason that the two groups are often linked. The Poles' soap ash, which is also known as potash,[159] is potassium carbonate. Made from the ashes of wood, potash provides the alkali that is required to help melt glass ingredients together and create a stable product. Since the glassmakers at Jamestown were using wood for fuel, they would eventually have a constant supply of the potash they needed in the ashes their furnaces produced. In the beginning, however, they would have need of some of the potash produced by the Polish laborers before they could start work. In England, glassmakers during this time period faced a worse problem. They had to purchase potash from European sources as they were being forced by legislation to convert to coal, which produced no wood ash, as their source of fuel.

As mentioned, a so-called trial of glass was returned to England at the end of 1608. It is not known for sure what comprised that test; it was probably no more than a glass ingot providing proof of the efficacy of Virginia's glassmaking resources. The glassmakers intended product is believed to have been window glass. There was an enormous window shortage in London as "*large expanses of glass were becoming fashionable for those who could afford them.*"[160] Window glass had to be imported from the continent at great cost to meet the demand because English glassmakers in the beginning of the 17th century could not make window glass profitably using coal furnaces. The Virginia Company felt that a window glass factory in Virginia would be a lucrative enterprise, despite the breakage that could occur during transport. There was a limitless supply of wood for fueling the furnaces and producing potash, as well as plenty of sand on the James River beaches to provide the needed silica.

Besides sand and potash, another ingredient was used in the production of glass—cullet or waste glass. Old broken glass or scraps of glass formed during the manufacturing process were thrown into the mix to reduce the melting point. This was economical for the glassmakers because they would not have to sustain high temperatures in their furnaces, the same reason that glass is recycled today. Over 7,000 fragments of cullet have been recovered along with other glassmaking debris in the fort. The fragments are all pieces of crown window glass, probably brought from a European window factory. Crown glass is blown glass that has been spun on the end of a long rod, called a pontil, into large flat disks that could be two to three feet in diameter. There was a lot of waste with this type of glass when the glazier cut the rounds into panes to lead into a window. The curved, raised edge pieces and the thickened center where the pontil had been attached, known as the bull's eye, were unusable. These waste elements from the round would be collected from the workshop floor to be sold as the commodity known as cullet.

The German glassmakers were producing green glass or *Waldglas*, which was the typical type of glass produced, using potash in the forest glasshouses of the 16th and 17th centuries. The green color is a result of the high amount of iron oxide in the impure beach sand that was the source of silica. Decolorizing agents that could neutralize the green color were known but have not been associated thus far with the making of forest glass.[161] Several pieces of one of these minerals, pyrolusite or manganese oxide, were found in association with the glassmaking artifacts in James Fort.[162] The properties of pyrolusite were known as early as the mid-16th century when metalworker Vannoccio Biringuccio described that the substance *"cleanses melted glass when it is mixed with it and causes it to change from green or yellow to white."*[163] The achievement of a

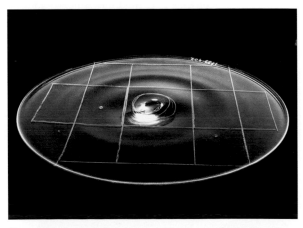

Figure 185. Crown glass round scored into panes of glass. The center "bull's eye" and the edge pieces are unsuitable for placing in a window and are discarded as cullet.

189

Figure 186. Close-up of pyrolusite brought by glassmakers to decolorize glass.

lighter glass would be highly desirable in the production of glass for windows, as this material would permit more light to penetrate the dimly lit 17th-century interiors. Biringuccio goes on to say that this material comes from Germany and Northern Italy.[164]

Also from Germany are the refractory clay crucibles that were used to melt the raw materials. The clay of these crucibles has quartz sand as a main ingredient and is fired to a near-stoneware consistency that creates "industrial strength" vessels able to withstand very high heat without breakage. One of the crucibles is marked twice on the base with a circular stamp bearing the initials PTV GER. Crucibles with this same mark have been recorded from excavations in Grossalmerode near Kassel, Germany. Indeed, the GER stands for Grossalmerode, which was a primary center of glass and crucible production for 400 years that peaked in the early 17th century. The initials PTV are believed to represent Peter Topfer who was listed as a leaseholder in the crucible production monopoly from 1621-1625. Topfer is named *"the elder"* in 1621, so he was most likely making crucibles prior to the 1608 glassmaking activity at Jamestown.[165]

With all the byproducts of glassmaking in the fort and additional subsequent efforts apparent in the glasshouse on Glasshouse Point,[166] there is yet no evidence that the German glassmakers ever succeeded in making anything beyond their trial. The main obstacle appears to have been the insufficiency of food supply in the colony, and the growing lack of confidence that the German craftsmen perhaps had that their English employers could sustain them. Immediately after the departure of the ship

Figure 187. Crucible base from bulwark trench stamped twice with a maker's mark PTV/GER, representing Peter Topfer, Grossalmerode, Germany.

carrying the glass sample to London in December 1608, John Smith sent the Germans to build a house for Powhatan because he had *"no victuals to imploy them"* in the fort. Without food in their stomachs, Smith says, *"few were able to doe any thing to purpose."*[167] While living with the Indians, the Germans were not only well fed, but they were led to believe that Powhatan was planning an attack on the fort to take advantage of the weakened condition of the colonists. Thinking that the settlement could not survive a double hit of hunger and an Indian assault, the Germans apparently decided that they would have a better chance of survival with Powhatan and agreed to smuggle arms and tools out of the fort for him. These intrigues consumed the better part of 1609, with the end result that all three Germans were dead at the hands of the Indians by the next spring. There would have been no time and little incentive for these glassmakers to make glass.

Conclusions

Just as in the children's choosing rhyme,
Tinker, tailor, soldier, sailor,
rich man, poor man, beggar man, thief,
doctor, lawyer, Indian chief,"

a wide range of occupations and social positions is reflected in the individuals at Jamestown during the first one-and-one-half years of settlement. The "Indian chief" is, of course, Powhatan who never set foot on Jamestown Island once the colonists arrived; but who, as leader of the vast confederation of Indian groups that surrounded the English colony, played a major role in the Jamestown story. But what is known about the rest of the individuals at Jamestown?

Most of the Jamestown experience is reflected through the eyes of the "rich men" and the individuals who had professions requiring university training such as the "doctors" and the "lawyers." These men, for the most part, were the literates – the ones who either wrote the accounts or were considered by their peers to be interesting enough to write about. An obvious exception to this is John Smith, a professional soldier, who left us the largest body of literature regarding the early years at Jamestown. *"As a writer, John Smith apologized for 'his owne rough pen,' yet he left to posterity . . . an invaluable, if one-sided contemporary history of early Virginia."*[168]

The men who couldn't write their own accounts have nonetheless left stories for us to interpret by way of the trash they generated while going about their everyday lives. In it we find remnants of their weaponry and tools, remains of their meals, fragments of their pottery and glassware, pieces of their jewelry and clothing, and bits of their musical instruments and games. Put all together, this material record presents a picture of life that is so much more than the static generalization of laziness and incompetence that has found its way onto the pages of the history books. This is about living, breathing individuals who risked their lives for various reasons to travel to a new frontier. Some of the reasons were for adventure, some for opportunity, some to escape overwhelming personal problems, and some because they probably had little choice. We know from the records that some came as servants – John Smith brought his page, Samuel Collier, who he sent to live among the Indians to learn their language, and Captain John Martin brought his scribe Anas Todkill who he had commanded to *"record his journies."*[169] A good number of the craftsmen and laborers were also probably in the colony under the sponsorship of some of the gentlemen who were accustomed to having their retinue of serving men around them. These servants came prepared to work as indicated by the archaeological remains.

So why did the colony almost fail? Why was Jamestown almost abandoned just three years after it was first settled? John Smith tells us that it was the Virginia Company's drive to achieve immediate returns for the investors that worked to the detriment of the colony's welfare. He stated that *"for in over-toyling our weake and unskillful bodies, to satisfie this desire ofr present profit we can scarce ever recover ourselves from one Supply to another."*[170]

The Virginia Company, which eventually lost its charter in 1624, would have done well to heed the words of Sir Francis Bacon:

> *"Planting of countries is like planting of Woods; for you must make account to lose almost twenty years' profit, and expect your recompense in the end: for the principal thing that hath been the destruction of most plantations, has been the base and hasty drawing of profit in the first years."*[171]

Epilogue

Jamestown Rediscovery is after all, more than an exercise in *merely digging things up* but rather an exercise in *historical* archaeology. This is a process that uncovers through excavation, Jamestown's past and tries to determine *why* those remains of the past wound up in the ground. The discovery part of the process is physical and clerical. The context and meaning part of the process is also physical and clerical, but essentially historical. So *Jamestown Rediscovery* is a constant interplay between the artifacts from the ground and written factual statements. Also a very significant part of the *Jamestown Rediscovery* historical archaeology process is its preoccupation with what might appear to be minutiae. Much of its discoveries appear to be microscopic examination of trivia, over-focusing on the things of so little value that even the first settlers relegated them to the trash heap. If the process stopped at artifact recovery and then mere "bean-counting," the process would indeed amount to systematic collecting and not a particularly insightful exercise. But exactly because the pure archaeological evidence can be a direct link with an unfiltered material past, a past that just so happens to have a partial documentary account of it, then transcending the trivial is possible. Happily that means that the process can address questions that meant something then and, more importantly, now.

For example, based on traditional historical interpretation, we might think we know that basically the beginnings of the United States, the world's sole remaining superpower, was originally in the hands of inept London businessmen who, totally ignorant of the real New World, sent 104 of the most incompetent, lazy, and poorly equipped people in England to ignorantly choose to begin the British Colonial Empire on a mosquito infested marshy peninsula that the Virginia Indians had long ago abandoned as uninhabitable. It was only the importation of more people to replace the dead that enabled the colony to take root. In other words, the Anglo-United States began as a greedy mistake and endured by coldly calculated human sacrifice. That may well be true. But not the whole truth.

Here is an historical archaeological view. Some of the artifacts of first Jamestown are in many respects the "fall out" of some of the things people did there on a daily basis from May 13, 1607 to about 1624; that is, whenever they were periodically healthy or inspired enough to do anything at all. They certainly did not do **nothing**. Specifically objects from pits, the moat, cellars, and a well, many likely thrown there in 1610-1624, clearly indicate that Jamestown was a very industrious place. For one thing we now know these men first built a fort, in the amazing space of three weeks, that was never captured in battle on the most defendable high ground of the most naturally fortified piece of ground along the James River. And indeed, people were making trade jewelry in precisely the designs and of the material, copper, that they already knew the natives would trade for food. They were also successfully experimenting with making glass, a commodity much needed in England, and they were busy making "survival" products like shot, bullets, iron tools and implements from spare armor, repairing guns, and refining ore in search of precious metals. Of course, much time seems to have been required to hunt, fish and repel incessant Indian guerrilla attacks. Even still these men were continually cutting down trees for palisades and to support houses. It is also clear that a number of people were doing a fair amount of digging: excavating clay pits, digging slot trenches for planting and/or repairing palisade timbers, digging postholes for the major timber supports for houses, excavating cellars for barracks and storage, a powder magazine and making coffins and digging graves. Based on the archaeological/historical discoveries then a Jamestown hard at work doing exactly some of the kinds of things they had to do to survive and the Company succeed, is hardly an illogical image.

Add to that, eyewitness descriptions of life at Jamestown for the same early years. While they do indicate that not everyone was exactly pulling his own weight, still at times there seems to have been many things going on that advanced the cause. For instance, the men cut much timber for clapboarding and wainscoting, and dug and collected sassafras roots and "*gilded*" soil to relade the homeward bound ships. Those activities were at least supposed to turn a profit for the sponsoring Virginia Company. They also pitched tents and built houses and collected bark or reeds to cover them and built two blockhouses nearby the fort. The church and the store seemed to be continually under repair or in rebuilding. Of course on special days they would attend church or court or entertain a visiting emissary from the Powhatan chiefdom. They bargained with seaman for food and for whatever luxuries they could get their hands on when there was a supply ship in port. They also cleared fields and planted crops with varying degrees of success as they attempted to raise horses, cows, hogs goats, sheep and chickens. This in the face of a major drought until 1613. They drilled with their muskets, took target practice, stood watch, and mounted ordinance. So, some were not idle. It is true that Captain John Smith lamented that certain gentlemen were not only not aiding the cause of settlement, but in fact spending all their time black marketeering and living high on the hog. These were the men he sarcastically called "...*the saint-seeming worthies of Virginia.*" Historians can dwell on these stories and read "fiasco." But artifacts with other documents say some Jamestonians were hard at meaningful work. These were the *saintly worthies* of Virginia. For their efforts, Jamestown could live on to become the first permanent English settlement in the new world. The Company failed but the Colony and the nation from which it grew, most certainly did not.

Endnotes

Prologue

[1] Edmund S. Morgan. *American Slavery American Freedom* W.W. Norton & Company, Inc. New York, 1975.

[2] Morgan. *American Slavery,* 48.

[3] *Ibid.,* 56.

[4] *Ibid.,* 70.

[5] *Ibid.,* 86.

[6] Alan Taylor. American Colonies, Penguin Books, New York, 2001, 130-133.

Chapter I

[7] Kathleen Deagan and Jose Maria Cruxent. *Columbus's Outpost Among the Tainos,* Yale University Press, 2002, passim.

[8] David B. Quinn, Ed. *Observations Gathered Out of "A Discourse of the Plantation of the Southern Colony in Virginia by the English, 1606" written by the honorable gentleman, Master George Percy,* Charlottesville, Virginia, 1967, 15.

[9] *Ibid.,* 16.

[10] Dennis Blanton. Personal communication, 1996.

[11] Philip L. Barbour. *The Complete Works of Captain John Smith,* London, 1986, Vol. I: 206.

[12] *Ibid.*

[13] Quinn. *Observations,* 22.

[14] Barbour. *Smith,* I: 210.

[15] Barbour. *Smith,* II: 325.

[16] Louis B. Wright. *A Voyage to Virginia in 1609: Strachey's True Reportory,* Charlottesville, Virginia, 1964, 63-64.

[17] *Ibid.,* 76.

[18] *Ibid.,* 79-81.

[19] Ralph Hamor. *A True Discourse of the Present Estate of Virginia, and the success of the Affaires there till the 18 of June, 1615,* in Barbour. *Smith,* Vol II: 242.

[20] Barbour, *Smith,* II: 138.

[21] Barbour, *Smith,* I: 35.

[22] Wright, *Voyage,* 79-82.

[23] *Ibid.*

[24] Barbour, *Smith,* II: 262.

[25] *Ibid.,* 324.

[26] *Ibid.,* 225; I. Noël Hume, *The Virginia Adventure,* (Knopf, New York, 1994), 274.

[27] *Algemeenrijksarchief's Gravenhage Colectie Leupe Supplement,* Velh 619.89. Michael Jarvis brought this chart to my attention and Jeroen van Driel gave valuable references.

[28] Barbour. *Smith,* II: 242, Hamor, *A True Discourse,* 242.

[29] Susan M. Kingsbury. *Records of the Virginia Company of London,* 1935, IV: 259.

[30] Barbour. *Smith,* II: 136.

[31] Rosemary Taylor, *Blackwall, the Brunswick and Whitebait Dinners,* (Blackwall, 1991). I am indebited to Ms. Taylor for providing a copy of this booklet.

[32] I am indebted to Daniel Brown for alerting me to the exact numbers.

[33] Barbour,. *Smith,* I: 205.

[34] Mary Abbott. *Life Cycles in England, 1560-1720, Cradle to Grave,* London and New York: Routledge, 1996, 135.

[35] Catherine Correll-Walls, *Jamestown Biographies Project,* a database of biographical information gathered from traditional sources such as first hand accounts, scholarly publications and British and Irish Manuscript collections.

[36] *Ibid.*

[37] Nell Marion Nugent. *Cavaliers and Pioneers*, Baltimore: Genealogical Publishing Co, Inc.1974, XXI.

[38] W. Stitt Robinson, Jr., *Mother Earth Land Grants in Virginia, 1607-1699*, passim.

[39] Martin does eventually get by grant 10 shares (1000 acres) of choice land in 1616 and stays in Virginia may mean his English prospects were not major. Brown, II: 943. Alexander Brown. The Genesis of the United States, Houghton Mifflin & Co., New York, 1891.

[40] Op cit, Correll-Walls above.

[41] Warner F. Gookin. "Who Was Bartholomew Gosnold?" in *William and Mary Quarterly*, 3rd Series, Vol.6, No. 3, 401.

[42] *Ibid.* The author is indebited to Nicholas Hagger, owner of Otley Hall, the Gosnold mansion, for suggesting sources for Gosnold's biography.

[43] Barbour, *Smith* I: 203.

[44] George Percy. *Observations gathered out of Discourse of the Plantations of the Southern Colony in Virginia by the English, 1606.* In Alexander Brown. *The Genesis of the United States*, (Boston: Houghton, Mifflin and Company, 1890), 152.

[45] *Ibid.*

[46] Correll-Walls, *Jamestown Biographies Data Base*, Jamestown Rediscovery Center, Jamestown, 2004.

[47] Barbour. *Smith* II; 140-142, 160-163, 190-191.

[48] FEMA, Flood Insurance Study and Flood Rate Map, Jamestown Island, Virginia, 1991.

[49] William Strachey, *Historie of Travell Into Virginia Britania*, Louis B. Wright and Virginia Freund, Eds., London: Robert Maclehose and Co., 1953: 37.

[50] Percy, *Observations*, in Brown, *148.*

[51] Strachey, *The Historie of Travell Into Virginia Britania (1612)* in Edward Wright Haile. *Jamestown Narratives*, 58.

[52] Frederic W. Gleach. *Powhatan's World and Colonial Virginia, A Conflict of Cultures.* Lincoln and London: The University of Nebraska Press, 1997, 91.

[53] Barbour, I: 173. Champlain, VA, 1998, 616.

[54] Correll-Walls, *Jamestown Biographies*, compilation.

[55] Helen C. Rountree. *The Powhatan Indians of Virginia, Their Traditional Culture*, Norman and London: The University of Oklahoma Press, 1989, 184-194.

[56] Strachey, *History of Travell*, in Haille, 619.

[57] Barbour, *Smith*, II: 258.

[58] *Ibid.*,151.

[59] *Ibid.*, 260-261.

[60] The Library of Virginia. *Virginia Colonial Records Project*, Survey Report # 01538, PRO, Class SP14/90, State Papers, Domestic, James I, Letters and Papers, 1611-1618, 421-456.

[61] Barbour, *Smith*, II: 262.

[62] Strachey, *History of Travell*, in Haile, 622; George Percy, *A True Relation of the procedings and occurrents of moment which have hap'ned in Virginia from the time Sir Thomas Gates was shipwrack'd upon the Bermudes, anno 1609, until my departure out the country, which was in anno Domini 1612,* in Haile, *Jamestown Narratives*, 509.

[63] Ralph Hamor, *A True Discourse of the Present State of Virginia*, Richmond, VA: The Virginia State Library, 1957, 40, 45. Barbour, *Smith* I: 63, 73.

[64] Strachey. *Historie of Travell*, in Haile, 622.

[65] *General Archives of Simancas, Department of State, Volume 2589, Folio 61,* Copy of deciphered letter of the Marquess of Flores to the King of Spain, August 1, 1612, in Brown, *Genesis*, 572.

[66] William Strachey. *"True Reportory of the Wreck and Redemption of Sir Thomas Gates, Knight"* in Louis B. Wright, *A Voyage to Virginia in 1609*, ed. Charlottesville: The University Press of Virginia, 1973, 64.

[67] Edward Arber, ed., *Captain John Smith's Works, 1608-1631*(Westminster: Archibld Constable and Co.:1895) xcv. I am indebted to the research of Catherine Correll-Walls for the reference of women at Jamestown.

[68] Pedro de Zuniga to Philip III, [23 February] 15 March 1609 in Philip Barbour, *The Jamestown Voyages Under the First Charter 1606-1609*, Cambridge: The University Press, 1969, II: 255.

[69] Strachey, *"True Reportory,"* 63.

[70] *Musters of the Inhabitants in Virginia 1624/1625* in Virginia M. Meyer and John Frederick Dorman, eds. *Adventurers of Purse and Person Virginia 1607-1624/5* (Richmond, VA: The Dietz Press, INC.,1987), 71.

[71] Brown, *Genesis,* II: 895.

[72] Douglas W. Owsley, Parvene Hamzavi, and Karin L. Bruwelheide, "Analysis of the APVA Skeletal Collection Jamestown, Virginia," January 1997.

[73] Thomas West, Lord De La Warre, "Letter to Salisbury," September 1610 in Haile, 466.

[74] Brown, *Genesis,* I: 393.

[75] *Ibid.*, 116.

[76] *Ibid.*, 116, 121-122, 125-127, 141.

[77] *Ibid.*, 143-145.

[78] *Ibid.*, 243.

[79] Frank Hancock, Jamestown Revisited, *A Medical Proposal with Circumstantial Considerations,* (Burlington, NC: The Hancock Press, 1998)

[80] Percy, *Observations*: 24-27.

[81] Brown, *Genesis*, I: 311.

[82] *Ibid.*

[83] Barbour, *Smith*, II: 223-224.

Chapter II

[1] Thad Tate, " Early Jamestown History," lecture, Yeardley House, February, 1994.

[2] William M. Kelso, *Jamestown Rediscovery Archaeological Project: The Search for the site of James Fort (1607)*, Association for the Preservation of Virginia Antiquities, Richmond, 1993.

[3] Richard Randolph. "Island of Jamestown" *Southern Literary Messenger,* Vol. III, 1837, 303; John L. Cotter, *Archaeological Excavations at Jamestown, Virginia*, National Park Service, Washington, D.C., 1958, 17.

[4] William M. Kelso, et. al, *Jamestown Rediscovery, Books I-VII*, Richmond, Virginia: The Association for the Preservation of Virginia Antiquities, 1994-2001.

[5] Louis B. Wright, *A Voyage to Virginia in 1609: Strachey's True Reportory*, Charlottesville, Virginia, 1964, 63-64.

[6] Ivor Noel Hume, *Fort Raleigh National Historic Site, 1991 Archaeological Investigation*, mss National Park Service Southeastern Ar-

chaeological Center, 25-26.

[7] Ransome True, ed., *17th Century Patents from the State Land Office, Richmond, Virginia*, #83, mss, Jamestown Rediscovery Center, Jamestown, Virginia.

[8] David B. Quinn, ed. *Observations Gathered Out of "A Discourse of the Plantation of the Southern Colony in Virginia by the English, 1606" written by the honorable gentleman, Master George Percy*, University of Virginia Press, Charlottesville, Virginia, 1967, 22.

[9] Philip L. Barbour. *The Complete Works of Captain John* Smith, Vol. I, London, 1986, 206.

[10] See Chapter I, 15.

[11] Barbour*, Smith*, II: 325.

[12] *Ibid.*, 324.

[13] Wright, *Voyage*, 79-81.

[14] Barbour, *Smith*, II: 242. *Ralph Hamor. A True Discourse of the Present Estate of Virginia, and the successe of the Affaires there till the 18 of June,, 1615.*

[15] Barbour, *Smith*, I: 157.

[16] Wright. *Voyages*, 79.

[17] *Ibid.*, 80-81.

[18] I am indebted to the research and master's thesis of Eric Deetz for the "discovery " of the mud and stud tradition at early Jamestown and his direction of the field work of Structure 165. Eric Deetz. *Architecture of Early Virginia: An Analysis of the Origins of Earthfast Tradition*. Master of Arts Thesis, University of Leicester, 2001; see also Rodney Cousins. *Lincolnshire Buildings in the Mud and Stud Tradition*, Heritage: Lincolnshire, 2000.

[19] Correll-Walls. *Jamestown Biographies Database*, Jamestown Rediscovery Center, Jamestown, Virginia, 2004.

[20] Jeffery P. Brain, *Fort St. George VI*. Peabody Essex Museum, Salem, Massachusetts, 2001, 8; Ivor Noel Hume. *Shipwreck!* Hamilton ,Bermudas, 1995, 16.

[21] I am always indebted to the unique and precise expertise of Bly Straube, Jamestown Rediscovery senior curator, for the identification and dating of the artifacts discussed in this book.

[22] Barbour, *Smith*, II: 317-318.

[23] *Lord De La Warre to Virginia Company of London, 7 July, 1610*, in Edward Wright Haile, *Jamestown Narratives*, Champlain, Virginia, 1998, 466.

[24] Wright, *Voyages*, 81.

[25] *Ibid.*, 64.

[26] *Ibid.*

[27] Susan M. Kingsbury, *Records of the Virginia Company of London*, IV: 1935, 259.

[28] Joann Bowen, *The Starving Time at Jamestown*, mss report, Jamestown Rediscovery Center, Jamestown, Virginia, 1999.

[29] Wright, *Voyages*, 71.

[30] *Lord De La Warre letter to the Earl of Salisbury, rec'd September in 1610*, in Haile, *Jamestown Narratives*, 466 .

[31] Barbour, *Smith*, I: 259.

[32] George Percy, *A True Relation of the Occurrents of Moment which have happened in Virginia*, in Haile, *Jamestown Voyages*, 505.

[33] This is a preliminary identification by veterinarians at Virginia Polytechnical and State University, Blacksburg, Virginia. Thanks to

[34] Smith's Map of Virginia, 1612. detail in Barbour, *Smith*, II: 140-141; Scott Weidensail. "Tracking America's First Dog," *Smithsonian Magazine*, March 1999, 45-57.

[35] Barbour, *Smith*, II: 232.

[36] Nancy Egloff. "Report on the Starving Time Population Figures" mss, Jamestown Yorktown Foundation, 1990; Catherine Correll-Walls. *Jamestown Biographies Project Data Base,* Jamestown Rediscovery Center, Jamestown, VA 2004.

[37] Barbour, *Smith,* passim.

[38] Bly Straube, personal communication, 2003.

[39] *Ibid.*, 83. For a discussion of other well references, see Chapter V.

[40] I am grateful for the advice of Jamestown Rediscovery staff archaeologist, David Givens, regarding point manufacture.

[41] I am grateful to Jamestown Rediscovery conservator, Michael Lavin, for an explanation of why copper preserves organic material.

[42] Barbour, *Smith,* II: 175.

[43] Gabriel Archer, *A Relayton of the Discover...y,* in Edward Arber, ed., *John Smith's Works* King's College, Birmingham, 1884, I: Iii.

[44] *Ibid.*

[45] I am indebted to Dennis Blanton, Director of the Center for Archaeological Research, College of William and Mary, for assessing the collection.

[46] Archer, *A Relayton,* I: Iii

[47] See Chapter I, 28.

[48] See Figure 26.

[49] I am indebted to archaeologist Danny Schimdt, who spent six weeks in the well shaft, half-submerged at times, to reveal its secrets and for his summary of the results: D. Schimdt, *Excavations Results and Interpretation STR170 at Jamestown*, mss APVA Jamestown Rediscovery Center, Jamestown, Virginia, 2003. Also for the arduous months of conservation of the well artifacts by Michael Lavin and Dan Gamble.

[50] See Chapter V.

[51] William M. Kelso, *Kingsmill Plantations*, (Academic Press), 1984, 5.

[52] Ivor Noel Hume, *The Wells of Williamsburg,* Colonial Williamsburg Foundation, n.d., passim.

[53] Wright, *Voyages,* 83.

[54] Dr. Jack Kane, hydrologist, personal communication, 2002.

[55] Wright, *Voyages, 4.*

[56] Eric Deetz suggested this strategy which ultimately led us to find the key west wall.

[57] John L. Cotter, *"Archaeological Excavations at Jamestown, 1934-1957"* APVA Lecture Series, Williamsburg, Virginia, October 20, 1993.

Chapter III

[1] The term Statehouse hereafter refers to the building site on the eastern end of a complex of foundations located on the extreme western edge of the APVA Jamestown property. The entire contiguous series of foundations attached to the Statehouse will hereafter be designated Statehouse Complex, an edifice that existed either intact or in partial or total ruin from 1665 until 1698. An earlier building located toward the eastern end of Jamestown and used for governmental functions, will be termed Berkeley's Row, although it was also called, at times during the 17th century, State house.

[2] Samuel H. Yonge, *The Site of Old James Towne, 1697-1698*

(Asssociation for the Preservation of Virginia Antiquites: Richmond, 1903) passim.

[3] H.R. McIlwaine, ed., *Journals of the House of Burgesses of Virginia, 1659/60-1693*, Virginia State Library, Richmond, 1904, 26.

[4] Yonge, *Old James Towne*, 18.

[5] The artifacts discussed here are described in greater detail in Bly Straube, *State House Ridge artifacts, 1903-2002*, (mss, APVA, Jamestown Rediscovery Center), passim.

[6] Louis R. Caywood, *Report on the Excavations at the Site of the Third Ridge and Fourth State Houses at Jamestown, Virginia, November 1-15, 1954*. mss, Colonial National Historic Park, Jamestown, Virginia.

[7] Joel L. Shiner, *Report on the Excavations in the Area of the Statehouse Group at Jamestown*. mss, Colonial National Historic Park, Jamestown, Virginia, 1955.

[8] Both Caywood and Shiner concluded that the burial ground beneath the Statehouse ruins predated the building of the Statehouse Complex probably by enough years to have erased all memory of it. Shiner concluded that the sometimes helter-skelter orientation of many of the graves might indicate that they were from the 1609-10 "Starving Time" winter.

[9] A serious re-examination of the Statehouse Complex and the burial ground that lay beneath were additional goals of the Jamestown Rediscovery excavations. The burials lived up to expectations in that physical and scientific analysis gave new insight into a sizable sample of the Jamestown popula-

tion, ca. 1610-1630 (Chapter VI).

[10] Cary Carson, Willie Graham, Carl Lounsbury, and Martha McCartney, *Description and Analysis of Structure 144, Jamestown, Virginia, A Report to APVA Jamestown Rediscovery*, (Colonial Williamsburg Foundation Research Division, 20 August, 2002) passim; Jamie May, *A Report of the Excavations of the Statehouse Ridge Complex, Structure 144*, (mss, APVA Jamestown Rediscovery Center) passim.

[11] Carson, *Structure 144*, 1-3.

[12] Carson, *Structure 144*, 1-4.

[13] Carson, *Structure 144*, 1-6.

[14] Carson, *Structure 144*, 1-8.

[15] Straube, *passim*. This may be evidence of the early structure Yonge felt he found, but no other architectural elements were found during the recent excavations.

[16] Carson, *Structure 144*, Chapter 4.

[17] Carson, *Structure 144*, 3-E-14.

[18] Warren Billings, personal communication, June 4, 2003.

[19] Warren M. Billings, *Jamestown and the Founding of the Nation*, Colonial National Historical Park, (Thomas Publications, Gettysburg, PA), N.D., 49.

[20] For a thorough discussion of the sucession of the five Jamestown churches, see Lyman G. Tyler, *Cradle of the Republic*, Chapter VII, 1906.

[21] Tyler, *Cradle*, Chapter VII.

[22] Tyler, *Cradle*, Chapter VII .

[23] "*M. J. Galt Report*" in John L. Cotter. *Archeological Excavations at Jamestown, Virginia*, Archeological Research Series Number Four, (Washington D. C., National Park Service, 1958), 222.

[24] Tyler, *Cradle*, Chapter VII.

[25] Billings, 49.

[26] Martha W. McCartney, *Biographical Sketches: People Associated with Jamestown Island*, An Archaeological Assessment of Jamestown, Virginia, Technical Report Series No. 5, (Williamsburg, Virginia), 164.

[27] McCartney, *Sketches*, 168.

[28] Martha W. McCartney, *Documentary History of Jamestown Island, Volume II, Land Ownership* (Jamestown Archaeological Assessment, Colonial Williamsburg Foundation, College of William and Mary, 2000), 116, 68.

[29] Cotter, *Excavations*, 112-121; Carl Lounsbury, *The Statehouses of Jamestown*, (Colonial Williamsburg Foundation: unpublished report, October 22, 1994).

[30] Instructions to Francis Wyatt, January 1638-39, CO 5/1354, PRO),

[31] *Patents from the State Land office*, APVA mss. Jameston Rediscovery Center, number 83.

[32] Warren M.Billings, *A Little Parliament*, (unpublished), 60.

[33] Cotter, *Excavations at Jamestown*, 77-79.

[34] McCartney, *Documentary History of Jamestown Island*, 44.

[35] Cotter, *Excavations at Jamestown*, 77-79.

[36] Warren M.Billings, *A Little Parliament*, (unpublished), 144.

[37] Martha W. McCartney. *A Narrative History of Jamestown Island*, Volume I, An Archaeological Assessment of Jamestown, Virginia, Colonial Williamsburg Foundation, College of William and Mary, 1999, 85.

[38] *Ibid.*, 85.

[40] McCartney, *Documentary History*, II: 404-424.

[41] William M. Kelso to Cary Carson, personal communication, April 29, 2002.

[42] McIlwaine, *Burgesses, 1619-1660*, 96, 101; *1660-1693*, 27.

[43] *Land Patents*, APVA, number 130: *"and bounded as followth Vizd beginning on the South side of the said house close to the wall where the said westernmost house joynes to the middle house, thence running S. wesly 34 degr 67 feet to high water mark, thence N. wesly 56 degr up the river side 120 feet, thence N. Ely 34 degr 181 ffeet & halfe, thence S. Ely 56 deg. 120 feet thence S Wly againe 34 degr through the said old State house and the partition wall dividing the sd westernmost house and middle house 114 feet and halfe to the place where it first began."*

[44] In his will of March 31, 1670 Stegg leaves to Ludwell his part of a house and furniture which they had bought from Henry Randolph. This should not be confused with the three-part "old State house complex" (Carson, *Structure 144*, 3-E, 14).

[45] Berkeley to Randolph: *"all that the remains, foundation and brick works of a certain house or messuage that was burned of 40 feet long and 20 feet broad being the westernmost pt of the ruined fabrick or buildings adjoining to the old State house which said messuage was formerly in the occupation of Richard Bennett Esqr* [the former Governor and last occupant] *together with the land whereon the said ruined messuage standeth, situated lying and being upon the river side in James city."*

[46] *"one messuage house or tenement of brick building of 40 feet long and 20 wide being the middle pt of that fabrick of building where was the old State house, together with the lands."* There

immediately followed the sale by Randolph of the other two Berkeley Row buildings.

April 7, 1671: Henry Randolph sold to Thomas Swann of Surry *"one messuage, house or brick building of 40 feet long and 20 wide being the easternmost end of that pile of building whereof the old state-house was pt and next adjoining thereto, which messuage was formerly in the occupation of Thomas Bayly."*

April 7, 1671: Henry Randolph sold to Thomas Ludwell of James City County *"one messuage or tenement of brick building of 40 feet long and 20 feet wide being the messuage of pt of that fabrick pile of building which contains three tenements, the middlemost whereof was the old State house which messuage was formerly in the occupation of Richard Bennett Esqr.*

[47] Carson, *Structure 144, 3-D-3.*

[48] Cotter, *Excavations at Jamestown,* 50-51.

[49] After various remote sensing tests, test holes excavated in a gridded pattern during the Jamestown Archaeological Assessment revealed a target there. It was concluded that there were no 17th-century features in the area. It is the opinion of the author that this testing was not extensive enough to lead to that conclusion.

[50] Rieley and Associates, *Assessment of Selected 17th-century Surveys at Jamestown Island, Virginia,* (unpublished report: APVA Jamestown Rediscovery Center, 2002).

[51] Cotter, *Excavations at Jamestown,* 45-47.

[52] The author feels that this can be the only explanation for such a lightly built partition bonded onto the main foundation with no evidence beneath nor along the partition of an earlier dismantled end wall.

[53] See Ludwell/Stegg, Randolph sale; Above.

[54] Cotter, *Excavations at Jamestown,* 50.

[55] Bly Straube, personal communication; I. Noel Hume and Audrey Noel Hume, *The Archaeology of Martin's Hundred, Site A, Pit 3, 1630-1640,* Figure 105, no. 4.

[56] William Waller Hening, *Statutes at Large,* (RWG Bartow: New York, 1823) 172.

[57] Warren M. Billings, *Sir William Berkeley, A Virginians Biography,* (unpublished) Chapter 11.

[58] John Clayton. To Robert Boyle. Boyle Papers 3a, Item 3 160-162. Archives of the Royal Society of London, London, England 1688. In McCarteny, *Narritive History,* 112-113.

[59] *(Executive Journals, Council of Colonial Virginia, 532).*

[60] Coits toss.

[61] I am especially indebted for the historical research of Bly Straube for sorting out many of the references to the evolving uses of the Statehouse Complex buildings.

[62] McIlwaine, *Burgesses,* 121-122: *July 6, 1680 ...'Whereas there is the ruines of two brick houses burnt in the late Rebellion...it's the opinion of his Excellencie & the councell that Coll. Bacon may have one of the houses on the same termes...the same which did belong to Mr. Auborne"*

[63] Billings, *A Little Parliament,* 144.

[64] *May 22, 1684 ..."Resolved in the affirmative The report of ye commt for contracting for the building the state house...it is Referred to Mr. Wm Sherwood to draw the articles between his*

Exlncy...And the Honble Collo. Phillip Ludwell for ye Rebuilding the state house."
May 22, 1684 ..."The petition of Collo. Nathaniell Bacon ...for a stack of building belonging to the Country, formerly granted to phillip Ludwell Esqr. for 50. yeares...[and]
Ludwell...declaring that he did voluntarily Relinquish the said lease or grant. Resolved that the said Building or Ruine of two houses be leased to the Honable Nathaniell Bacon Esqr. For fifty yeares...under the same conditions as...June, 1680...November 1682."
May 23,1684 ..."the two houses to be granted to Coll. Bacon, Returned from his Exlncy and Councell with their Assent, that a lease shall be drawn."
[65] *PRO Colonial Office, Class 5, Vol. 1407, 267-340*
[66] Hening, *Statutes,* 86.
[67] APVA, *Land Patents,* number 152.
[68] (Sainsbury 1964:16:513, 516,)
[69] Billings, personal communications, June 4, 2003.

Chapter IV

[1] Douglas W. Owsley, Ashley McKeown, William M. Kelso, Karin S Bruwelheide, Jamie May and David Hunt. *Two Early 17th-century Burials from James Fort, Jamestown Island, Virginia,* 2003, (unpublished report) National Museum of Natural History, Smithsonian Institution, Washington, D.C., APVA Jamestown Rediscovery Center, Jamestown, Virginia.
[2] Philip L. Barbour, *The Complete Works of Captain John Smith (* London, 1986), I: 208.
[3] Owsley, et al., *Two Early Burials,* 39.
[4] Paul Budd and Janet Montgom-ery, *Combined Pb-, Sr- and O-isotope Analysis of Tooth Enamel from JR102C (a 17th-century individual from Jamestown, Virginia, USA) and related samples,*(ArchaeoTrace Gibraltar House, Halifax UK), unpublished report, APVA Jamestown Rediscovery Center, Jamestown, Virginia.
[5] Owsley, et al., *Two Early Burials,* 35.
[6] David B. Quinn, ed., *Observations Gathered Out of "A Discourse of the Plantation of the Southern Colony in Virginia by the English, 1606" written by the honorable gentleman, Master George Percy,* (Charlottesville, Virginia, 1967) 15.
[7] *Ibid.*
[8] Catherine Correll-Walls, *Possible Identity of JR 102 C,* (unpublished report: APVA Jamestown Redis-covery Center, Jamestown, Virginia, 2003).
[9] Catherine Correll Walls. *Jamestown Biographies Data Base,* (unpublished report: APVA Jamestown Redis-covery Center, Jamestown, Virginia, 2004).
[10] Barbour, *Smith,* II: 139.
[11] Quinn, *Observations,* 25.
[12] Virginia M. Meyer and John Frederick Dorman, *Adventures of Purse and Person,* 3rd edition, (Richmond, Virginia: Order of the First Families of Virginia, 1987), 586.
[13] Barbour, *Smith,* I: 20.
[14] Samuel H.Yonge. *The Site of Old Jamestown* (Richmond, Virginia: APVA, 1903), 72.
[15] Barbour, *Smith,* II: 181.
[16] I am indebted to Janet Long, anthropologist/sculptor and National Museum of Natural History anthropologist, David

Hunt, for their talented work in reconstructing the face of JR102C.

[17] Lucy Tomlin Smith, *The Itinerary of John Leland, 1535-1543,* (Carbondale, Illinois: Southern Illinois University Press, 1964), 47, 49, 59.

[18] Quinn. *Observations,* 26.

[19] See Nancy Oestreich Lurie, "Indian Cultural Adjustment to European Civilization," in James Morton Smith, ed., *Seventeen Century America,* (Chapel Hill: University of North Carolina Press 1959), 33-60.

[20] Owsley, et al., *Two Early Burials.*

[21] Emily Williams. Archaeological conservator, Colonial Williamsburg Foundation, letter to Elliott Jordan, March 15, 1998, APVA Jamestown Rediscovery Center, Jamestown, Virginia.

[22] Barbour, *Smith,* II: 192.

[23] I am indebted to Dr. Harry Hager and Bruce Wilson for providing the CT scan at Williamsburg Community Hospital and Marc McAllister of Innova, International, Dallas, Texas for processing the CT data into a stereo-lithography file, and Accelerated Technologies for building the skull model.

[24] Tonia Deetz Rock, *Report on Burial 1046 at Jamestown, Virginia* (unpublished report: APVA Jamestown Rediscovery Center, Jamestown, Virginia 2003).

[25] Barbour, *Smith,* I: 33.

[26] Warner F. Gookin and Philip L. Barber, *Bartholomew Gosnold: Discoverer and Planter,* (London, 1963), 49-177.

[27] Edward Wright Haile, *Jamestown Narrative,* (Champlain, Virginia, 1998), 185.

[28] This important artifact was identified by the combined efforts of senior curator Bly Straube, conservator Michael Lavin, scholars James Lavin and arms expert, Claude Blair.

[29] *Ibid.*

[30] *"Drill Postures"* an engraving by T. Cockson, English, 1615-1620, The British Museum.

[31] Barbour, *Smith,* I: 206.

[32] I am indebted to Dr. Ashley McKeown who, with a generous grant from crime novelist, Patricia Cornwell, and under the direction of Dr. Douglas Owsley, Smithsonian institution, spent two years in residence at Jamestown during the burial study and taught us all some of the science and art of forensic anthropology and skeletal biology. I must also gratefully acknowledge the field supervision of senior staff archaeologist, Jamie May, and her archaeological analysis of the burial site.

[33] I am indebted to Catherine Correll-Walls who found the very generous architectural historian Philip Aiken who in turn connected me with the gracious owner of Shelley Manor, Andrew Scott, who then led me to Shelley Church.

[34] John L. Cotter, *Archaeological Excavations at Jamestown, Virginia,* (Washington D.C.: National Park Service, 1958) 219-225.

[35] Douglas W. Owsley, Parvene Hamzavi and Karin S Bruwelheide, *Analysis of the APVA Skeletal Collection Jamestown, Virginia* (unpublished report: National Park Service, 1997).

[36] Nancy Egloff, *Report on the Starving Time Population Figures*

(unpublished report, Jamestown Yorktown Foundation, 1990); Catherine Correll-Walls, *Jamestown Biographies.*

[37] Joel L. Shiner, *Report on the Excavations in the Area of the Statehouse Group at Jamestown, Research Project N. 105* (Colonial National Historical Park, Jamestown, Virginia, June 16, 1955).

[38] David W. Stahle, et al., "The Lost Colony and Jamestown Droughts," *Science,* April 24, 1998.

[39] Ashley H. McKeown, Douglas W. Owsley, and William M. Kelso, *Jamestown Rediscovery Statehouse Burial Ground Research Design* (unpublished report: APVA Jamestown Rediscovery Center, Jamestown, Virginia, 1993; revised 1996, 2000, 2004).

[40] Ashley H. McKeown, *Statehouse Burial Ground Summary Report,* (unpublished report: APVA Jamestown Rediscovery Center, Jamestown, Virginia, 2003).

[41] Bly Straube. *Artifacts from Ludwell Statehouse Group Burials,* (unpublished report: APVA Jamestown Rediscovery Center, Jamestown, Virginia, 2002).

[42] *Ibid.*; Ivor and Audrey Noel Hume. *The Archaeology of Martin's Hundred, Part II* (Philadelphia and Williamsburg: University of Pennsylvania and the Colonial Williamsburg Foundation 2001), Figure 96, 2.

[43] Egloff, *Starving Time.*

Chapter V

[1] George Percy [1608?] "Observations gathered out of a Discourse of the Plantation of the Southerne Colonie in Virginia by the English, 1606," *The Jamestown Voyages under the First Charter 1606-1609.* Volume 1. Philip L. Barbour, ed. (London: Cambridge University Press, 1969), 144.

[2] Carville V. Earle, "Environment, Disease, and Mortality in Early Virginia," in *The Chesapeake in the Seventeenth Century*, Thad W. Tate and David L. Ammerman, eds., (New York, NY: W.W. Norton & Company, 1979), 103.

[3] Barbour II: 212 and 324.

[4] William Strachey, "A True Reportory of the Wreck and Redemption of Sir Thomas Gates, Knight," *A Voyage to Virginia in 1609*, Louis B. Wright, ed. (Charlottesville, Virginia: University Press of Virginia, 1964), 99.

[5] *Ibid.,* 82.

[6] William Strachey, "For the Colony in Virginea Britannia. Lawes Divine, Morall and Martiall, etc, 1611, *Tracts and Other Papers*, Peter Force, ed. (Washington: Wm. Q. Force, 1844),15.

[7] Pumps have been used on ships for emptying water from the bilge since the early 16th century. The author thanks Ron Coleman for his thoughts on the pump.

[8] Brown, I: 492.

[9] Barbour, II: 262.

[10] *Ibid.*

[11] A court case dated July 12, 1624 discusses the "Tobacco wch was growne wthin the fforte." While apparently the area set aside for the

Virginia Company's tobacco crop, Ensign John Utey claims to have "planted some Tobacco for his owne use wth[in] the palizadoe" H.R. McIlwaine, ed., Minutes of the Council and General Court of Virginia. (Richmond, Virginia: Virginia State Library, 2nd Edition, 1979), 18-19.

[12] The Maine was located on land adjacent to Jamestown known as the Governor's Land. Alain Charles Outlaw, *Governors Land: Archaeology of Early Seventeenth-Century Virginia Settlements,* (Charlottesville, Virginia: University of Virginia Press, 1990), 160-161.

[13] William Kelso and Beverly Straube, *Jamestown Rediscovery VI* 2000, 40 - 41.

[14] Although it is documented in Spanish colonial contexts as early as 1600 [Kathleen Deagan, *Artifacts of the Spanish Colonies of Florida and the Caribbean, 1500-1800,* Volume 1 (Washington, D.C.: Smithsonian Institution Press, 1987), 47], this ware is usually found on Jamestown area sites in contexts dating to the second quarter of the 17th century (Ivor Noël Hume and Audrey Noël Hume, The Archaeology of Martins Hundred, (Williamsburg, Virginia: The Colonial Williamsburg Foundation 2001), 331.

[15] Ivor Noël Hume, *Shipwreck! History from the Bermuda Reefs,* (Hamilton, Bermuda: Capstan Publications, 1995, 41).

[16] John G. Hurst, David S. Neal, and H.J.E. van Beuningen, *Pottery Produced and Traded in North-west Europe 1350-1650*, Rotterdam Papers VI (Rotterdam: Stichting "Het Nederlandse

Gebruiksvoorwerp", 1986), 69 – 73.

[17] Thomas Carltle, "History of Friedrich II of Prussia V3." http://www.worldwideschool.org/library/books/hst/prussia/History_of_FriedrichI.../chap13.htm. (October 2001).

[18] David Gaimster, *German Stoneware 1200 – 1900.* (London: British Museum Press, 1997), 368.

[19] Jeremy N. Green, *The Loss of the Verenigde Oostindische Compagnie Retourschip "Batavia," Western Australia 1629.* BAR International Series 489, (London, England: B.A.R., 1989), 138. These medallions differ from the medallion from Structure 170 in that they incorporate the lions of Jülich and Berg on the shield rather than using them as supporters.

[20] *Ibid.,* 109.

[21] John Davis, *Pewter at Colonial Williamsburg.* (Williamsburg, Virginia: Colonial Williamsburg Foundation, 2003), 2.

[22] Worth Bailey, "Notes on the Use of Pewter in Virginia during the Seventeenth Century," *William and Mary College Quarterly Historical Magazine*, Second Series, Volume 18, Issue 2 (Apr., 1938), 232.

[23] Davis, 234.

[24] Anthony North, *Pewter at the Victoria and Albert Museum._*(London: V&A Publications, 1999), 140.

[25] John Davis, personal communication, 2002.

[26] Walter R. Brown, *The Stuart Legacy: English Art 1603-1714.* (Birmingham, Alabama: Birmingham Museum of Art, 1991), 99.

[27] Virginia M. Meyer and John F. Dorman, eds., *Adventurers of Purse and Person, 1607-1624/25.* (Rich-

mond, Virginia: Dietz Press, 1987), 37.

[28] In the 1625 census, only Richard Pierce and Richard Kingsmill are recorded as owning houses out of the 18 individuals listed at Neck of Land. By 1636 Richard Pierce had accumulated 12 headrights, which gave him the right to patent 600 acres of land on the east side of the Chickahominy River (Martha McCartney, *Documentary History* III, 271).

[29] There was little standardization in spelling in the 17th century, with words and names often being spelled as they sounded.

[30] J.C. Hotten, *The Original Lists of Persons of Quality, 1600-1700.* (Baltimore, Maryland: Genealogical Publishing Company., 1980), 179.

[31] Meyer and Dorman, 5 – 6.

[32] *Ibid.*, 25.

[33] McIlwaine, *Minutes of the Council*, 96.

[34] *Ibid*, 97.

[35] Kingsbury, III: 612.

[36] Humphrey Barwick, *A breefe discourse, concerning the force of all manuall weapons of fire, 1594.* (Norwood, New Jersey: Walter J. Johnson, 1974), 23.

[37] Leonid Tarrasuk and Claude Blair, eds. *The Complete Encyclopedia of Arms & Weapons* (New York: Bonanza, 1986), 83-84; Arturo Puricelli-Guerra, "The Glaive and the Bill," *Art, Arms, and Armour: An International Anthology*, Volume I: 1979-1980, Robert Held, ed., (Chiasso, Switzerland: Acquafresca Editrice, 1979), 9.

[38] David Blackmore, *Arms and Armour of the English Civil Wars.* (London: The Royal Armouries, 1990), 81.

[39] Kingsbury, III: 99.

[40] Two bills were excavated from an area known as Pasbehegh (44JC298) that was part of the land set aside under Governor George Yeardley in 1618. Known as the Governor's Land, it was occupied by tenants and Virginia Company employees. Another bill was found at Flowerdew Hundred, a plantation owned by Yeardley from 1618 – 1624.

[41] Puricelli-Guerra, 11.

[42] The shot carried the caliver, a firearm smaller and lighter than a musket.

[43] Strachey, *Lawes Divine, Morall and Martiall*, 32.

[44] Barbour.

[45] The author thanks Erik Goldstein for his thoughts on the breastplate modification.

[46] Strachey, *Lawes Divine, Morall and Martiall*, 15.

[47] William M. Kelso, *Kingsmill Plantation 1619 – 1800: Archaeology of Country Life in Colonial Virginia.* (New York: Academic Press, 1984), 155.

[48] *Ibid.*, 154-156.

[49] Dave Givens, personal communication, 2004.

[50] Noël Hume and Noël Hume, II.

[51] William M. Kelso, Nicholas M. Luccketti, and Beverly A. Straube, "A Re-evaluation of the Archaeological Evidence produced by Project 100: The Search for James Fort," Colonial National Historical Park, mss., 1990.

[52] Howard Gill, "The Blacksmith in Colonial Virginia," (Colonial Williamsburg Foundation, mss., 1965), 343.

[53] John Rolfe, *A True Relation of the State of Virginia Lefte by Sir Thomas*

Dale Knight in May Last 1616.
(Charlottesville, Virginia: University
Press of Virginia, 1957), 10.
[54] The Ancient Planters of Virginia,
"A Brief Declaration (1623)" in
Edward Haile, ed., *Jamestown
Narratives.* (Champlain, Virginia:
Roundhouse, 1998), 894.
[55] Spade nosings have been
documented on archaeological sites
in Maine dating as late as the early
18th century [Robert L. Bradley
and Helen B. Camp, *The Forts of
Pemaquid, Maine: An Archaeological
and Historical Study.* Occasional
Publications in Maine Archaeology
Number Ten (Augusta, Maine:
Maine Historical Preservation
Commission, 1994), 217-219].
[56] Noël Hume and Noël Hume, II:
347 n.283 and 434 n.477; Audrey
Noël Hume, *Archaeology and the
Colonial Gardener,* Colonial
Williamsburg Archaeological Series
7 (Williamsburg, Virginia: The
Colonial Williamsburg Foundation,
1974), 72-75.
[57] Outlaw, 129.
[58] Henry Mercer, *Ancient Carpenters'
Tools.* (Mineola, New York: Dover
Publications, 2000), 1-2.
[59] Similar axes have been found at
other sites near Jamestown,
including the Drummond Site at
Governor's Land (ca. 1620), the
Buck Site (ca. 1630-50), and Site B
at Martin's Hundred (ca. 1623-40).
[60] Jay Gaynor, "'Tooles of all Sorts
to Worke': A Brief Look at
Common Woodworking Tools in
17th-Century Virginia,"*The
Archaeology of 17th-Century Virginia.*
Theodore R. Reinhart and Dennis
Pogue, eds., (Richmond, Virginia:
Archeological Society of Virginia ,
1993), 338-339.

[61] David Harvey, "The Archaeo-
logical Evidence of Tools Used in
Seventeenth-and Eighteenth-
Century Virginia," *Eighteenth-
Century Woodworking Tools.*
(Williamsburg, Virginia: Colonial
Williamsburg Foundation, 1997),
87.
[62] Gaynor, 334.
[63] Kenneth Schwarz and Carl
Lounsbury, personal communica-
tion, 2003; Sue Margeson, *Norwich
Households: The Medieval and Post-
Medieval Finds from Norwich Survey
Excavations 1971-1978.* (East
Anglian Archaeology Report No.
58, 1993), 146.
[64] Randle Holme, *The Academy of
Armor & Blazon,* The Third Book
(Chester: Printed for the author,
1688), 284.
[65] William Strachey, "For the
Colony in Virginea Britannia.
Lawes Divine, Morall and Martiall,
etc, 1611, *Tracts and Other Papers* ,
Peter Force, ed. (Washington: Wm.
Q. Force, 1844), 18.
[66] Alison Sim. *The Tudor Housewife.*
(Stroud: Sutton Publishing Limited,
1996), 50.
[67] Noël Hume I:181.
[68] Norman F. Barka, "The Archae-
ology of Piersey's Hundred,
Virginia, Within the Context of the
Muster of 1624/25," *Archaeology of
Eastern North America Papers in
Honor of Stephen Williams.* James B.
Stoltman, ed. (1993), 313-335.
[69] Al Saguto, personal communication, 2002; June Swan, *Shoes.*
(London: B.T. Batsford Ltd., 1982),
12.
[70] McCartney, Documentary
History III, 193.

Chapter VI

1 Ralph Hamor, "A True Discourse of the Present Estate of Virginia," The Complete Works of John Smith 1580-1631, in Phillip L. Barbour, ed. (Chapel Hill, North Carolina: The University of North Carolina Press, 1986), II: 239.

2 Barbour, *John Smith* II: 225.

3 Brown, I: 83.

4 *Ibid.*, 83.

5 The Ancient Planters of Virginia, "A Brief Declaration (1623)" in Edward Haile, ed., *Jamestown Narratives.* (Champlain, Virginia: Roundhouse, 1998), 894.

6 John Smith inherited this position from Thomas Studley who died August 28, 1607.

7 Barbour, *John Smith,* III: 272.

8 George Percy [1608?] "Observations gathered out of a Discourse of the Plantation of the Southerne Colonie in Virginia by the English, 1606," *The Jamestown Voyages under the First Charter 1606-1609.* Volume 1. Philip L. Barbour, ed. (London: Cambridge University Press, 1969), 111., Sir Walter Cope to Lord Salisbury, August 13, 1607.

9 *Ibid.*, I:176, Newport to Lort Salisbury, July 29, 1607.

10 Derek Keene, "Metalworking in Medieval London: an Historical Survey," *Historical Metallurgy* 30:2 (1996):96,

11 Barbour, *John Smith* II: 157.

12 *Ibid.,* 158.

13 *Ibid.,* 184.

14 Barbour, *John Smith* III: 271.

15 Barbour, *John Smith* II: 184.

16 Barbour, *John Smith* II: 215.

17 *Ibid.,* 888.

18 Barbour, *John Smith* I: 226; Barbour, *John Smith* II: 266, 267, 215-216; Brown: 488; Strachey, *Travels* [Haile 687-688].

19 Hening (1823) Statutes: 135.

20 Justine Bayley (1996) "Innovation in later medieval urban metalworking," *The Journal of the Historical Metallurgy Society*, Volume 30, Number 2: 70.

21 Martincamp flasks found in association with evidence of metalworking at the site of the 1585 settlement on Roanoke Island, North Carolina, are believed to have been used as receivers.

22 Jacqueline Pearce, personal communication, 1999; Stephen Moorhouse "Medieval Distilling-Apparatus of Glass and Pottery," *Medieval Archaeology* VI, (1972), 120.

23 Jacqueline Pearce, personal communication, 1999.

24 An earthenware alembic was excavated from an early 17th-century context at Martin's Hundred, an area adjacent to Jamestown (Ivor Noël Hume, *Martin's Hundred*, 1982, A Delta Book, 101-102).

25 Jacqueline Pearce, personal communication 1999; Moorhouse "Medieval Distilling-Apparatus of Glass and Pottery," *Medieval Archaeology*, VI: 96-97.

26 Moorhouse, 87.

27 Marion Campbell, "Gold, Silver and Precious Stones," English Medieval Industries, John Blair and Nigel Ramsey, eds. (London, England: The Hambledon Press, 1991), 151.

28 Diana Scarisbrick, *Tudor and Jacobean Jewellery* (London: Tate Publishing, 1995), 38.

[29] Barbour, *John Smith* I: 209

[30] McIlwaine, Minutes of the Council and General Court, 154

[31] Barbour, *Jamestown Voyages*, 232.

[32] Barbour, *John Smith* I: 209.

[33] Barbour, Jamestown Voyages, 231.

[34] Robert Johnson, "The New Life of Virginiea 1612," in Peter Force, ed. *Tracts and Other Papers John Smith* (Washington, D.C.: Peter Force, 1836), Volume 1, 4:12.

[35] In 1620 Captain Nuce built a *"faire Well of fresh water mantled with bricke, . because the River and Cricks are there* [in what is now Newport News,] *brackish or salt"* (Barbour, *John Smith* II: 310).

[36] McCartney, Narrative History, 92.

[37] Barbour, *John Smith* II: 199.

[38] Brown I: 83.

[39] David Parsons, "Stone," English Medieval Industries, John Blair and Nigel Ramsey, eds. (London: The Hambledon Press,1991), 25.

[40] Barbour, *John Smith* II:162

[41] Adrian Oswald, *Clay Pipes for the Archaeologist,* British Archaeological Reports 14 (1975), 76.

[42] Colin Andrew Tatam "The Clay Tobacco Pipe Industry in the Parish of Newington, Southwark, London," *The Archaeology of the Clay Tobacco Pipe* XIII. Ed. By Peter Davey, ed., BAR British Series 239, (1994), 5; D.J. Markell "The Clay Tobacco Pipes," *Excavations in Poole 1973-1983,* Ian P. Horsey, ed. (Dorchester: Dorset History and Archaeological Society,1992), 159.

[43] Oswald: 96

[44] Willliam Harrison, *Great Chronologie,* as quoted in Oswald, 1975: 3.

[45] Paul Hentzner, *Travels in England During the Reign of Queen Elizabeth (1612).* London: Cassell and Company, Ltd., 1901), 42.

[46] D. Rhodes *Clay and Glazes for the Potter. Pennsylvania:* Chilton Book Company (1973), 20.

[47] Adrian Oswald, "Marked Clay Pipes from Plymouth, Devon," *Post-Medieval Archaeology* 3, (1969), 138-139.

[48] David Jones, Ipswich Museum, personal communication December 1998.

[49] Compact Oxford English Dictionary (Oxford: Clarendon Press, 1998), 1310:546.

[50] Jacqueline Pearce, *Border Wares,* (London: HMSO, 1992), 41.

[51] William Shakespeare, *Much Ado About Nothing* I: iii, 53-54.

[52] Carole Rawcliffe, *Medicine and Society in Later Medieval England,* (Alan Sutton Publishing, 1995),160.

[53] F.P. Wilson *The Plague in Shakespeare's London,* (Oxford University Press, 1999), 9.

[54] Eleanour Sinclair Rohde, *The Old English Herbals,* (New York: Dover Publications, 1971), 72.

[55] Kathleen Epstein, *British Embroidery* (Austin, Texas: Curious Works Press,1998), 55.

[56] William Shakespeare, *Much Ado About Nothing,* III, iv, 56-57.

[57] Kathy Lynn Emerson, *The Writer's Guide to Everyday Life in Renaissance England* (Cincinnati, Ohio: Writer's Digest Books, 1996), 14.

[58] David R. Ransome, "Wives for Virginia," *William and Mary Quarterly,* Third Series, 48:1 (Jan 1991), 16.

[59] William Love arrived in May 1607 (Barbour, *John Smith* II: 142); Thomas Hope, William Ward, John

Powell, William Young, William Beckwith, and Lawrence Towtales arrived in January 1608 (Barbour, *John Smith* II: 162).

[60] Barbour, *John Smith* II: 170, 192.

[61] *Ibid.,* 172.

[62] *Ibid.,* 41 and 155.

[63] Kay Staniland, "Getting There, Got It: archaeological textiles and tailoring in London, 1330-1580," *The Age of Transition,* David Gaimster and Paul Stamper, eds., (Oxford: Oxbow Books, 1997), 240.

[64] Jane Ashelford, *The Art of Dress,* London: The National Trust (1996), 27.

[65] Francis Perkins, gentleman, arrived at Jamestown on the first supply in January 1608 along with his son Francis whom John Smith lists as a laborer (Barbour, *John Smith* I: 223). Within 3 days of their arrival, a fire consumed all of their possessions except a mattress that had not yet been unloaded from the ship. In a March letter written to a friend in England, he asks for £10 worth of used clothing *whether it be large or small garments, doublets, trousers, stockings, capes or whatever may appear fit . . . since . . . everything is needed and whatever may be sent will be useful* (Brown: 176-177).

[66] Molina was held prisoner at Jamestown from 1611 to 1613. While there he managed to smuggle out his observations of the colony, hidden in the sole of a shoe, to the Spanish ambassador to London (Brown II: 646).

[67] Randle Holme, *The Academy of Armory & Blazon.* The Third Book (Chester: Printed for the Author, 1688), 284, 290.

[68] Bridget McConnel, *The Collector's Guide to Thimbles,* (London: Bracken Books, 1996), 6.

[69] *Ibid.,* 10.

[70] R.F. Tylecote, Á contribution to the metallurgy of 18th and 19th century: Brass pins," *Post-Medieval Archaeology* 6, 190.

[71] Geoff Egan and Hazel Forsyth, "Wound Wire and Silver Gilt: changing fashions in dress accessories c.1400- c.1600," Gaimster and Stamper, eds., 222.

[72] Chris Caple, "Factors in the Production of Medieval and Post-medieval Brass Pins," *Trade and Discovery: The Scientific Study of Artefacts from post-Medieval Europe and Beyond,* Duncan R. Hook and David R.M. Gaimster eds. British Museum Occasional Paper 109 (1995); 226

[73] Starch, made of boiled wheat, was introduced into England in 1564 by Dinghen van den Plass, a Dutch woman [Jane Ashelford *The Art of Dress.* (London: The National Trust. 1996), 33].

[74] John W. Shirley, "George Percy at Jamestown, 1607-1612," *The Virginia Magazine of History and Biography,* 57:3 (July, 1949), 235.

[75] Barbour, *John Smith* II: 232.

[76] Holme, 291.

[77] A parallel is depicted in the Journal of the British Archaeological Association 14 (1858) 262-266.

[78] Sue Margeson, *Norwich Households: The Medieval and Post-Medieval Finds from Norwich Survey Excavations 1971-1978.* East Anglian Archaeology Report No. 58 (1993), 22.

[79] Geoff Egan, *Lead Cloth Seals and Related Items in the British Museum,* British Museum Occasional Paper 93 (1994), 1.

[80] *Ibid.,* 4.

[81] Egan, personal communication 1994.

[82] Shirley, 237.

[83] Brown, II: 115.

[84] On at least two occasions John Smith complains about the condition of the tents that the first colonists were provided: *our Tents were rotten* (Barbour, *John Smith* I :35); and *in foule weather we shifted into an old rotten tent* (Barbour, *John Smith* III: 295).

[85] Kingsbury IV: 450.

[86] Sheelah Ruggles-Brise, *Sealed Bottles.* (New York: Charles Scribner's Sons 1949), 162. This mark was adapted by Virginians for use on their personally marked wine bottles. Interestingly, this practice does not extend to English individuals or merchants.

[87] Robert Stenuit, "Early relics of the VOC trade from Shetland: The wreck of the flute *Lastdrager* lost off Yell, 1653," *The International Journal of Nautical Archaeology and Underwater Exploration* (1974) 3:2: 243-244.

[88] Egan, *Lead Cloth Seals,* 1994: 78.

[89] Egan personal communication 1999

[90] Geoff Egan, "England's Post-Medieval Cloth Trade: A Survey of the Evidence From Cloth Seals," *Trade and Discovery: The Scientific Study of Artefacts from Post-Medieval Europe and Beyond.* British Museum Occasional Paper 109, 1995: 319.

[91] Egan, *Lead Cloth Seals,* 110.

[92] Alison Sim, *The Tudor Housewife.* (Phoenix Mill: Sutton Publishing, 2000), 50.

[93] Egan, *Lead Cloth Seals,* 106.

[94] Ivor Noël Hume, *Martin's Hundred.* New York, New York: Dell Publishing Company, 1982:

190-191.

[95] Egan, *Survey,* 319.

[96] Kathy Lynn Emerson, *Everyday Life in Renaissance England From 1485-1649* (Cincinnati, Ohio: Writer's Digest Books, 1996), 22.

[97] Shirley, 237.

[98] Shakespeare, *Taming of the Shrew* iv.i.49.

[99] The English ell was 45 inches whereas the Dutch ell was 27 inches (Egan, *Lead Cloth Seals,* 145).

[100] *Ibid.,* 113.

[101] Barbour, *John Smith,* III: 295.

[102] Barbour, *John Smith,* II:164.

[103] Barbour, *John Smith,* I: 225-226.

[104] Barbour, *John Smith,* II: 193.

[105] Brown, I: 43.

[106] Brown: 888.

[107] Barbour, *John Smith,* II: 163.

[108] Picard, 307.

[109] Barbour, *John Smith,* II: 164.

[110] Christopher Newport," A Description of the Now Discovered River and Country of Virginia (1607)," *The Virginia Magazine of History and Biography* XIV (Richmond, Virginia, 1907), 374, 376.

[111] Barbour, *John Smith,* II:111.

[112] John C. Pearson, "The Fish and Fisheries of Colonial Virginia," *The Williams and Mary Quarterly* 22:3 (July 1942), 220.

[113] William Strachey, *A True Reportory of the Wreck and Redemption of Sir Thomas Gates, Knight (1610)* in *A Voyage to Virginia in 1609,* Louis B. Wright, ed. (Charlottesville, Virginia: The University Press of Virginia, 1964), 64.

[114] Joanne Bowen and Susan Trevarthen Andrews, "The Starving Time at Jamestown," Unpublished ms., 2000.

[115] Barbour, *John Smith,* II: 104.

[116] Leonard Mascall, *The Booke of*

Fishing with Hooke and Line (1590). New York, New York: DeCapo Press, 1973), 18-23.

[117] Dame Juliana Berners *A treatyse of fysshynge with an Angle (1496)*. (The University of Oregon: Renascence Editions, 2002) (http://darkwing.uoregon.edu/%7Erbear/berners/berners.html).

[118] Mascall, 23.

[119] Barbour, *John Smith,* I: 147.

[120] Barbour, *John Smith,* II: 213.

[121] Noël Hume, Martin's Hundred, 427-428.

[122] Barbour, *John Smith,* II: 138.

[123] Barbour, *John Smith,* II: 212.

[124] Brown, 492.

[125] Barbour, *John Smith,* I: 263.

[126] Sassafras was believed in the 17th century to be a cure for scurvy, yellow jaundice, and *the French disease (*syphilis). The London surgeon John Woodall who sent a fully equipped surgeons chest to Jamestown in 1609 noted that *the best of these rootes grow in Virginia.* (John Woodall, *The Surgions' Mate* (1617) Bath England: Kingsmead Press, 1978, 56.

[127] Brown, I: 107.

[128] The Compact Oxford English Dictionary (Oxford: Clarendon Press, 1998): 671, 943.

[129] Gabriel Archer "The descripton of the now-discovered river and country of Virginia, with the likelihood of ensuing riches by England's aid and industry," *Jamestown Narratives*, Edward Wright Haile, ed., (Champlain, Virginia: Roundhouse, 1998), 119.

[130] Brown, I: 107.

[131] Edward Maria Wingfield, "A Discourse of Virginia," in Jocelyn R. Wingfield, *Virginia's True Founder* (Athens, GA: The Wingfield Family Society, 1993), 319.

[132] The Ancient Planters of Virginia, "A Brief Declaration," in Haile: 894.

[133] The London Virginia Company, "Instructions by way of advice, for the intended Voyage to Virginia," in Jocelyn Wingfield, 295.

[134] Barbour, *John Smith,* II: 225.

[135] Wingfield, "A Discourse" in Jocelyn Wingfield: 327

[136] Barbour, I: 41.

[137] Barbour, II: 172.

[138] William Thorndale, "Drew Pickayes (1564-1607)" *The American Genealogist.* 70: 3, No. 279,131-132.

[139] *Ibid.,* 225.

[140] Barbour, *John Smith,* II:189

[141] Barbour, *John Smith,* I: 35.

[142] In 1986 a socketed chisel was successfully produced in an experimental bloomery using limonite derived from surface deposits within 20 miles of Jamestown (David Harvey, "Reconstructing the American Bloomery Process," *The Colonial Williamsburg Historic Trades Annual*, I: 19-37).

[143] Howard B. Gill "The Blacksmith in Colonial Virginia," Unpublished ms on file Colonial Williamsburg Foundation, 1965, 6-7.

[144] Gill, "Blacksmiths", 110.

[145] This work, called Project 100, was initiated by the National Park Service to find evidence of the first fort. The conclusions were that no trace had been found (John L. Cotter *Archeological Excavations at Jamestown, Virginia*. Second Edition. Special Publication No. 32 of the Archeological Society of Virginia, (1994), 11-17.

[146] Gill, "Blacksmith," 109.

[147] William M. Kelso, Nicholas M.

Luccketti, and Beverly A. Straube, "A Re-Evaluation of the Archaeological Evidence Produced by Project 100," mss submitted to Colonial National Historical Park, 1990.

148 Brown 1890: 328.

149 Barbour, *John Smith,* II: 311.

150 One was recovered from Pit 1 (ca. 1610) and one was found in the well (Structure 170) discussed in the previous chapter.

151 David B. Quinn. *The Roanoke Voyages 1584-1590.* London: Hakluyt Society, (1955), 831.

152 Barbour, *John Smith,* II: 225.

153 J. C. Harrington, *A Tryal of Glasse,* Richmond, VA: The Dietz Press (1980), 10; Charles E. Hatch, "Glassmaking in Virginia, 1607-1625," *William and Mary College Quarterly* Second Series, 21:2 (April 1941), 128-129.

154 Barbour, *John Smith,* II: 191

155 Barbour, *John Smith,* II: 190

156 Barbour, *John Smith,* II: 181

157 Germany, particularly the area of the Kaufunger Wald in the northern part of the County of Hesse, was well known for its glass production in the 16th and 17th centuries. On the other hand, the Baltic areas of Poland were England's sources of pitch and tar in this period. In addition, references to glass production at Jamestown ceases after 1610, by which time the Germans are dead, whereas pitch, tar, and soap ashes continue to be exported to England.

158 Eleanor S. Godfrey, *The Development of English Glassmaking 1560-1640.* Chapel Hill: The University of North Carolina Press (1975) : 212

159 Potash was a rare and costly commodity in 17th-century England and glassmakers had to compete for it with other industries such as the making of soap and saltpetre.

160 Godfrey: 204.

161 *Ibid.,* 160.

162 This identification was made by Dr. Brent E. Owens, Geology Department, College of William and Mary.

163 Vannoccio Biringuccio *The Pirotechnia.* The M.I.T. Press (1959), 113.

164 There are residual deposits of pyrolusite in Augusta and Shenandoah counties in Virginia but there was no mining done in these areas during the early colonial period (Charles Palache et al. *The System of Mineralogy of James Dwight Dana and Edward Salisbury Dana.* Seventh Edition (New York: John Wiley and Sons, Inc., 1951) I: 564.

165 Hans-Georg Stephan, personal communication, 1998; Hans-Georg Stephan (1995) *Grossalmerode.* Glas- und Keramikmuseum Grossalmerode, 44, Figures 24 and 25.

166 J. C. Harrington, *A Tryal of Glasse* . Richmond, VA: The Dietz Press, Incorporated, Second Printing, 1980.

167 Barbour, *John Smith,* II: 192

168 Barbour, *John Smith,* I: lxi

169 Barbour, *John Smith,* I: 221

170 Barbour, *John Smith,* II: 190.

171 Brown "Bacon's Essay of Plantations," II, 799.

Illustration Credits

Figure 1, 2, 71a, 72, 74, 75, and the base photo of Figure 77. Colonial National Historical Park, Jamestown, Virginia.

Figure 6. Jan Steen, 'Skittle Players outside an Inn' © National Gallery, London. National Gallery Picture Library, London.

Figure 7. Hendrik Corneliz Vroom, 'Portuguese Galleon' (c. 1600). Tiroler Landesmuseum Ferdinandeum, Innsbruck.

Figure 10A. John Woodall, folding plate at the end of the chapter entitled, 'A note of particular ingredieces for a surgeon's chest' from Surgeon's Mate, 1639 edition (first published in 1617). By permission of the Director of Information Services and University Librarian of the University of Bristol, England.

Figure 11a. 'Portrait of Sir Thomas Gates' from the original portrait by C. Jansen, now in the possession of Sir Leonard Brassey, Bart., Apethorpe Hall, near Peterborough, England. The portrait appeared in Wedells, Virginia Historic Portraiture, 1930.

Figure 11b. 'Thomas West, Lord De La Warre' in Alexander Brown, Genesis of the United States, 1011.

Figure 12A. 'Portrait of George Percy,' Virginia Historical Society, Richmond, Virginia.

Figure 13. Philips Wouverman, 'River Landscape with a Tent' in The Netherlandish Painters of the Seventeenth Century, Phaidon Press Ltd. London.

Figure 14. Map of Virginia 1608. Archivo General De Simancas (Ministerio de Cultura de Espana, M.P. y D IV-66).

Figure 15. Sidney King, 'Jamestown in 1619,' Colonial National Historical Park, Jamestown, Virginia.

Figure 16. Algemeen Rijksarchief, Den Hag, Netherlands.

Figure 17A. John Speed, 'Map of London, 1610' in A Tudor Atlas. By permission of the British Library.

Figure 17b. 'Sir Walter Raleigh's House' 1873, William Whiffen Collection, Tower Hamlets Local History Archives, Bancroft Library, London.

Figure 23A. Diego Rodriguez de Silva y Velazquez, 'Felipe III, A Caballo' (Philip III, On Horseback') (c. 1583). By permission, Ministerio de Educacion, Cultura y Deporte, Museo Nacional del Prado, Madrid, Spain.

Figure 23B. Artist unknown, oil on canvas, 'Portrait of King James I,' Colonial Williamsburg Foundation.

Figure 25. Artist unknown, 'The Somerset House Conference,' 1604, oil on canvas, plate 680, National Portrait Gallery, Picture Library, London.

Figure 28A. John White, 'Indian Elder or Chief' in Volume II, The American Drawings of John White, c. 1585. © Copyright British Museum.

Figure 61a, 61c, 62, and 70. Samuel Yonge, Photos and drawings from The Site of Old James Towne 1607-1698, copyright 1930, The Association for the Preservation of Virginia Antiquities.

Figure 68. Colonial Williamsburg Foundation, 'Conjectural Drawing of Structure 144' from 'Description and analysis of Structure 144, Report to APVA Jamestown Rediscovery,' August 2002.

Figure 71b. Cary Carson, 'Conjectural Drawing of Structure 112' for Colonial National Historical Park, Jamestown, Virginia.

Figure 87. The British Museum, Map Room.

Figure 88. Jacob Willemsz the Younger, 'Officers of the White Banner 1648,' Gemeente Musea Delft Collection Stedelijk Museum Het Prinsenhof.

Figure 89. 'Captain Gosnold Trades With Indians,' Americae pars decima, Openheim, 1619. Courtesey of the Virginia Historical Society.

Figures 95a, 98a, and 131. Tom Roberts, Drawing of Well, © The Richmond-Times Dispatch.

Figure 96. Jan Steen, 'The May Queen' (c. 1648-51), from the John G. Johnson Collection, Philadelphia Museum of Art.

Figure 100. David Teniers the Younger, detail from 'The Village Holiday' or 'Dance of the Peasants' (c. 1650), Virginia Museum of Fine Arts, Richmond. The Adolph D. and Wilkins C. Williams Fund. Photo: Ron Jennings. © Virginia Museum of Fine Arts.

Figure 101a (left). Photo: Gavin Ashworth. Courtesy of the Chipstone Foundation.

Figure 101b (right). Jug, Grenzau, Germany, 1618. From the Zais Collection in the Kunstgewerbemuseum, Cologne, Germany (now lost).

Figure 102. Gerard ter Borch, 'Guardroom' from the John G. Johnson Collection, Philadelphia Museum of Art.

Figure 105. Abraham Diepraam, 'Barroom' (c. 1665). Rijksmuseum, Amsterdam.

Figure 107. Randle Holme, 'Black Bill' from The Academy of Armory and Blazon, (printed for the author, 1688), PL06804. By Permission of the British Library.

Figure 112. Jacob de Gheyn, illustration plates from The Exercise of Armes (first published in The Hague, 1607). Dover Pictorial Archive Series, 1999 edition, Dover Publications, New York.

Figure 115. Gabriel Metsu, detail from 'The Interior of a Smithy' © National Gallery, London. National Gallery Picture Library, London.

Figure 119. Detail from illustration BL966628, The Oxford Illustrated History of Tudor Britain. By Permission of the British Library.

Figure 120B. Alain Outlaw, detail from 'Agricultural Tools' in Governor's Land: Archaeology of Early Seventeenth-Century Virginia. Virginia Department of Historic Resources.

Figure 125. Detail from illustration E1175 (3), 966.b.28, in The Oxford Illustrated History of Tudor Britain. By Permission of the British Library.

Figure 128. Jacob Duck, 'A Woman Ironing.' Centraal Museum, Utrecht.

Figure 129b. Ivor Noel Hume, detail from Figure 87 in Volume II of The Archaeology of Martin's Hundred. Colonial Williamsburg Foundation.

Figure 130a (left). 'Youth's Shoe' (c. 1605-13), the Parrott Collection, Aylesbury Museum, Buckinghamshire County Museum, England.

Figure 130b (right). Jan Steen, 'The Village School.' The National Gallery of Ireland.

Figure 132. Jan Steen, 'Skittle Players outside an Inn' © National Gallery, London. National Gallery Picture Library, London.

Figures 133, 139, 140, 149, 151, 152, 157, 160, 170, 172, 175, 176, 179. Randle Holme, illustrations from The Academy of Armory and Blazon, (printed for the author, 1688), the British Library.

Figure 134. Cornelis Pietersz Bega (Haarlem 1631-1664), 'The Alchemist,' oil on canvas, Eddleman Collection, Chemical Heritage Foundation, Philadelphia, Pennsylvania, USA.

Figure 143. Hendrick Terbrugghen, 'Boy Lighting His Pipe with a Candle,' Castle Dobo Itsvan Museum, Eger, Hungary/Electa Archive, Milano.

Figure 144. Andrian Brouwer, 'The Smokers' from The Friedsam Collection, Bequest of Michael Friedsam, 1931 (32.100.21). Photo: © 1989, The Metropolitan Museum of Art.

Figure 146. Tudor Earthenware Fuming Pot, IT.328. Picture Library, Museum of London.

Figure 148. Jan Steen, 'Die Liebeskranke' ('The Lovesick Woman') Inv. Nr. 158, Bayerische Staatsgemaldesammlungen, Alte Pinakothek Museum, Munich.

Figure 150. Quiringh van Brekelenkam, 'Interior of a Tailor's Shop' Inn' © The National Gallery, London. National Gallery Picture Library, London.

Figure 159. Anthony van Dyck, 'Portrait of a Man' from the Marquand Collection, The Metropolitan Museum of Art, Gift of Henry G. Marquand, 1889, (89.1511 1), Photo: © 1984, The Metropolitan Museum of Art.

Figure 163. British School, 'William Style of Langley' c. 1636. Tate Gallery, London/Art Resources, New York.

Figure 171. John White, 'Atlantic Sturgeon' c. 1585. © Copyright British Museum.

Figure 184. 'Glass Spinner' from A Diderot Pictorial Encyclopedia of Trades and Industry, plate 245, Crown Glass XI. Dover Pictorial Archive Series, Dover Publications, New York.

Figure 185. 'Specimen of Crown Glass' c. 19th century. Science and Society Picture Library, Science Museum, London.